I0099547

Memorial Book of the Community of Chorzel
(Chorzele, Poland)

Translation of
Sefer zikaron le-kehilat Chorzel

Editors: L. Losh, Association of Former Residents of Chorzele

Published in Tel Aviv, 1967

Published by JewishGen

**An Affiliate of the Museum of Jewish Heritage—A Living Memorial to the Holocaust
New York**

Memorial Book of the Community of Chorzel Poland
Translation of *Sefer zikaron le-kehilat Chorzel*

Copyright © 2019 by JewishGen, Inc.
All rights reserved.
First Printing: January 2019, Shevat 5778
Second Printing: March 2019, Adar II 5779

Translation Project Coordinator: Susan Kittner Huntting
Translated by Jerrold Landau and Miriam Leberstein
Layout: Joel Alpert
Cover Design: Rachel Kolokoff Hopper

This book may not be reproduced, in whole or in part, including illustrations in any form (beyond that copying permitted by Sections 107 and 108 of the U.S. Copyright Law and except by reviewers for public press), without written permission from the publisher.

Published by JewishGen, Inc.
An Affiliate of the Museum of Jewish Heritage
A Living Memorial to the Holocaust
36 Battery Place, New York, NY 10280

JewishGen, Inc. is not responsible for inaccuracies or omissions in the original work and makes no representations regarding the accuracy of this translation. Digital images of the original book's contents can be seen online at the New York Public Library website.

The mission of the JewishGen organization is to produce a translation of the original work, and we cannot verify the accuracy of statements or alter facts cited.

Printed in the United States of America by Lightning Source, Inc.
Library of Congress Control Number (LCCN): 2018967232
ISBN: 978-1-939561-75-6 (hard cover, 334 pages, alk. paper)

JewishGen and the Yizkor Books in Print Project

This book has been published by the **Yizkor Books in Print Project**, as part of the **Yizkor Book Project** of JewishGen, Inc.

JewishGen, Inc. is a non-profit organization founded in 1987 as a resource for Jewish genealogy. Its website [www.jewishgen.org] serves as an international clearinghouse and resource center to assist individuals who are researching the history of their Jewish families and the places where they lived. JewishGen provides databases, facilitates discussion groups, and coordinates projects relating to Jewish genealogy and the history of the Jewish people. In 2003, JewishGen became an affiliate of the **Museum of Jewish Heritage—A Living Memorial to the Holocaust** in New York.

The **JewishGen Yizkor Book Project** was organized to make more widely known the existence of Yizkor (Memorial) Books written by survivors and former residents of various Jewish communities throughout the world. Later, volunteers connected to the different destroyed communities began cooperating to have these books translated from the original language—usually Hebrew or Yiddish—into English, thus enabling a wider audience to have access to the valuable information contained within them. As each chapter of these books was translated, it was posted on the JewishGen website and made available to the general public.

The **Yizkor Books in Print Project** began in 2011 as an initiative to print and publish Yizkor Books that had been fully translated, so that hard copies would be available for purchase by the descendants of these communities and also by scholars, universities, synagogues, libraries, and museums.

These Yizkor books have been produced almost entirely through the volunteer effort of researchers from around the world, assisted by donations from private individuals. The books are printed and sold at near cost, so as to make them as affordable as possible. Our goal is to make this important genre of Jewish literature and history available in English in book form, so that people can have the personal histories of their ancestral towns on their bookshelves for themselves and for their children and grandchildren.

A list of all published translated Yizkor Books in the project with prices and ordering information can be found at:
http://www.jewishgen.org/Yizkor/ybip.html

Lance Ackerfeld, Yizkor Book Project Manager
Joel Alpert, Yizkor-Book-in-Print Project Coordinator

JewishGen
Yizkor Book Project

This book is presented by the
Yizkor Books in Print Project
Project Coordinator: Joel Alpert

Part of the
Yizkor Books Project of JewishGen, Inc.
Project Manager: Lance Ackerfeld

These books have been produced solely through volunteer effort
of individuals from around the world. The books are printed and
sold at near cost, so as to make them as affordable as possible.

Our goal is to make this history and important genre of Jewish
literature available in English in book form so that people can have
the near-personal histories of their ancestral towns on their bookshelves for themselves and for their children and grandchildren.

Any donations to the Yizkor Books Project are appreciated.

Please send donations to:
Yizkor Book Project
JewishGen
36 Battery Place
New York, NY 10280

JewishGen, Inc. is an affiliate of the
Museum of Jewish Heritage
A Living Memorial to the Holocaust

Preface for the Translation

When asked as a teenager if I wanted anything from my paternal grandparents' home after they had both died, the only item that was important to me was a photo of my great-grandparents (p. 157) from "the old country." I was named for my great-grandmother and often stopped to stare back at the photo hanging on the wall, trying to imagine their lives and if I detected a family resemblance. Many years later, as an adult and Jewish educator particularly curious about the world in which they lived, I learned they raised their family in Chorzele, Poland and discovered the Chorzele Yizkor Book. But my inability to read Yiddish and my limited Hebrew severely frustrated my research. Thus, It was an honor to be able to fund this English translation in an effort to widen the audience within my family - and beyond - for stories about life in this part of Poland before the war.

Susan Kittner Huntting
Sarasota, FL
December 24, 2018

Acknowledgements for the Translation

My deepest thanks go to those whose experiences and expertise made this volume possible. In 1967 the former residents of Chorzele and their families compiled their memories. I imagine that was a cathartic act for them while it also gave future generations a precious glimpse into their rich pre-war world. Lance Ackerfeld, with the Yizkor Book Project of JewishGen, diligently managed and advanced the pace of this work. Miriam Leberstein (Hebrew) and Jerrold Landau (Yiddish) gave the world an invaluable gift by translating these stories to English. Last, but surely not least, I want to thank my father, David Kittner (1918 – 2014) for modeling the importance of family and giving me roots, wings and the resources to make this translation possible.

Special thanks to the National Yiddish Book Center in Amherst, Massachusetts and the New York Public Library for supplying the images used in this book.

Susan Kittner Huntting
Sarasota, FL
December 24, 2018

Dedication for the Translation

This translation is dedicated to those who came before and their many and proud descendants: my great-grandparents from Chorzele, Yitzhak and Golde Kitnik; their children, some of whom perished with them and others who left for the US and Israel; their children's children, including my father and his five siblings; their great-grandchildren, my sister and cousins; and our next generations. May all their lives be blessings.

Susan Kittner Huntting
Sarasota, FL
December 24, 2018

Explanation of the Cover Design

by Rachel Kolokoff Hopper

Photo and Illustration Credit: Front cover photo of dried wildflowers and front cover illustration by Rachel Kolokoff Hopper

When I read the *Memorial Book of the Community of Chorzel* to gather inspiration for the cover design, I was struck by the recurring theme of family, but also by the wide spectrum of emotion that is shared; love, loss, longing, joy, sorrow, peace, contentment, and finally horror.

I wanted the cover to give expression to these emotions and also to serve as a memorial to the community of Chorzel. A vibrant community that was once full of family before its people were destroyed and wiped from the earth by the Holocaust.

The illustration which covers the entire back and front covers of the book is a layered blend of a photograph of dried wildflowers merged with a Hebrew manuscript from the Yizkor book (page 21). It is meant to bring fond memories of an old way of life, long ago, when it was a peaceful time for the Jews of Chorzel.

The front cover photo is from the interior of the book and is of the Cantor Yisrael–Menashe Wald and his family. As they stare at us from the past, it reminds us of all the precious lives that were lost in the evil of Nazi Germany.

The back-cover photo is also from the interior of the book. It shows Chorzel as it was before the destruction.

I hope this cover does justice to the once vibrant Jewish community and people of Chorzel.

We must never forget.

Notes to the Reader:

We apologize ahead of time for the poor quality of images in the book. Often these images had been scanned from the original Yizkor books which were of poor quality to begin with, being copies of old photographs. Each transfer results in loss of quality. We have done the best we could, given the original material and the resources and technology at hand. Even though images often appear of higher quality on computer screens, that does not transfer to high quality images in print. A reader can view the original scans on the web sites listed below.

Within the text the reader will note "{34}" standing ahead of a paragraph. This indicates that the material translated below was on page 34 of the original book. However, when a paragraph was split between two pages in the original book, the marker is placed in this book after the end of the paragraph for ease of reading.

Also please note that all references within the text of the book to page numbers, refer to the page numbers of the original Yizkor Book.

The original book can be seen online at the New York Public Library site:

https://digitalcollections.nypl.org/items/03bf4e00-64aa-0133-694c-00505686a51c

or at the Yiddish Book Center web site:
https://www.yiddishbookcenter.org/search/collection/%22NYPL-Yiddish%2520Book%2520Center%2520Yizkor%2520Book%2520Collection%22

In order to obtain a list of all Shoah victims from Chorzel, the reader should access the Yad Vashem web site listed below; one can also search for specific family names using family name option. These lists are continually updated by Yad Vashem, so it is worthwhile to periodically search these lists.

There is much valuable information available on this web site, including the Pages of Testimony, etc.
http://yvng.yadvashem.org

A list of this book and all books available in the Yizkor-Book-In-Print Project along with prices is available at:
http://www.jewishgen.org/Yizkor/ybip.html

Geopolitical Information:

Chorzele, Poland: 53°16' North Latitude, 20°54' East Longitude

Alternate names: Chorzele [Pol], Chortzel [Yid], Khozhele [Rus], Chorzellen [Ger], Khorzel, Khorzele, Khorzhel, Khozhel

Period	Town	District	Province	Country
Before WWI (c. 1900):	Chorzele	Przasnysz	Płock	Russian Empire
Between the wars (c. 1930):	Chorzele	Przasnysz	Warszawa	Poland
After WWII (c. 1950):	Chorzele			
Today (c. 2000):	Chorzele			

Jewish Population: 950 (in 1857), 1,549 (in 1897)

Russian: Хожеле / Хоржеле / Хоржева. Yiddish: כאָזשעל. Hebrew: לה'חוז / חורזיל

Chorzele is 16 miles N of Przasnysz, 49 miles W of Łomża, 70 miles NE of Płock, 70 miles N of Warszawa.

Nearby Jewish Communities:
Janowo 10 miles WNW
Przasnysz 16 miles S
Baranowo 18 miles ESE
Krasnosielc 20 miles SE
Myszyniec 20 miles ENE
Nidzica 20 miles WNW
Szczytno 21 miles N
Kadzidło 24 miles E
Mława 24 miles WSW
Maków Mazowiecki 29 miles SSE
Ciechanów 29 miles SSW
Czarnia 30 miles E
Ostrołęka 30 miles ESE

BALTIC SEA

LITHUANIA

RUSSIA

Vilnius ●

● **Chorzele**

POLAND

BELARUS

GERMANY

● Poznan

Warsaw ●

● Lodz

● **Czestochowa**

● **Zabrze**

● Prague

● Krakow

CZECH REPUBLIC

● **Jordanow**

UKRAINE

SLOVAKIA

250 miles

0

0   250 Km   500 Km

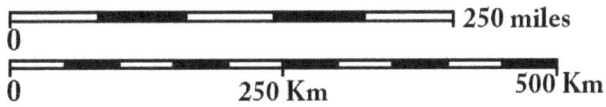

POLAND - Current Borders

Hebrew Cover of the Original Yizkor Book

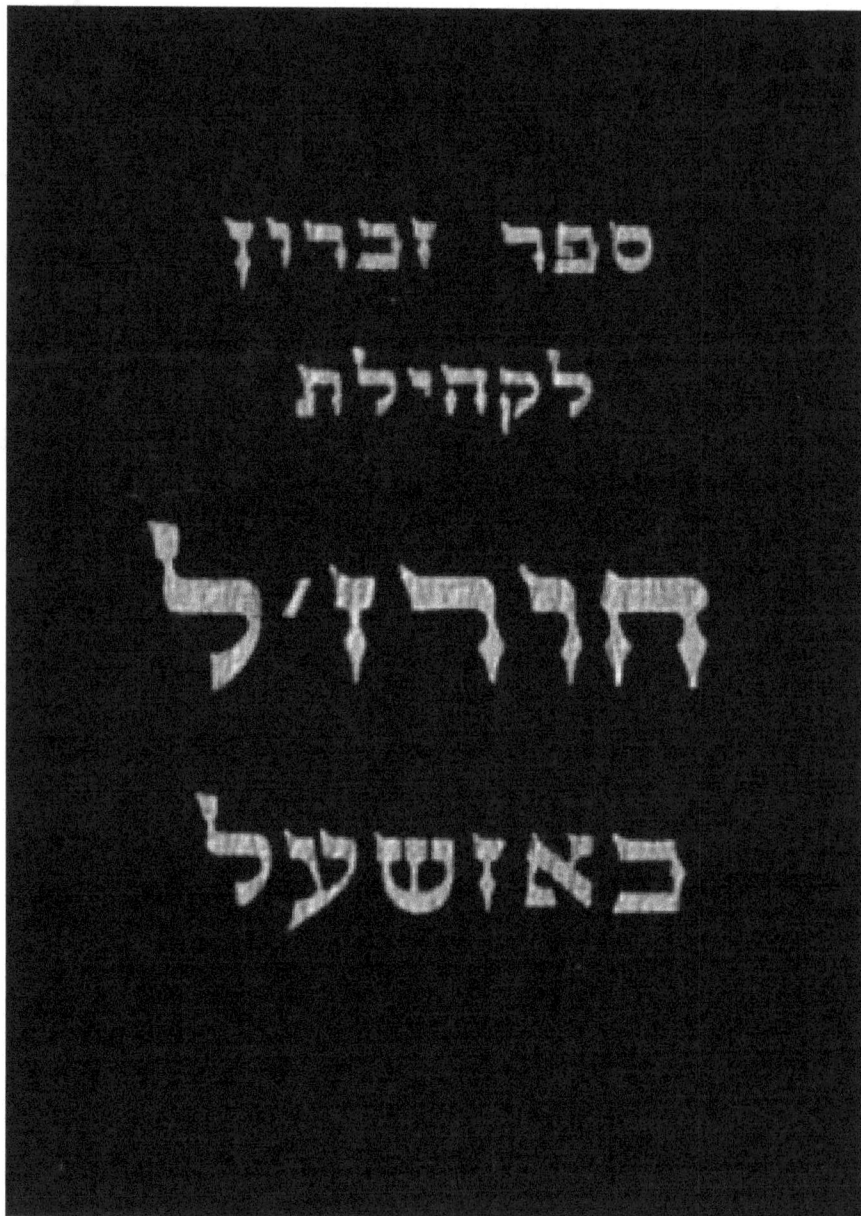

ספר זכרון
לקהילת
חורז׳ל
באזשעל

Translation of the Cover of Original Yizkor Book

Memorial Book

Of the Community of

Chorzele

Table of Contents

Part Two [Yiddish]

Part Three [Yiddish]
Documents and Lists

Footnotes
1. "We do not erect monuments for the righteous; their words are their memorial" (Jerusalem Talmud Shekalim 2:5
2. Nahum Sokolow - a Zionist leader, author and Hebrew journalist
3. Pioneer Youth
4. Interest Free Loan

Family Notes

[Page 6]

Entrance to the town (from the side of the bridge)

Market Square (1917)

[Page 7]

Foreword
by M. Carmi
Translated by Jerrold Landau

... Remove the shoes from your feet, for the place upon which you are standing is holy... (Joshua 5:15)

This Yizkor Book is the fruit of the collective labors of the natives of Chozele in Israel, to give expression to the world of experiences tied to our past, and to carry the feelings of agony and sorrow that we hold in our hearts in memory of our dear martyrs who perished in the Holocaust during the time of the Second World War. Approximately 50 of our townsfolk who live in Israel contributed their articles and memories to this book, and we all worked for the common goal to the best of our ability, with love and a fundamental connection to the subject that is more dear to us than anything, in order to erect in this manner a monument and memorial to our community that was destroyed to its foundations.

As is known, our town Chorzele is located on the border that separates Poland (originally Russia) and Eastern Prussia (Germany), two worlds that are far apart from each other not only from an historical and geopolitical perspective, but also from a general Jewish and social–Zionist perspective. Even though the town was always under Polish (Russian) rule, it was influenced to a significant degree in its economic life by the German side. However, it was always a typical Polish (Russian) town in its essence – with rabbis, scholars, honorable communal activists, wealthy and poor people, observant people and free–thinkers, Zealots and heretics, *maskilim* and ignoramuses, philanthropists and misers, merchants and tradesman, people interested in improving the world and Zionist pioneers. From among the 280 Jewish families (approximately 1,300 individuals) who lived in Chorzele during the 1930s, most had a Zionist outlook. It is a fact that approximately 150 complete or partial families made *aliya* to the Land of Israel during that period.

The memory of our dear ones who did not succeed in being with us in Israel is holy. To perpetuate their memory, we have undertaken this holy work of publishing a memorial book. Oh, dear former residents of Chorzele: read this book and teach its chapters to your sons and daughters who did not know our community from up close. Teach them to know the wellspring from which our ancestors drew their strength to stand up to the vicissitudes of faith and adversity during the Jewish exile, the power and initiative that was buried within the lives and deeds, private and public, of the Jews of Chorzele. Also, those Jews, some of whom had the foresight to succeed in abandoning their native town while there was still time, to make *aliya* to the Land of Israel and to demonstrate all the aforementioned traits in building and creativity, in the defense forces (Haganah) and in the War of Independence.

Would it be that the memory of the holy and pure natives of our town who did not merit such shall remain within us forever, and may their souls be bound in the bond of the lives of the generation who continues in actualizing the renaissance of Israel.

[Page 8]

... Listen to this, oh elders, and hear, all the residents of the earth, could this have happened in your days and in the days of your fathers; tell your children about this, and your children to their children, and their children to the following generation.

(Joel 1)

... And I will send portents in the heavens and the earth, blood, fire, and pillars of smoke. The sun will turn to darkness and the moon to blood before the advent of the great and awesome Day of the Lord; and everyone who calls the name of God will escape because Mount Zion and Jerusalem will be a refuge as God said, and to the survivors whom God has called.

(Joel 3)

[Page 11]

One Does Not Make a Monument to the Righteous…
(*Shekalim* Chapter 2, 8)

by HaRav Efraim Sokolower
Translated by Jerrold Landau

To the memory of my parents of blessed memory: My father the rabbi and gaon Rabbi Mordechai Chaim Sokolower, the head of the rabbinical court of Chorzele, died on 15 Kislev, 5697 (1936). My mother the *rebbetzin* Esther Rachel, died on 4 Tammuz, 5678 (1918).

It is the general custom among the entire world, among all circles, to erect a monument over the graves of one's dear ones. Everyone attempts to set up a fine monument, to the best of his ability.

This holy custom has a pure, ancient source. Its source is in the Torah with our matriarch Rachel of blessed memory. It says (Genesis 35) – "And Jacob erected a monument over her grave, that is the monument of the Grave of Rachel, to this day." Our sages explain (as quoted in Rashi, Vayechi, verse 7), that Jacob of blessed memory buried Rachel along the way, and did not even bring her to Bethlehem to bring her to the Land, so that she could be of assistance to her children: when Nebuzaradan[1] brought them to exile, and they would pass by, Rachel would come out of her grave, weep, and beg for mercy on their behalf, etc. It is perhaps for this reason that Jacob erected a monument over her grave, so that the Children of Israel would know and recognize the place, and therefore be able to pray there at the time of need, when they find themselves in a situation of trouble.

To this day, the holy custom of visiting the graves of one's forebears is well rooted: from afar, from across the ocean, children and close family members come to the graves of their ancestors, to pray over their grave. To ward off any tribulation, they rush to the cemetery to beg for mercy. When a joyous occasion occurs in the household, on the eve of a wedding of children, they visit the graves of their forebears. For in all generations, the monument atop the grave is the link that binds, or more accurately – strengthens – the natural bond between parents and children. On the other hand, it is thanks to the monument that the children know and feel that their parents are still in a certain place. Even though the distance is very far, and they cannot see them for any price in the world – despite this, something lives within them.

It is told regarding one of our great sages, Rabbi Yochanan, who said, "This is a bone of my tenth son" (Berachot, 5). After his ten children died in his lifetime, he would always carry in his pocket a small bone of his last son who died, and this small bone gave him something through which to remember and not forget that once he had something so precious: ten dear and precious children (apparently, there is some small feeling of comfort through this).

[Page 12]

We, the relatives of the martyrs of the Holocaust years, enter into the third decade after the third destruction in our history. This destruction was so fundamental, and turned into a destruction of the entire nation: entire communities were destroyed completely, and the nation was immersed in a general mourning. The entire nation was submerged in individual mourning. Silenced by the depth of the destruction, for a long period we were unable to come together and join up for a communal memorial uniting the mourning of each individual family of our town Chorzele. However, the general destruction is slowly being forgotten. The general feeling that enveloped the entire House of Israel in every place is weakening from year to year. The terrible tragedy of the murder of six million Jews — men, women, and children — no longer makes an impression in the world. People have already become accustomed to these words, and their meaning has turned into a mere linguistic expression.

With this situation, a feeling was awakened and grew in our hearts, which gave us no rest (from time to time, or at times, even more often), imbuing us with longing for family– parents, children, brothers and sisters! During those moments, we began to search for some memorial in order to assuage our soulful longing. Among ourselves, we looked afar, one thought chasing another, perhaps at least giving us some hope that at one point we will be able to visit the graves of our forebears. Even at a moment where this hope seems to us like a fantasy, for our sorrow there is no memorial at all, not even a "tiny bone" of our dearly beloved, for they were destroyed completely and not even a small amount of ash remain.

Even those of our dear ones who merited to be given a Jewish burial before the Holocaust or during the Holocaust – even those who merited having a monument erected over their graves – can we ever visit their graves? Even if I was given the possibility of visiting Chorzele once, if only to see the grave of my revered father, the final rabbi of Chorzele, and the grave of my revered mother the *rebbetzin* of blessed memory (who died at the age of 37), I would not be able to unite with their spirit and soul next to their graves for a brief moment. Since this possibility was removed from us (the possibility of fulfilling the tradition of erecting a monument and visiting the graves of one's forebears) we only have one way to do so, in accordance with the words of our sages written at the outset of my words, "We do not make a monument for the righteous, as their words are their memorial." Even though this statement implies that there is no need to make monuments for the righteous, for they leave behind their words and good deeds, we must interpret this statement in its simplest meaning, for to our sorrow we are unable to make these monuments for our holy, righteous martyrs. The connection to our city and community that once was, to our beloved Chorzele, has been severed completely. There is no possibility, just as there is no desire or hope, heaven forbid, to renew our connection with that accursed land that does not exist for us anymore. Similarly, there is no possibility of erecting monuments to the Holocaust victims of our community, for there is no trace of them. They did not merit, and we did not merit Jewish burials. Therefore, we must forge a new connection to all of our dearly beloved ones, may their memories be a blessing. Their words and their deeds are their memory.

The publication of a memorial book to the martyrs of our city is a great and fine thing. This book will serve as a memorial monument for generations. Whenever we look into it, we will be inspired to remember our relatives in our hearts, and this memory will draw us closer to their spirits and souls. When the righteous Joseph was in Egypt, oppressed in body and spirit, young in years, of refined soul and noble spirit, he fell into impure and cruel hands. Before his eyes stood the image of his elderly father, and since he saw the image of his father, his spirit was strengthened to withstand all the obstacles and oppression in his path. This memory gave him the power and encouragement to gird himself and continue on in the tradition of his dear father, as he received it during his childhood.

[Page 13]

This memorial book will adorn every house of our fellow townsfolk, and will stand constantly before our eyes in honor and glory. Indeed, I lived in Chorzele for only limited periods of time, but I still managed to gain from its essence and peer at what was inside. Within this tiny town there were great scholars, pious people and people of good deeds, those who pursued charitable and benevolent deeds in a wondrous fashion, and those who engaged in communal work in a faithful and dedicated manner, people through whom the entire community was blessed. I was especially impressed that I found a religious intelligentsia there, consisting of young and old, God fearing and wholesome, who were fully honorable to God and their fellows – great scholars, enthusiastic Hassidim, engaged in the realities of the world, who knew how to speak pleasantly, and relate with love and appreciation to their fellows.

These images will stand before our eyes always, and their holy memories will light up our paths in life, so that we can continue the golden chain – we and the coming generations.

May their souls be bound in the bonds of life.

Translator's Footnote

Nebuzaradan was the commander of Nebuchadnezzar's army. See http://www.jewishvirtuallibrary.org/jsource/biography/nebuzar.html

An Image and an Essence that was Lost
by Z. K–N
Translated by Jerrold Landau

This survey was constructed from a joint conversation that took place between six of our townsfolk with the purpose of dredging up from their memories facts and names that would capture the image and essence of the town in a fundamental fashion. The six are: Shlomo Levavi (Herzog), Hagar Levavi (Adler), Gershon Shniadover, Nachman Lenanter, Yosef Nesher (Adler), and Moshe Carmi (Weingort).

The Town in General

Before the Second World War, Chorzele belonged to the Warsaw Wojewoda, district of Plock, Pszanysz Powiat. It was situated on the Orzyc River and the Narew Stream, near the border between Poland and East Prussia.

[Page 14]

The border was about two kilometers from the town. The final railway stop in Polish territory (Warsaw – Ostrów Mazowiecki – Ostrołęka, Chorzele) was about three kilometers from the town. A German town and the Flamberg railway station were on the other side of the border.

The town had a population of 3,800 just before the Second World War, of whom approximately 1,300 were Jews, and the rest were Poles (Catholic Christians). There were four Jews on the town council: Avraham–Michael Adler, Tovia (Tevel) Fater, Shmuel Szniadower, and Mendel Przysusker.

Moshe–Aharon Gwyazda, Aharon–Motel Bekerman, and Mendel Kac participated in the civic public committee for tax matters.

Relations between the Jews and Christians worsened during the final years prior to the Second World War on account of the anti–Semitic propaganda. Christian shops were opened, and "pickets" began to appear next to the Jewish shops. The picketers were young Christians who warned the farmers to refrain from purchasing from Jews. Once when Zalman Milsztejn pushed aside a picketer next to his shop, he was captured together with several inciters, dragged to the center of the market, where he was soundly beaten.

There were two priests in the town. One was older, and had good relations with the Jews. The second was younger and claimed that one must not purchase from Jews, but it was forbidden to beat them. On one occasion before a fair, when rumors spread that a pogrom was about to take place, the Jews sent a delegation to the police chief. The police chief accepted bribes and promised to calm the storm. He summoned policemen from the area and, before the fair, arrested all those suspected of organizing the disturbances. A detailed plan regarding the carrying out of the disturbances was found in their hands. This plan included the dividing up of the Jewish girls and Jewish property amongst themselves.

The Community and Communal Institutions

Between the two wars, Avraham–Michael Adler was the head of the community. The following were among the prominent communal activists: Mordechai Mendel Frajdman, Aharon–Mottel Bekerman, Tovia (Tevel) Fater, and Mendel Przysusker.

The Tomchei Aniyim [Support for the Poor] Society was directed by Reb Moshe–Shimon Adler, an important man who himself assisted the poor through discreet gifts. He also set up credit for them in the grocery stores, and provided them with firewood for the winter. He would purchase the wood in the summer so it would get dry. He himself would collect the money to cover the provisions from amongst the residents. During the German occupation from 1915–1918, he would smuggle flour and bread for those in need. Once, some of the pious members of the city council came to him and threatened that if his daughter participated in a theatrical production, they would forbid his *shechita* (he was a *shochet*). The members of the troupe acted with wisdom and promised Reb Moshe–Shimon 30% of the income of the performance for the benefit of Tomchei Aniyim. He allowed his daughter to participate as an actress despite the danger to his status as a *shochet*.

The Linat Tzedek Society[1] was founded during the time of the First World War. With the outbreak of the war in 1914, all the residents of the city fled after it was burned down through the actions of warfare. When they returned during the German occupation, many diseases broke out among them. Then, the Jewish–German physician Dr. Levi Leiser recommended the founding of the Linat Tzedek. Its founders included Elimelech Cytryniasz, Libe Adler (the wife of the *shochet* Moshe–Shimon Adler – both of them tended to the sick day and night). Between the two wars, Sara–Masa Szniadower (chair), Hagar Adler, Gitel Kowal, Rachel Jochet, and Sara Jochet were active in Linat Tzedek.

[Page 15]

The Chevra Kadisha Society tended to all matters of burial and supervision of the cemetery (there was only one cemetery in the town). The trustees of the Chevra were A. M. Bekerman, Tevel Fater, and, may he live, Meir–Yaakov Weingort. Mordechai–Mendel Farberowicz served as the "Kohen Shamash" – chief administrator.

Houses of Worship and Shtibels

There was one synagogue in the town, where services were held only on Sabbaths and festivals. There were also two *Beis Midrashes*, the old and the new, where services were held every day. The Old *Beis Midrash* housed the *Chevrat Mishnayot* [Mishna Study Group], headed by Reb Kalman Ajzensztadt. The New *Beis Midrash* was the spiritual center of the city, where people would debate holy and secular questions and administer general communal issues.

During the High Holy Days, the younger generation would worship together with their parents in the synagogue. The *Shacharit* service was led by Shalom Margolis, and the *Musaf* service by Yosef Cohen.

During the times of elections to the Zionist congresses, the activists of the parties and movements would post all sorts of notices in the *Beis Midrash*, but the *gabbaim* [trustees] would remove them.

Reb Wolf Tyk would study in one of the *Beis Midrashes* all day. Reb Yaakov Korzniak, one of the frequenters of the *Beis Midrash*, would awaken the people every Sabbath for the recital of Psalms.

Hasidim from the Ger, Aleksander, Nowyminsk, and Sochaczew courts existed in town. All of them had separate *shtibels*, but their influence on communal life in the town was not noticeable. When their rebbes would come to visit the Hasidim, all the Hasidim would gather together, without concern as to whose court the rebbe belonged to.

Institutions of Study and Education

As time went on, more than ten *cheders* with different rebbes existed in the town. Reb Aharon–Leib, Reb Ozer, and Reb Zalman–Meir taught the young children. Reb Feivish, Reb Ben–Zion, Reb Avraham–Yitzchak Hablyn, and Reb Mordechai–Mendel Frajdman taught Chumash. Reb Yechiel and Reb Ben–Zion taught *Gemara*. There were also *cheders* that taught Talmud, Hebrew, and arithmetic, founded by Reb Moshe Kalman's and Reb Hershel Gliksberg. The children learned to write a bit of Hebrew from Reb Yidel the teacher and Reb Motel the teacher.

A government Jewish school with two grades existed in 1918–1919, with Velvel Rabinowicz as the principal. Reb Yosef Nesher (Adler) taught Hebrew and singing in this school.

[Page 16]

A four–grade government school existed from 1920–1930. After the end of the fourth grade, the students transferred to the fifth grade of the government Polish School. The teachers in the Jewish school were Y. Fajgenbaum and Mrs. Cytryn. The government annulled the aforementioned order in 1930, and all the classes of the Jewish school merged with the government Polish school.

Children of the Talmud Torah with *gabbai* Meir–Yaakov Weingort (second from left), the teacher Natanke Yochanan's (first on left), Yechiel David the *shamash* (first on the right), Yankel Todres the translator (second from right)

Rabbis and Clergy

The following is a list of rabbis who occupied the rabbinical seat of Chorzele from 1904[2] until the liquidation of the community:

Years of tenure	Name	Notes
1897–1899	Rabbi Kowalski	Moved to Włocławek
1901–1912	Rabi Rozenstrauch	Moved to Olkusz
1912–1914	Rabbi Brunroth	Moved to Ciechanów
1916–1937	Rabbi Sokolower	Passed away
1937–1942	Rabbi Fajncajg	Perished in the Holocaust

[Page 17]

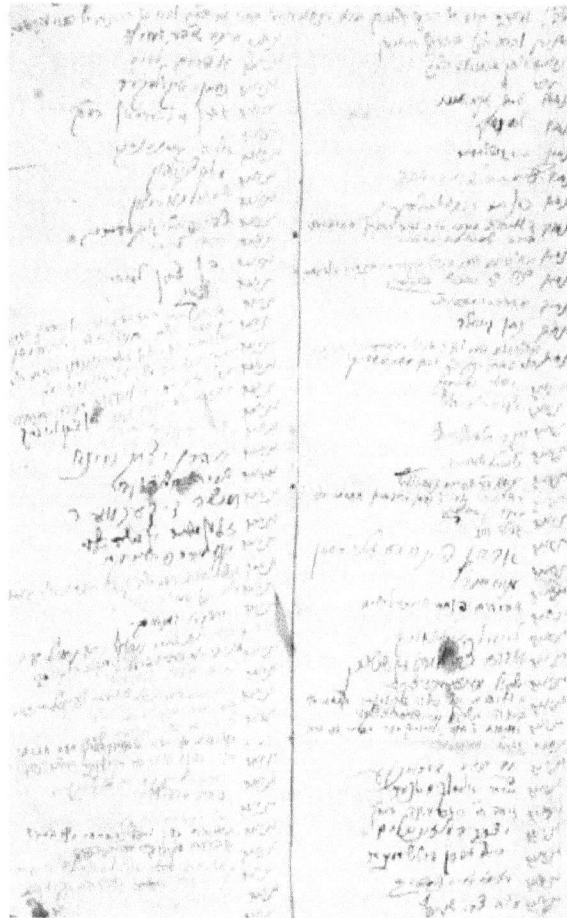

The sale of *chometz* [leavened products] document from the eve of Passover

[Page 18]

The following is the list of people, no longer alive, who served in holy positions in our town:

Cantors: Reb Moshe–Shimon Adler (the *shochet*), Reb Yisrael–Menashe Wald.

Rabbinical judge: Rabbi Hersh (Tzvi) Gliksberg

Shochtim [ritual slaughterers]: Reb Yosef Cohen, Reb Avraham Sziniak.

Circumcisors: Reb Mordechai–Mendel Frajdman, Reb Yosef Cohen, Reb Yitzchak Meir Richter, Reb Avraham Sziniak.

Gabbaim: Reb Chaim Rozencwajg, Reb Tanchum, Kowal, Reb Matis Sokolower, Reb Michael Berent, Reb Mordechai–Mendel Frajdman.

Shamashim: Reb Shlomo the son of Rabbi Weingarten, Reb Hershel (Jofak) and his son, Reb Yechiel–David.

The Zionist Movement

Before the First World War, Reb Fishel Lachower of blessed memory disseminated the ideas of Zionism and enlightenment in town. The first Zionist pioneers [*chalutzim*] made *aliya* in 1909: Mordechai Ajzensztat of blessed memory, Simcha Adler, Eliezer Mar–Chaim.

The first Zionist organization was set up after the war in 1918 by the emissary Y. Hendler of Maków. All of the Zionist parties and movements in the city joined this organization later.

The following is the list of Zionist organizations and the active members who stood at their helm:

a. Mizrachi (the strongest movement in the town): Mordechai–Mendel Frajdman, Avraham–Michel Adler, Moshe–Aharon Gwiazda, and Meir–Yaakov Weingort.

b. Hechalutz: Moshe Leib Davidson and Yosef Lenanter (the founders), Yaakov Frankel, Yehuda, Richter, Pesia Student.

c. Gordonia: Artzia Lichtensztejn, Moshe Rosenblum.

d. Poale–Zion: Nachman Lenanter, Gershon Szniadower, Simcha Sokolower.

e. Beitar: Bunim Adler (Nesher), Zisha Gerlic.

f. Al–Hamishmar (group 1): Shepsl Frankel, Shlomo Hertzog, Avraham Kac, Moshe Jochet.

g. Et–Livnot (group 2): Aharon–Leib Grzebialka, Eli–Leib Fater.

h. Agudas Yisroel: Ben–Zion Sokolower, Shmuel Najer

The majority of the residents of the town supported the activities of the Zionist movement, with the exception, of course, of the Bund, which organized itself in 1918/20. Its activists were Aharon–Yitzchak Gliksberg, Leizer Nyborski, Moshe Kowal, Aharon Lewiner, Moshe Cwyrkowski.

The activities of the Keren Kayemet [Jewish National Fund] and Keren HaYesod were conducted jointly by all the Zionist organizations who were represented in the civic council. The chairman of the council was Mordechai–Mendel Frajdman. His assistants were Avraham–Michel Adler and Aharon–Motel Bekerman.

[Page 19]

Economic Life

All the local industrial enterprises were in Jewish hands. These included the beer distillery, the brick kiln (owned by the brothers Mendel and Pinchas Przysusker), the wool workshop (owned by Shimon Szniadower), the oil factory, and the flourmill (owned by Mordechai Lichtensztejn).

There were three Jewish estate owners in the nearby area: the Cwyrkowsky brothers, M. Richter and partners (the Zimna Woda Estate).

A significant portion of the Jewish population was involved with traditional commercial endeavors with the residents of the other side of the Prussian border. In 1933, the year of Hitler's ascension to government, the border was closed definitively to such enterprises, especially for the Jews.

The open commerce with the residents of Prussia included used clothing, dried mushrooms, strawberries, and other fruit. Before the First World War, during the Czarist rule, the Jews of Chorzele were occupied in leasing ponds in Prussia for the purposes of fishing. They would reach as far as Astrachan on the Caspian Sea for fishing purposes.

Before the First World War, Moshe Aharon Gwyazda established a loan fund. During the period of German rule (1915–1918) the fund was turned into a bank, which was under the supervision of the Jekopo Center in Warsaw between the two world wars.

Moshe Aharon Gwyazda was always the living force behind the bank. The bank granted loans to all Jewish residents who were in need of such, especially the small–scale businessmen and tradesmen.

Those active in the bank included Mordechai–Mendel Frajdman of blessed memory, Mordechai Przysusker of blessed memory, and, may he live, Shlomo Levavi.

Between the two world wars, the situation of the Jews of Chorzele was similar to that of the Jews in other towns of that nature in Poland. Before and immediately after the First World War, the situation was particularly bad. This forced many of them to seek new sources of livelihood overseas. This also explains the situation that there were only about 1,300 Jews in the town just before the Second World War.

A significant number of the Jews of Chorzele escaped to Russia along with the Red Army that was retreating from the area at the beginning of the First World War. Most of them never returned to the town, but rather immigrated later to other countries, including England, Switzerland, Israel, the United States, Argentina, and others. These émigrés included Rabbi Goodman (England), Rabbi Botchko (Switzerland), Rabbi Sokolower (Israel).

Cultural Activities

The town library was founded during the time of the German occupation (1915–1916) by a group of activists from among the youth: Alter Cytryniasz, Itche Koszniak, Hagar Adler, Yosef Adler,

[Page 20]

Liba Przysusker, Hershel Jochet, and Shlomo Herzog. The library included several hundred books in Yiddish and Hebrew, and its committee displayed initiative and effort in various cultural areas, including performances, question evenings, a dramatic group, etc. Those active in the dramatic group included Moshe Cwyrkowski (the scenery director), Yosef Tyk (the stage manager), Gershon Szniadower, Leizer Neuborsky, and others.

There was also a Tarbut hall in the town, where the youth would gather every Sabbath between *Mincha* and *Maariv* to sing Israel and popular songs, and spend time together.

The following were among the important guests who visited the town for matters of Zionism, culture, and education: Rabbi Milikowsky (1916), Melech Ravitch (1928)[3], Dov–Ber Malkin (1931), Dvora Lachower (1932). Their visits instigated a cultural–societal awakening among the majority of the residents of the town, even though the visitors targeted their visits to the specific group to which they were affiliated.

Translator's Footnotes

1. A lay run society to tend to the sick, especially during the night.
2. From the table below, it appears that the date 1904 is an error in the original text.
3. See http://www.yivoencyclopedia.org/article.aspx/Ravitch_Melech

In Memory of the Town and its Residents
by Moshe Carmi
Translated by Jerrold Landau

The town of Chorzele did not stand out in any way from amongst the other towns of Poland, in which vibrant Jewish life took pace. Its only outstanding feature was that it was in a remote area, and was a border town on the border between Poland and East Prussia.

The bridge over the Orzyc River is found at the main entrance to the city, where the flourmill of Mottel Lichtensztajn (known as Mottel Zeigermacher – the Watchmaker – even though he never worked as a watchmaker) was located, as well as the flourmill of Berl Brener. Ruda Road, which was a sort of "information center" for those who were entering and exiting the town, was nearby. From this road, one would reach a square yard, around which there were shops, primarily owned by Jews (except for two or three gentile shops). This square was the center of the town, where the market days took place twice a week, as well as the monthly fair. Military parades and festive celebrations of the Polish population, including religious ceremonies, took place there. The rest of the streets of the city spread out from that square. The streets were not called by their official names, but rather by the names of their prominent residents, such as the Street of Reb Tevel Fater and the city rabbi, Rabbi Sokolower; or the street of Reb Avraham Shaar and Moshe–Aharon Gwyazda.

On the route from the square toward the border, one would pass the Great Synagogue and the *mikva* [ritual bath]. After Szirota's grocery store, the road led to the beer brewery of the brothers Mendel and Pinchas Przysusker, and further on, to the edge of the city (the dunes), where Chaitsha and Rachtsha Herzog and Yechezkel Segal lived.

[Page 21]

It apparently seems that the lives of the Jews of the town were lead calmly. However, each individual family was a world unto itself. Despite the fact that Chorzele was not graced with many wealthy people, those who were considered wealthy stood out with their great amount of property only in comparison to the majority of the Jews of the town who had meager possessions. Nevertheless, the town was known for the generosity of all its residents. The community concerned itself with the poor people who came to Chorzele to collect donations, and established a guesthouse for them with the assistance of Shimon Szirota. The *gabbai* of the Great Synagogue, Reb Chaim, would concern himself with all poor people, ensuring that they received a warm meal from a householder every day of the week, and especially on Sabbaths and festivals. It can be said that there was not one resident of the city who went hungry, for assistance would be offered immediately upon finding out about any dire situation. For the most part, two householders would go out to collect money for the needy person. Despite the difficult economic situation of the majority of the Jews of Chorzele, everyone would give due to an internal impetus. There were barely any incidents of refusal.

Those active in the Y. L. Peretz Library (1930)

*

The societal life of the town was centered primarily around the following movements:

Mizrachi – encompassed all the areas of life in the city, and conducted publicity on behalf of the Zionist idea among the Orthodox circles. The crowning achievement of its Zionist activity was the effort on behalf of the Jewish National Fund [Keren Kayemet], to which Mordechai–Mendel Frajdman was especially dedicated. The Mizrachi members founded a synagogue that also served as a meeting place for the young men of the city who wished to find a symbiosis between religion and Zionism, as well as for people who were especially active in communal life.

[Page 22]

Agudas Yisroel set up a *hachshara* camp for agricultural work on the farm of the Jews Cwyrkowski. Ben–Zion Sokolower, the son of the rabbi, and Shmuel Neuer were especially active on that front.

The Hechalutz movement stood out in its Zionist activity and its organization of all communal matters in the town. Its influence was especially noticeable in forging the character of the youth. Hechalutz activists included Yerachmiel Segal of blessed memory, Yehuda Richter, Yaakov Frankel, Avraham Weingort of blessed memory, and others.

The influence of the Bund was not very large in our town, even though some members of the working intelligentsia with left leaning tendencies were members. They had a headquarters and a library named for Y. L. Peretz.

The Beitar movement was organized by Bunim Adler. After he made *aliya*, it was headed by Zisha Gerlic, Nathan Rosenblum, and Meir Shaar.

Zisha Gerlic

There were organizations for offering assistance and support, such as Bikur Cholim [Visiting the Sick], and Linat Tzedek (both made great efforts for the needy). The Chevra Kadisha [Burial Society] especially stood out. Its members left their workplaces at any time of need to pay the last respects to any deceased person, without any expectation of remuneration. Over many years, the heads of the Chevra Kadisha included Tevel Fater, Aharon–Mottel Bekerman, Meir–Yaakov Weingort, and Chona Kowal. The annual Chevra Kadisha feasts that took place on the 11th of Adar were major events. The important people of the city and many guests were invited.

[Page 23]

Chorzele had a special connection with the position of the town cantor. When the Cantor Moshe–Shimon was no longer able to fulfil his role on account of his age, Menashe Wald was accepted as cantor. His sweet voice and enthusiastic prayers, which were literally an outpouring of the soul, were the pride of the town. The synagogue was filled to capacity during his prayers.

*

Most of the residents of the city earned their livelihoods from the grain and foodstuffs trade. They would purchase produce from the farmers of the area, and supply in return everything that was needed in the villages. The manufacturing enterprises included a beer brewery and the brick kiln of the Przysusker brothers.

The shops for the sale of textiles were noted for their strong economic position. Mendel Farberowicz, Szafran, Avraham–Michel Adler, and Baharb were known as wealthy individuals.

Some of the residents of the town earned their livelihoods from shoemaking and tailoring. There were also two carpenters, Leizer–Itzel and Fishel.

*

It is worthwhile to note that, for the most part, the town had Zionist leanings, and a large portion of the residents actualized the Zionist imperative of *aliya* to the Land of Israel. Thanks to that, a large number of Jews of Chorzele live in Israel today, and are represented in many branches of economics and industry, as well as in a variety of social circles.

Memorial Candle

I will mention a number of individuals who are particularly etched in my memory:

Cantor Reb Yisrael–Menashe Wald

Reb Yisrael–Menashe Wald and his family, including two sons Shalom and Chaim, came to Chorzele from the large city of Warsaw, where he was an honorable merchant. He became a cantor when he lost his livelihood. He was accepted as cantor of the town after a try out on one Sabbath in the Great Synagogue. His voice was sweet, and since he was a great fearer of Heaven, his prayers were suffused with religious devotion. When he reached the prayer "*Hineni Heani Mimaas*"[1], he would place his head on the podium, tremble from fear of G–d, and his tears would dampen his *machzor*. However, when he reached the phrase, "and chastise the Satan" he would straighten out with pride, as he shouted to overcome the forces of evil...

[Page 24]

Cantor Yisrael–Menashe Wald and his family

The Lachower family

Great love was felt and is still felt by our townsfolk toward the Lachower family. The well–known writer and researcher Fishel and his intelligent, diligent sister Dvora came from this family. For many years, Fishel Lachower bore the idea of writing a memory book for our town. When he was finally free to actualize this idea, his work was interrupted by his death.

The Lachower family in Israel gave us the aforementioned manuscript of Fishel to look over. With their permission we are publishing its first page here – "The town" (page 25), which was definitely referring to Chorzele.

*

Dvora Lachower was given open expressions of love and appreciation when she came from the Land of Israel as representative of the Keren Kayemet LeYisrael [Jewish National Fund], and arrived in Chorzele for a brief visit with her family and friends. Dvora was very active in our organization in Israel. She delivered a memorial speech that was full of content and emotionally arousing every year on the memorial day of our destroyed community.

[Page 25]

The Town

Life in that town was still quiet in those days. In the surrounding towns, the sound of the piping of the locomotives could already be heard. The railways already crisscrossed the land, making lines through the flat land. However, this town was still virtually invisible, hiding among the dunes, forests, and bogs.

Here, if a sound is heard calling out, it is the voice of the *shamash* of the synagogue summoning the people to the worship of the Creator, or, to differentiate, the bells of the Catholic church that have been ringing morning and evening for generations, summoning the believers to prayer and supplication.

To go travel from the district capital to the town one passes through seven hills on an unpaved road. A Jew could set out from there with his wagon laden with merchandise on Thursday morning, but might not arrive in the town for the Sabbath. On such a Sabbath, the Jews would not rest. After the Sabbath day meal, they would walk to the Sabbath boundary[2], where they would wait by the road and look afar. Those who did not go lay down on their beds for their Sabbath afternoon nap, but their sleep was disturbed. They were not at ease after such a fitful nap. Both groups, those that went and those that did not, hastened to make *Havdalah* after the Sabbath. On such a Sabbath, one does not add from the holy to the profane [i.e. delay the departure of the Sabbath] – it is similar to one who marries a widow or a divorcee where one does not add on to the *ketubah*[3]. They would stand near the bridge, and wait there until midnight. They would go home at midnight, but another watch would come to listen for any sign or sound of a wheel outside the city. It once happened that a wagon that set out from the district city on Thursday did not return until Monday. On Monday, the horse returned with the bit in its mouth, neighing, but without its rider. He fell with his wagon into an uncovered pit, and the entire weight of the wagon was on top of him, and did not get up after his fall.

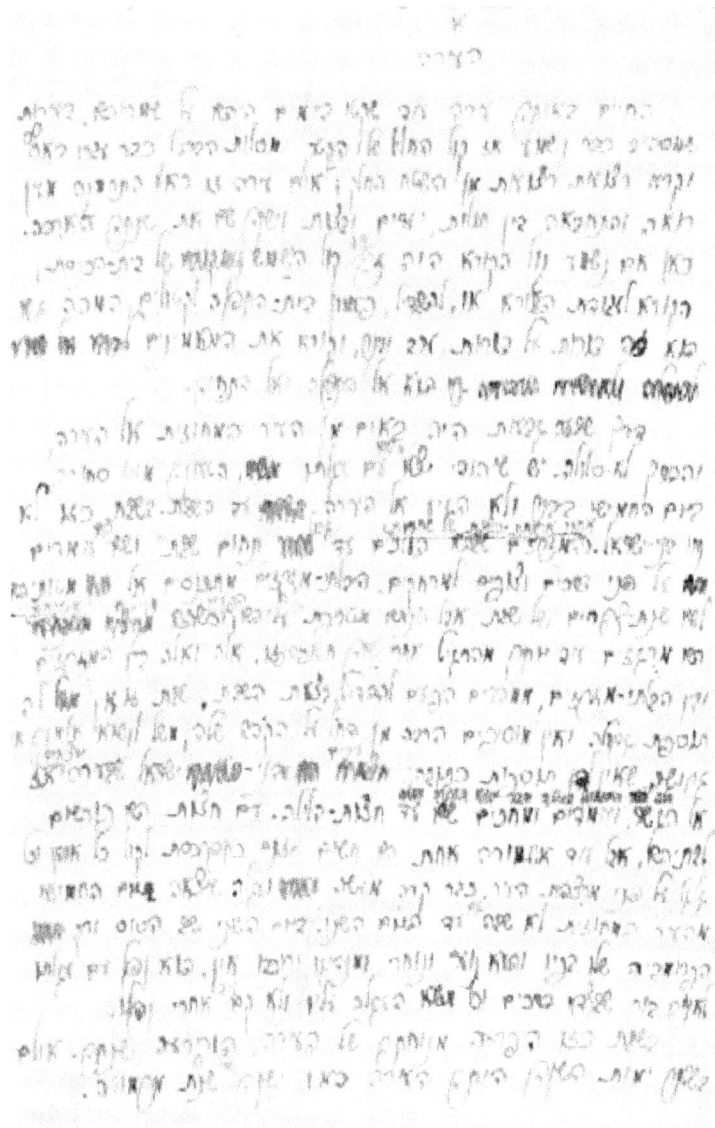

Manuscript from the estate of Fishel Lachower ("The Town")

On such a Sabbath, the town's rest was disturbed. However, on the rest of the days of the years, the town was as it always was from year to year.

[Page 26]

Fishele the Carpenter

Fishele the Carpenter was short in stature, but had a great and important profession. Most of the carpentry for the Jews of the town was done by him. He never earned enough to live on despite being busy with his work from early morning until sunset. Nevertheless, he did not admit to his poverty so as not to have to rely on others. He was blessed with two traits: self–respect and honesty, both of which he lived up to zealously. When he was a candidate for *aliya* to Israel, he refused to fill out the *aliya* questionnaire, for it was against his internal convictions. Therefore, he remained in the Diaspora.

Avraham Weingort

Avraham Weingort

Avraham Weingort was born in 1915 to Miriam and Reb Meir–Yaakov. He displayed talents for his studies during his youth, and he was sent to a Yeshiva in Warsaw. However, when he returned home, he was completely imbued with the Zionist idea, and he dedicated himself to the establishment of Hechalutz. Since he was also active in all the other areas of communal and cultural life in the town, he was greatly beloved by the residents of the town, young and old, on account of his fine traits. Even his political rivals held him in esteem. For some reason, he was unable to make *aliya* together with his parents in 1935. He only received his certificate two years later, and then he made *aliya*. He began to work in the Nesher beer brewery in Rishon Letzion.

He immediately volunteered for Haganah activities, and earned for himself a good name and honorable status in the moshava. He was among the first to respond to the call of the Jewish community to enlist in the Brigade. He joined the Maccabee division. When he went out for training practice in the area of Latrun, the commando who was driving in a Polish Army vehicle had an accident. He died in that accident. This is how one of the best and most famous Jews of Chorzele perished.

Reb Pinchas Eichelbaum

Reb Pinchas Eichelbaum was one of the prominent individuals of our town. First of all, he stood out with his love of his fellow, and affection he displayed to all the residents of the town. He was of the stock of those Jews who added grace and goodness to the life of the town. Indeed, through the hearts beating inside of them, simple Jews left their mark on the life of the town with their modesty and discreetness.

[Page 27]

Pinchas Eichelbaum as a soldier in the Russian Army (center)

Reb Pinchas was a member of Mizrachi, and he regarded it as a great merit when the possibility of making *aliya* opened up for him and his family. His aforementioned special traits and unique abilities also stood out in the Land.

He was among those who was satisfied with his lot, that he had arrived in the Promised Land.

May his memory be a blessing.

Reb Yosef–Chaim Mar–Chaim

Reb Yosef Chaim Mar–Chaim was one of the important householders of the town. He conducted a forestry business of significant size, excelled in his scholarship, and was known as an expert in the Torah. He made *aliya* to the Land of Israel together with his wife Golda, who was his life partner. They settled in Mekor Chaim near Jerusalem.

He dedicated himself completely to the study of Torah through all his days in the Land of Israel. He would frequent the home of the chief rabbi, Rabbi Kook, of holy blessed memory.

Reb Yosef–Chaim and his wife died, and were buried in the holy city of Jerusalem. They left behind a large family, who were very active in many areas.

[Page 28]

The Przysusker Family

Reb Mendel Przysusker

Reb Mendel, the son of Reb Avraham Przysusker, from one of the oldest and most well–rooted families of our town, managed together with his brother a large tract of land, a brick kiln and a beer brewery known as the Briz. The entire family, including his children Yaakov–Meir (with his wife Sheindel and their children), his son Mordechai, his daughters Miriam, Fruma, Dvora, Rivka, and Sara–Chana, his sister Esther with her husband Reb Mordechai–Mendel Frajdman, his sister Perl with her husband Reb Chaim Rozenzwajg, his brother Pinchas Przysusker with his wife Krusa, all centered around these businesses, which were located in the courtyard of the family of Reb Mendel Przysusker.

Reb Mendel lost his wife Chaya Perl when he was still young, but he remained a widower and did not marry again despite the urging of his family, his friends, and the Hasidim who were close to him. Despite the fact that he was Orthodox and Hasidic, his connection with his first wife was one of great love that cannot be described in words and could not be severed with the vicissitudes of fate.

Reb Mendel was one of the people suffused with Jewish grace and glory, who imparted Jewish splendor throughout Poland. His appearance commanded respect. He was a wise, upright, and successful businessman. He was accepted and honored by all the townsfolk. He was involved with all aspects of communal life, simple in his mannerisms, and friendly with the common folk. He would frequent government offices where they respected his opinions and ideas. Reb Mendel was an uncompromisingly religious man, but he was above Jewish and Hassidic zealotry. He was especially careful about the commandments between man and his fellowman. He never crossed a border, and never set foot on German soil. He would explain this by stating that he found in an obscure book that the German nation descends from Amalek, and one should be careful not to enter into their domain.

Reb Mendel stood out in his longing and pining for the Land of Israel, but his wide–branched business endeavors and his strong family ties prevented him from making *aliya* and settling there. He died at the hands of the Nazi enemy, and perished along with the members of the community that he served during his lifetime with pride, benevolence, and comfort.

We can speak about Reb Pinchas and Krusa Przysusker in one breath, for they were not only husband and wife, but they were also forged from the same material – both were upright and pure, refined, truthful, and careful about physical and spiritual cleanliness. Both were modest people, who were satisfied with little. They worked at their share in the common family business to meet their basic needs. Their expenses were not great since they did not have children. They lived a simple lifestyle, as is fitting for modest people who are satisfied with organized family life, in the work of one's hands, and in the labor of one's hands.

[Page 29]

Reb Pinchas and Krusa Przysusker

Reb Pinchas and Krusa Przysusker belonged to the group of good, simple people, who symbolized all that was good and sublime in the Jewish towns of Poland.

*

Mordechai Przysusker (Biren), the young son of Reb Mendel and Chaya–Perl was treated specially by his sisters who raised him, for he was orphaned from his mother Chaya–Perl when he was still a baby. Chaya–Perl was an intelligent, dear woman, beautiful and beloved by all who knew her. When the child grew up and became a lad, he was already graced with special traits – expertise and sharpness, natural intelligence, and a friendly manner with people. These traits stood out especially when he became a young man and began to direct the wide–branched family businesses. He was especially talented in matters requiring constant contact with the authorities. Despite his many business endeavors, Mordechai found time to take care of communal matters. He was especially dedicated to issues with running the public bank and the fire fighters organization.

When he made *aliya*, he became involved in the establishment of the first beer brewery in the Land (Nesher in Rishon Letzion), which he directed for many years. Even here, despite being very busy with his business, he dedicated all his free time to the organization of former residents of Chorzele.

Mordechai Przysusker (Biren) was the chairman of the organization, and he was the one who laid the foundations for its proper functioning. He made great efforts to establish the charitable fund of the former residents of Chorzele, and to perpetuate their memory in a special grove in the Martyrs Forest in the mountains of Jerusalem. Until his last day, he stood at the head of all activities of the organization. His memory will be guarded by us forever.

Translator's Footnotes

1. "Here I am, poor in worthy deeds" recited by the cantor prior to the *Musaf* service on the High Holy Days.

2. See http://www.halachipedia.com/index.php?title=Techum

3. The *Ketuba* is the marriage contract that specifies an amount to be paid upon dissolution of a marriage. There is an additional amount specified that does not apply to the marriage of a widow or a divorcee. The author is evidently trying to display his halachic prowess with these analogies.

[Page 30]

The Legend of Chorzele...
by Simcha Adler
Translated by Jerrold Landau

Tidbits from the Table of Memories...

I, Simcha Adler, the son of Reb Moshe–Shimon, prayer leader and ritual slaughterer (*shochet*), have come here to tell a bit about myself and a lot about my town. My story will survey the way of life in Chorzele during my era.

I was nine months old when my parents arrived to settle in Chorzele in 1893. (We came from a town called Grabowo in Greater Poland.) That year, the community of Chorzele had a population of approximately 150 families. From that time, I recall the old *shamash* in the synagogue, Todros. Was he the first (the synagogue did not seem old)? Was the rabbi who served there at that time the first?

Who were the first settlers, and when did they arrive? Were they border smugglers? — for Chorzele was on the border of East Prussia, and much of its livelihood came from that manner. The only manufacturing enterprise was the "Broiz" founded by Grandfather, whom I knew in his old age. He was the first of the Przysuker dynasty.

When I grew up, I started to get to know the town, its houses, its streets, the "Marek" that was square as a final *Mem*. It had a well in the middle, which was rarely used in those days, other than in the event of a fire. I got to know the river, the wooden bridge, and the nearby forest. All of this created a homey feeling. This feeling was strengthened by the mannerisms of the people, as if they were responsible for each other.

We lived for a few years in the courtyard of Mendel Sporn, and then moved to live in the courtyard of Reb Yossel Meir Leib's, where we were neighbors with his son–in–law Reb Kalman Ajzenstat. My father of blessed memory needed a large yard for the slaughter of fowl. He would make a small hole in the ground, and cover it after the slaughter with dirt that he took from the oven. This is how he maintained cleanliness and hygiene[1], for only a few feathers fluttered about and circled over the ground when the wind caught them.

Simcha–Yaakov Sporn
One of the first *Haskalah* [enlightenment] adherents of Chorzele

Even as the family grew, we lived in two rooms, another small room, and a kitchen, where the maid's cot was located. There were no windows in the small room. There were two beds in it, in which four children slept. There was no room for a chair. A small crate was attached to the wall, which had four "Kopelech"[2] into which Father was very insistent that we place our heads when we slept. The straw upon which we slept was changed once a year. What was taken out was called "*Shetshk*e". We had to soften the straw before going to sleep, for it had become hard as a rock after a night of sleeping upon it. My brother Aharon liked to sleep very late, and he was a big "pest" during his childhood – his hand was in everything and everyone's hand was upon him. (Father would say about him: when the "*mazik*"[3] is asleep, it is good for him and good for the world.)

[Page 31]

Around 1898, the rabbi of the city moved to serve in the city of Turek. As he left, the splendor of the Czortkow Hassidim departed, and they divided up into a *shtibel*, and a *minyan* that took place in the Broiz house every Sabbath. Rabbi Koblaski, the son of the rabbi of Grabowo, came after him. Father had originally been the prayer leader and *shochet* in that town, and he was the one who recommended the new rabbi.

In its time, the Large *Beis Midrash* was full of studying youths. The writer Fishel Lachower was among them[4]. People came from other places so they could be imbued with his influence. I met several of them many years later in London, who spoke about him with reverence. He later came to Włocławek on the recommendation of Nachum Sokolow, where he supported Rabbi Reines in the founding of Mizrachi.

I recall a large fire that began near the house of Yankel "Einbinder" [the binder] and quickly spread to the "Stadales", which burned like boxes of matches, for their roofs were covered with straw and the wind blew from the side. After this event, the town purchased fire extinguishing machines that operated as a well. Four men would stand on each side to operate it. The rubber pipe would be placed into the well in the Marek, from which it would draw water to put out the fire. The families that suffered from the fire were hosted in private houses as well as the small *Beis Midrash.* Yankel "Einbinder" came to live with us until his house was rebuilt. That is how we became friendly with him. Later, I would often visit him to read the books that he had for binding.

This was the era of the *Haskalah* [enlightenment]. The influence of Peretz Smolenskin[5] (in his book: A Wanderer on the Path of Life), Mapu, and Mendele Mocher Sefarim was felt greatly. Those who received influence from them wished to impart this influence to others. Their method was to gather the workers together and lecture to them on Sabbath afternoons in the *cheder* of Yidel Melamed [the teacher]. They commenced the activity with *Pirkei Avot*[6], and they did not encounter opposition since this was connected to tradition. Then they would conduct a public prayer service next to the prayer leader's podium. Simcha Yaakov Sporn and Moshe Ajzensztat were among the first and most active of the *Haskalah.*

In our town, as in all towns, the heads of the *Haskalah* movement were autodidacts – that is, lads (in most cases boys from well–off families) who gained their education through reading and self–study. Since they were free from the worries of livelihood of their families (they were bachelors), so they dedicated all their time to reading everything that came their way. Some of them had the opportunity to obtain books in various branches of the sciences, fine literature (in Hebrew, Yiddish, Russian, Polish, and German) as well as textbooks for language study (including French). The enlightened lads were thirsty for knowledge, not only for themselves, but also to raise the cultural level of their surroundings.

[Page 32]

My brother Avraham–Michel (eighteen years old) began the activity. He was very attached to the *aggadaic* [lore] stories of the Talmud. He listened to such wonderful stories with great attention. This continued until Father became ill with a severe case of typhus that lasted for several months. Then Yidel stopped giving his lessons in the *cheder* for fear of infection. Later, they continued for some time to meet in the small *Beis Midrash*, until the endeavor was canceled due to lack of energy to continue.

Moshe Ajzenstat, one of the *Maskilim* of the town

The *Haskalah* was associated with the following names: Avraham–Michel was called the *Maskil*, and his friend Yaakov Brzoza was called the *Choker* [Researcher]. Avraham–Michel attempted to learn Russian from Kirpichnikov's grammar book. It would not have made sense to study Polish, the language of the people, since Russia was the governing power, and the petitions were in Russian.

The merchants and shopkeepers learned to speak Polish through their contact with the gentiles (most of whom were farmers, and Polish language skills were not of a high level). They did not have to write in Polish, and it was not worthwhile to keep themselves from Torah study in order to learn that language.

Rabbi Rozenstrauch, a worldly, intelligent man, came to us after Rabbi Koblaski. The lads from various places did not return to the *Beis Midrash*, and it became almost empty. It was the era of pogroms in Russia, and there was an impetus to leave and wander off to America. The rabbi attempted to continue with tradition and to conduct a Yeshiva in his home, but few people attended. He also attempted to interfere with the founding of the library that was our ideal, and for which we struggled. The rabbi also lashed out against the fact that we would read *Hashiloach*, even though he himself read the Russian newspaper *Rusikai Viedamasti* daily to demonstrate his status as an erudite person who knows the language of the land. He later moved to Olkusz. He only succeeded in establishing two things in Chorzele: turning the roof of the entranceway into the Women's Gallery, and setting up the Fish Hut next to the fields of the gentiles. The Fish Hut is certainly still standing today.

During those times, several young mothers lost their lives from typhus. My mother died on Tisha B'Av 1902. The wife of Yankel Einbinder, the wife of Shalom Einbinder, and other women whose names I do not recall also died at that time. My mother of blessed memory had lost her mother and father by the time she married Father. She would send me with packages of soup to the houses of a sick child whose father was in America (I took care to carry out my mission in secrecy, so that the neighbors would not find out about it). My mother was tall, of thin build, dark haired, with fiery eyes. She conducted her household as a woman of valor. She was loved and held in esteem by all the members of the town. She died at the age of 35.

[Page 33]

I was ten years old, and I did not understand the tragedy that had taken place in my life. I knew that I was now an orphan, and this would arouse mercy. The children had pity on me in the *cheder* as well, and were not cruel to each other for a certain period. As was the custom, our maid was fired immediately after the death of my mother. Sara and Miriam, the two daughters of our neighbor Kalman, took care of us five children. There was a great closeness among the neighbors. They participated in the concerns of the family, and took part in their joyous occasions as well as any tragedy and illness that afflicted the heart.

In the meantime, my brother Avraham–Michel was taken into the army, and Father brought his third wife into the home. Avraham–Michel returned from the army after four years (he had served in Tsaritsyn[7]). In 1910, I went to Palestine as a *chalutz* [Zionist pioneer] with two other people from our town. These were days of fear for the Jews of Russia, when the Chornaya Sutniya began to attack Jews, and the government secretly supported the attackers. Jews began to escape to America and any other country that would accept them. Jews who had a connection to Palestine or who were unable to travel to lands farther away due to lack of means also traveled to Palestine.

The youth made their own accounting and began to rebel against the placidness of their parents. The romanticism of Zionist pioneering attracted the youth – a return to the land and becoming proficient in productive trades in the Land of Israel. The Zionist congresses had their influence, for they were in accordance with their spirit. The word "Zionists" penetrated and took root in our city as well. An additional word began to be tossed around on the Jewish street, a word that made our good Jewish mothers very afraid: "Socialists." It too took hold among us.

A portion of the rabbi's livelihood came from *shechita* (ritual slaughter). The rabbinical teacher also benefited from it. In addition, the rabbi and the cantor received a stipend from every wedding that took place, as well as from rabbinical judgments that for the most part took place in the presence of "arbitrators." The rights to receive the income of two kopecks from selling every portion of yeast was in the hands of Dovka, a widow who owned a general store in the market. Her fame came from her son–in–law (*Dovka's Eidem*), who was the only groom in town who came from Lithuania ("*der Litvak*").

The *gabbai* of the synagogue, and perhaps also of the *Beis Midrash*, was Reb Aharon Yechiel, a grain merchant and the in–law of Yehoshua Herzog. At the conclusion of services on weekdays, the *shamash* would walk through the congregation with the *pushka* (charity box), as everyone donated coins for the upkeep of the synagogue. There was a small box with a hole for coins next to the door on one of the walls of the synagogue. "*Matan Beseter*" [discrete gifts] was written upon it. When the elderly Todros, the *shamash* of the synagogue died, Shlomo the Rabbi's, the son of the rabbi who had been buried in our town cemetery, took his place. Hershele Yupak served as the *shamash* of the synagogue.

[Page 34]

The Names of the Bride and Groom...

There were days when "*Tateshe*" [Daddy] returned home from visiting his Rebbe. He would enter his house and declare, "Mazel tov, our daughter is engaged." Those days passed with "a sigh." Then the function of the *shadchan* [marriage broker] became obvious. Every Jew was able to become a *shadchan*, whether he occupied himself in that role for his own benefit, or whether to save a Jewish soul from singlehood, especially if she was the daughter of well–off parents... The *shadchan* had his eyes in his head as he attempted to solicit the interest both sides, to get them to meet, and to allow those who "speak of their honor" to get to know each other knowingly or unknowingly.. If interest develops, the lad would met the girl for a stroll, and a conversation would be conducted in the third person: "What does she say? Or "Her mother is very nice..."

In the interim, the parents would discuss the matter of dowry and the years of support during which the groom would be supported at the table of his father–in–law, and the dwelling that would be given to him upon his marriage. When they reached an agreement, they would write the *tenaim* [pre-marital agreement]. One condition would state that if the groom rescinds the offer of marriage, he would pay a fine for the anguish caused to a Jewish girl.

After the engagement, the groom would be invited to the house of his future father–in–law for a Sabbath. The lad would bring a present to the bride (*charuzim*), and the groom would receive a gold watch with a chain from his future father–in–law. The free side of the watch would be attached to a hole in the vest. The groom would button the hole for security and place the watch in his pocket. This aroused the desire to take out the watch on frequent occasions, to give a light push with the thumb to the pin when the cover would jump off and open on its own. He would briefly examine the many lines showing the minutes, the small hand that moved constantly, and be amazed at this wonder that he was wearing...

The parents did not agree that love would be a fundamental factor in the marriage. They would say, "There is no assurance that those in love will continued with their pleasantness. Love blinds. It can come after the wedding." They would discuss the honor of the woman, and also denounce her. However, the woman was non–understandable to them. They did not make efforts to understand her, and that which they did not understand – they denigrated. For religious reasons, they continued with family connections where "he found"[8], for "regarding divorce – the altar sheds tears"....

World literature during that era, which was read in translation, was secular, romantic, and poetic. Love was the daughter of the heavens, and we fell in love with love. We loved its beauty, with purity and splendor. The feminine creation – the young maiden, enchanted us in all her pleasant mannerisms, with her eyes and her hair, her face and her small mouth. With our youthful dreams, we dreamt of our happiness to find such a woman... Master of the World! How much grace did you impart to the daughters of Eve.

The groom would be called to the Torah on the Sabbath prior to his wedding. He would receive the maftir *aliya*. As he descended from the *bima*, the woman from the gallery would throw raisins at him as a good omen and for good fortune. The friends of the bride would gather on the Sabbath to spend some time with her, to encourage her, and to make her happy. They would drink wine,

[Page 35]

lick up everything, and dance. They would feel the bride's gown and hair, and speak about the wedding day with a sense of jealousy and compassion.

Then the wedding day arrived.

All the relatives from near and far came to the wedding, for this was a family event. If anyone was lacking in funds for the return trip, they would ask the in–laws...

The wedding took place in two houses. The bride was in one house, dressed in a white dress, with a double veil on her head. She sat at the side, and her friends surrounded her. She did not dance. She did not taste any food all day, for it was a fast day for her. There was a great deal of preparation taking place around her. Soon the musicians and the jesters would arrive to play the "*oyfshpiel.*" Instead of jesting, the jester would talk about issues of the day in a voice full of emotion and devotion, "It is your day of judgment, bride, so weep..."

The house was full of guests. The girls would come in attractive, red velvet dresses with long sleeves. The cuffs would spread out in the fashion of flower leaves, covering the hands until the arm (the fingers looked like full sheaths). Every girl's neck was decorated with lattice over the chest. Her hair was done with a strand in the center of the head. A braid would surround the head in the form of a wreath. She would be wearing golden earrings. Who can describe the grace and beauty of the girls on that day!

The girls danced the waltz, polka, and polka mazurka with each other. This was a natural dance, with vocalization, as if fitting for young girls. The dresses would flutter as they circled, as if they were crinolines. Their faces were beaming. How rare were the opportunities to dance...

The mothers arrived later. The breasts of even the thinnest and most delicate of them were prominent. They danced enthusiastically and clutched their heads with importance. Their dance was a bit awkward. They jumped as if they were doing the hip hop. Their faces beamed with joy.

The groom was in the second house. The lads sat next to him, drinking wine and cracking nuts, until the groom was taken to the *bedekin* [veiling ceremony]. He approached the bride, lowered the double veil, and covered her face. Then came the turn of the jester. He spoke about the preciousness of women in general, and of the bride in particular, who followed the footsteps of her praiseworthy, important, honorable, pure and pristine mother, a woman of valor in the conduct of her house, and a dedicated mother to her children. The fortunate mother who reached this great day, to bring her daughter to the wedding canopy so she will become a housewife... The entire family listened to the slickness of the jester. The mother enjoyed it more than anyone. She wept.

They brought the groom back to his place. He remained there until the groomsmen and musicians arrived to lead him to the *chupa* next to the synagogue. The groomsmen led the groom in a procession in which they all joined. The musicians played joyous songs known to everybody.

The groom was stood under the *chupa*, facing east. He covered his eyes with a fine, white, folded, handkerchief. The musicians who accompanied the bride played once again. Those assembled received candles, which were lit one from the next. The mothers of the groom and bride held the bride, and together

[Page 36]

led her around the groom seven times. They would then stand her to the left of the groom. The cantor sang "*Mi Adir*"[9].

The *shamash* poured a cup of wine for the rabbi, who recited a blessing over it. They gave the groom to drink, but he only took a taste. The mother lifted the veil from the bride and put the cup to her lips. She tasted the wine. The rabbi then told the groom to recite the formula word for word as he placed the ring on the index finger of her right hand: "Behold you are married to me with this ring in accordance with the law of Moses and Israel." The rabbi read the *ketuba* [marriage document] in the Aramaic language, and recited the *Sheva Brachot* [Seven Blessings]. At the end, the *shamash* placed a glass on the ground, and the groom broke it with one stroke, as a sign of his strength. Those gathered broke out with a blessing of "Mazal Tov!"

Then, everyone returned to the home where long tables were set up for the meal. The musicians played their melodies, such as "Tirel Lirel Lumpapa!" This was joyous. The bride took hold of the groom's arm, for he was now her husband and support. When they arrived at the home, they were brought into a room where they remained alone for the *Yichud* [ritual seclusion as part of the wedding ceremony].

They would bring the groom to sit with the men (even there, the men would sit separately from the women). When it came time once again for the *Sheva Brachot*, they would bring in the bride and seat her next to the groom. After the Grace After Meals, they would fill two cups of wine. The person reciting the blessings would pour one cup into the other, and give them to the bride and groom to drink. Then the jester would appear and recite the list of gifts as a "gift sermon." He would sing with such breaths as if pieces of rubber were stuck in his throat, as he praised the gifts as "gifts fit for a king." "So and so from the bride's side, a pair of silver candlesticks for candle lighting, the gift announcement."; "so and so from the bride's side, a spice box for *Havdalah*, the gift announcement." Dra-a-a-sha Gesha-a-ank, Dra-a-asha Geshank."[10]

They would then arise to dance the Mitzva Dance. This was the dance of the elders. They would place their hands on the shoulders of their fellow and close the circle, with the bride in the center. Someone would take a red handkerchief out from his back pocket with a flourish and give the edge to the bride to hold. When they stopped dancing, the bride disappeared. The guests began to disperse, wishing each other, "We should meet at happy occasions."

The next day, the grandmothers would gather to take part in the mitzvah. They would walk with bent backs. They would be wearing a type of hairdo with a bonnet that waved as they walked. A strand of velvet was tied under their chins, so it would not move. This added a sense of grace and honor to their appearance...

The grandmothers cut the bride's hair. From that time, she would wear a wig. At that time, her own hair would disappear, for the wind played with them as if playing a trick. They would make sure that the wig would match the color of her hair. At that time, the procedures of the bride ended, and the procedures of a wife began..."

The *Sheva Brachot* lasted for an entire week. A light meal was served. The main thing was those two glasses of wine, that were poured from one to another before a blessing was recited over them. They would spend some time singing secular songs. Somebody would sing: "With no money one cannot be proud," a popular song in those days.

[Page 37]

The Child and the Yoke of Commandments...

The course of life went on. A child was born with "Mazel Tov!" Children were sent from the *cheder*s to the home of the new mother to read *Shir Hamaalot*[11]. The children were given packets of nuts.

On the Sabbath eve prior to the circumcision, they would make a *Shalom Zachar*. Friends would come, eat salted chickpeas and drink beer. For the bris, they would bring in the chair of Elijah the Prophet, upon which the *sandek*[12] would sit enwrapped in a *tallis*. This honor would be given to the family elder. The baby would be taken from his mother's bed and given over to the *kvatter*. The *kvatter* would transfer the baby onward until he reaches the *sandek*'s lap. The *mohel*, with his flowing beard, would begin with the blessing over the wine. Those who were finicky would keep their distance to the extent possible. When they heard the screams of the baby, they knew that he had entered into the covenant of Abraham our Forefather. Someone was honored with the mitzvah of *metzitza*, and the *mohel* would place several drops of wine into the baby's mouth. The *mohel* would declare the name of the baby and state: This young one will grow up! In your blood you shall live, and it is said to you, in your blood you shall live[13]! The father, enwrapped in his *tallis*, recited the blessing regarding the bringing of the child into the covenant of Abraham our Forefather. They baby would be returned to his mother's bosom. They would sit down to eat and drink.

They would bring a cradle into the house and lay the baby down in it. If he cried for a short time, they would rock the cradle until he calmed down. However, if he cried for an extended period, the mother would try to comfort him with a song:

At my child's cradle

Stands a golden goat

The gold will do business

With raisins and nuts.

Another song from Goldfaden's[14] repertoire is as follows:

In the Holy Temple

In a corner room...

As customary, the mother would nurse the baby. However, under certain circumstances, the baby would be fed from a bottle with a nipple on top. There were cases where they would hire a healthy village woman to nurse the baby, when there was a risk to life.

Another child, and another child came. If the situation allowed for it, a maid would be hired to supervise the children's hygiene and clothing.

In his fifth year, a boy would be brought for a term, that is to study from Passover until Sukkot, or vice versa. There were two teachers of young boys in our town: Avraham–Leib and Aharon–Yankel (the latter was a Hassid, and the Hassidic children studied with him). Avraham–Leib served as the Torah reader in the synagogue on the Sabbath. (He was our teacher).

[Page 38]

The father would bring the child to the *cheder*. The first time, the teacher would open the siddur with the large letters, and tell the child to look at them. He would hold the pointer at the *aleph*, and say to him, "Be a good boy and learn quickly." Suddenly, several kopecks would fall on the siddur. This was a present from the good angel who loves good kids. Then the father would leave and the child would be greeted by the other children, some with encouragement and some with anger.

At *cheder*, the child would learn to read the *aleph beit*, to recite *Modeh Ani* and the *Krishma* – the *Shema*. After two years, he would know how to pray from the siddur. He would then transfer to the "*Stelmach*" [wheelwright] to learn *Chumash* and *Rashi*. Then he would transfer to Feivish to study Gemara, where he would study the case of the ox who gored the cow in Tractate *Bava Kama*, or Tractate *Gittin*, *Ketubot*, or *Kiddushin*. There were Talmudic discussions such as "He said, and she said" which the mind could not grasp. They would be misty, and the answers were not clear. Suddenly the teacher would be standing next to you, and ask, "So, where are you holding?" I would awaken as if from a slumber, and a pall would fall upon me. He certainly sensed that I was not listening, and was daydreaming.

A law was issued by the Russian government that the *cheder* children must attend a school for two hours a day to learn Russian. The teacher was an elderly, weak Pole, and there were several children in his class. He taught the gentile boys and girls in the morning, and continued with us in the afternoon, when he had no more strength. We did not learn a lot.

In the winter, when the day was short, we would return to *cheder* in the afternoon. We would bring a kopeck for kerosene, and sit there until a late hour. We would make a paper lantern to light up the way home, like the pillar of fire.

There was another *cheder*, unique in its type. This was the Talmud Torah for poor children. The fathers of the town made sure that all Jewish children would know how to pray and recite Psalms. The Talmud Torah was next to the large *Beis Midrash*. The teacher was a short, stout Litvak [Lithuanian] who would laugh with an open mouth. He would sleep on a bench in the *cheder*, and eat at different homes on a rotation basis. He did not like potatoes, only noodles and egg drops. He would beat his students for his enjoyment. He would lay the child on the bench, put his head between his legs, pull down his pants, and whip him with a four–thong whip until the child thrashed with all his might. Those who experienced this would wail for several hours. Nobody protected the children of the poor people...

The parents sent their daughters to Yidel the teacher learn how to read and write in Yiddish, and then to the Blind Mottel. The laundry iron press was next to his *cheder*, and the noise did not interfere with the studies.

We studied with the aim of gaining knowledge. We learned how to write in Yiddish with the orthography of that time. We also learned arithmetic (addition, subtraction, multiplication) without a teacher. We helped each other, and we developed the aspiration to study other languages in an external fashion.

[Page 39]

The last of my teachers was David–Leib. He was sickly, and died several months after I finished learning with him. His father of blessed memory, who was a great scholar, reviewed the Talmudic lesson with me twice a week. In the morning, I went to the *Beis Midrash* to study a page of Gemara on my own. I continued on to study *Tanach* [Bible] and used all of the commentaries, including the Malbim[15]. This was not acceptable to the parents, who did not look favorably on the study of *Tanach*.

I was called up to the Torah when I reached Bar Mitzvah. My father recited the *Baruch Sheptarani* blessing[16], and I entered the yoke of commandments...

To Greet the Sabbath...

The townsfolk were busy with the worries of earning a livelihood all the days of the week. A large part of the livelihood came from the market days, when villagers would come to buy and sell. Our yard was filled with farmers' wagons who entered via the gate on the Bridge Street side. The farmers settled themselves into the home of Yosel-Meir Leib's (Pani Mankarsz) and smoked strong machorka[17]. The house was full of thick, sharp smoke that burned the eyes. The members of the household were busy in their iron implements shop that day. There was a large rock in the yard. They would place the iron rod on the rock, in accordance with the correct measure, and cut it with a chisel on one side and a heavy mallet. They would bend the rod back and forth until it broke. The echo of the banging and the clanging of the iron filled the yard with noise. (The grandson Mordechai was affected by the noise and became deaf.)

On Thursday, there was extra hustle and bustle as people did their shopping for the Sabbath. People who could afford it would by a chicken or a duck, aside from the meat for the *cholent*. They would buy the fish on Friday from the brothers Eli-Beinish and Heinich, who were assisted by Shmuel Zilarsz. The fish would be sold in the market directly from the barrels, in which they had been brought the previous day from Germany. Pike and bream were the desired species which were enjoyed by everyone. They would make excellent gefilte fish from these types of fish. It would be a disgrace if the only fish that arrived for the Sabbath were smelts.

On Friday afternoons, young and old would stream to the bathhouse and the *mikva* [ritual bath] which were located behind the large *Beis Midrash*. Prior to this, they would cut their nails, place the cuttings into paper, add three pieces of wood, and burn them. One does not cut one's nails on Thursday, because the nails begin to grow on the third day, would be the Sabbath. One must watch out for this...

On the other days of the week, the *mikva* served the mothers and brides. The *tikern* (the widow of Todros the *shamash*) lived close by. The bathkeeper, his wife, and their son who was ill with tuberculosis lived in one room. The entrance to the *mikva* was through that room. When the door was opened, one would see the residents walking around naked. The *mikva* had a pipe through which the hot water was brought in from the large, wood-fueled, oven. People entering the bathhouse would strip, put their clothes on a shelf, take a flask of water, soap themselves, pour the water over their heads, then go to immerse.

Some bathed in a bathtub to warm up their bones (there were two round, wooden bathtubs). They would be filled with almost boiling water. People would sit in them with their head and feet remaining outside. The champion who succeeded in sitting in this heat for five seconds was "The deaf Baruch." He would say, "Oy" and "Ha" with great enjoyment...

[Page 40]

From time to time, a steam bath would be set up in the second room of the *mikva*. They would purchase a *beziml* [little broom] at the entrance, ascend three steps, take a flask of cold water, hold the *beziml*, which has now become very hot, over the head, and use it to whip all parts of the body. Everyone shouted in chorus, "Ay! Ay!" and suddenly, "Enough!, Enough!" They quickly come or slide down. When they went home, they would hide in their clothes and cover their face in such a way that they could only see the eyes and the nose, red as a turkey.

Evening began to fall on Friday. Girls with their hair adorned with a white or blue band, tied like bird wings to their heads, with two braids like two snakes winding down their backs could be seen outside. The movement slowly increased. As if at the same moment, everyone burst forth from their houses to go to the various houses of prayer: some to the synagogue, some to the *Beis Midrash*, and some to the *shtibel*s or other *minyanim*. The last of them arrived, and the streets emptied. The Sabbath fell upon the town.

The Sabbath Queen...

The mother recited the blessing over the candles that were placed in the silver candelabra passed down the generations as an heirloom. The mother, bedecked in jewelry, lit the candles. She moved her hands over the candles in three circles, placed her fingers over her eyes, and recited the blessing in a whisper.

The Sabbath would be greeted in the houses of worship with "*Lecha Dodi Likrat Kala*". Chona Schneider used to lead the Friday night service in the synagogue. When the congregation began to go home, the *shamash* would bang the *bima* twice and announce, "Jews, there is a guest here for the Sabbath." The guest would be immediately snatched up.

The *shtibel*s had also concluded the evening service. The Hassidim were wearing their *zipicha*, their *gartel* around their waste, their velvet cap on the heads, and a red scarf around their necks, even though an *eruv* had been set up for the Sabbath. Here and there, someone wearing a *streimel* could be seen.

The *eruv* permitted people to go outside the city for a distance no more than the Sabbath boundary (2,000 cubits), but whom would think about going to the Sabbath boundary? The distance to the forest was not even that of the Sabbath boundary. Yisraelka Tyk, who would go out on Sabbath afternoons to check that there was no breach in the cemetery fence, did not venture outside the boundary.

When they returned home on Friday night, the men would announce loudly, "*Gut Shabbos.*" Father recited "*Shalom Aleichem Malachei Hasharet*" with feeling, and it seemed that the angels were present even though they could not be seen or felt. This was the additional soul that entered to dwell within us on the Sabbath day, which would see it and sense it.

[Page 41]

It was immediately noted that there is a woman in the house, and one is obligated to declare her glory, therefore one begins: "A woman of valor who can find, for her worth is more than pearls."

Two *challos*, a bottle of wine, and cups were already placed on the table in order to fulfil the commandment of having a set table for the Sabbath. Kiddush was recited on the wine. The *Savri Rabanan* phrase was recited silently. The hands were washed with a cup that held no less than ¾ of a quart. *Hamotzie* was recited, the bread was cut, a piece was broken off and salted, and was eaten. After the fish, the hymn *Kol Mekadesh Shevii Karaui Lo*[18] was sung. After the meat and the tzimmes, the Grace After Meals was recited. If at least three males over the age of Bar Mitzvah were present, the leader would recite in Yiddish: My masters, let us recite Grace," and those present would respond, "We will bless He from Whom we have eaten." The rest would be recited silently. The lips would move until they stopped and closed.

Early in the morning on the Sabbath day, the members of the Psalm Recital group would gather in the large *Beis Midrash*. These were common folk. They did not understand the meaning of the words, but rather enjoyed the reward of performing a mitzvah with the mere recital. They would also worship early, and then clear the place for the second *minyan*.

The Hassidim in the *shtibel*s worshipped late, according to their custom. They stood out in this matter, for they were Hassidim.

A Kohen was called up first to the reading of the Torah. If no Kohen was present, they would call up a Levite in his place, and the Levite would also receive the Levi *aliya* as a Levite[19]. The rabbi would receive the third *aliya*. An important, honorable man would receive the sixth *aliya*. Maftir would be given to a Bar Mitzvah boy or a groom prior to his wedding.

At lunch, after the fish, Father would distribute a small cup of 40% liquor that was purchased from the Russian Monopol. His opinion was that one does not drink liquor, but rather only tastes it on the Sabbath. The main course would be *cholent* and *kigel*[20]. It was good to rest after such a sumptuous meal. And who did not know that it is a pleasure to rest on the Sabbath... After the nap, the Sabbath fruit would be eaten: apples, pears, plums, cherries, etc. Tea with *kichel* would be eaten, and a berry cake would be eaten.

Grandmother would read *Tzena Urena*[21] silently in Yiddish. Her voice sounded weepy, as she recited: "And God said to Moses, go speak to the Children of Israel."

The Third Sabbath meal would be eaten, and we would go to the *Mincha* and *Maariv* services.

The women would sit at home, waiting until nightfall. Then they would recite: God of Abraham, of Isaac, and of Jacob, in Your love...[22]. They would wait until three stars appear in the sky as a sign that the Sabbath has ended.

Lights were lit at home. The men came home and said, "Good week!". *Havdalah* was recited: He who differentiates between holy and profane. When there was no older child, the wife held the four–wicked braided candle. The spice box from the hutch was on the table. The husband recited over the wine "Behold my God of salvations." When he got to "And the Jews had light, joy, gladness, and honor" those assembled answered "so may it be for us." He put down the cup, recited the blessing over the spices, and smelled them. He put his fingers to the candles, looked at is fingernails, and recited the blessing "Who creates the light of the fire." He lifted up the cup, drank from it, and wished everyone a good week once again. Women were not given the *Havdalah* wine to drink lest they grow a beard...

[Page 42]

It was a proper Hassidic custom to conduct a *Melave Malka* [post Sabbath meal].

The Feast of Unleavened Bread – Passover...

When Adar comes, joy increases. When Purim ended, matzo baking would start. We would bake at the home of Rachel–Leah, who brought us milk every morning. The kneading woman [*kneterke*] sat in a room. She kneaded the dough. Twelve women wearing white aprons that covered their entire body stood face to face on both sides of the table that was supported by stilts. They would roll the dough until it was thin and round. The dough would be given to the *redler* who made holes along the matzo with a studded roller. Then it would be given over to the *sheiber* who placed it into the baking oven, from which kosher for Passover matzos emerged.

All the furniture was taken out of the houses and placed in the yard. The double windows would be removed. The rooms would be whitewashed. The aroma of spring encouraged and awakened the desire to act, do, and help.

The search for leaven would be conducted on the night before the festival Crumbs of bread would be placed in several corners. Father would take a wooden cooking spoon in one hand and a bundle of duck feathers in the other hand. I would hold the candle. Father would recite the blessing for the search for leaven, and we children would go and seek out the leaven. He would sweep the leaven into the cooking spoon with the feathers, cover it with a cloth, tie it, and burn everything completely.

After the search for leaven, we would go to the wooden bridge at the Orzyc River, where we would immerse the new tableware that would be used for the first time on this festival. We would draw water for the matzo *shmura* with a special pitcher, to use for baking the next day, the eve of the festival. At home, the Passover dishes would be taken down from the *piekelek*.

I had the job of taking down all the books to air them out, including the large, leather bound set of Talmuds and about a hundred other books. They had to be removed from the shelf and checked page by page due to the suspicion that crumbs of *chometz* might have fallen into the pages while eating or reading.

On the morning of the eve of the festival, prior to 9:00 a.m., we would quickly eat three rolls of bread with coffee. 9:00 a.m. would be the transfer time. We would have to eat on the porch, for the inside was already sealed off from *chometz*.

We would go to bake matzo *shmura*. Here, the men did all the work: they kneaded, rolled, etc. They recited verses and sang. The matzo *shmura* was very expensive, and was designated only for father, and only for the Seder nights.

In the afternoon, we would eat potatoes with borscht. This borscht would be brought from the cellar, where there was a barrel of beets that had been picked for some time, had become sharp and sour, with the taste of good wine.

We would go to Fiszlender to get a haircut (he lived in a one room attic). Many people would be waiting.

[Page 43]

He received a "*machinka*" from his daughter in America, but he did not know how to use it, so he continued to work with scissors. He was not the only Jewish barber in the town. There were people in the town who grew their hair like monks. There was also Notka Yaakov–Pesach's who had a haircutting machine. I would say to him, "Notka, I am already big, and I want you to leave me a *grzyba*."[23]

I went to the son of Chaim to purchase a hat that he had brought from Warsaw. He would look at me, measure my head size with his glance, and say, "Number 32 will fit you." It did not fit. He would put two fingers on one side of the hat, two fingers on the other side, and pull it forcefully until they had made a knock. He put the hat back on my head and said, "It fits you," as he pulled me to the mirror on the wall.

At home I found out that they brought a new coat from Feivel–Berl. I was fortunate, for he was the best tailor, and he would sew for me. At Father's order, they would make it wider, so it would also fit me five years hence. I went to the synagogue with the new coat and hat, and felt like a scarecrow in the fields...

There was a spring wind, and an encouraging feeling. The prayers were recited by Father in the festive melody that was unique to him. I believe that the festivals have their own additional soul.

At home, all the preparations for the Seder were made. Father would wear his *kittel*. There would be a large pillow on the chair to lean upon, as a sign of royalty. Everyone sat around the long table in a crowded fashion. Many exacting preparations had been made. The *maror* [bitter herbs] was checked to ensure they were strong, and the *charoses* was checked to see it has been made properly. There were three matzos on a plate, covered with a cloth. Everything was set up in accordance with the laws of Passover: the shank bone, the *karpas*, etc., some on the right side and some on the left.

Father was a scholar, but he nevertheless reviewed the laws, even though he knew them well, to ensure that no error would be made, Heaven forbid, in any of the minutiae of the Seder.

We would wait impatiently. We were very hungry. The weakness penetrated to the heart, but we sat patiently, with appreciation and reverence for everything that Father was doing. He began by explaining the essence of the festival, the exodus from Egypt. We did not rush, for it is a mitzvah to tell the story at length.

We filled the cups of wine. Father recited Kiddush out loud, and we recited it after him. The youngest present asked the four questions. Every word was a question. When he finished, we all broke out in unison in the recitation of "We were slaves." Only someone who has read books about those who were captive or sold as slaves could understand, "and today we are free" in its unique sense.

We recited the *haggadah*, and stopped to listen to explanations and commentary, until we finally reached the meal. The first course was a hardboiled egg in salt water. We ate with an appetite. However, I suddenly got a stomach ache. The pain grew worse, and I writhed. However, I had to continue on.

Father took the *maror* with his fingers. The portion was the size of an olive [*kezayit*], which is equivalent to a small egg. He swallowed it, and it got stuck in his throat. We were afraid. Avraham–Michel stuck his finger into Father's mouth,

[Page 44]

to take remove *maror*. There were tears in Father's eyes. However, he quickly resumed the Seder as if nothing had happened.

The Seder continued until after midnight. We drank the four cups in accordance with the law. We ate the *afikoman* (a custom that turned into a law because it was a custom). Wearily but with excitement, we recited *Chad Gadya*.

Throughout the festival we played with nuts: *nis* and *druit*, or seven *gribelech*, three next to three and one on top. We tossed a nut from afar. If it fell on top, we would take everything. If it feel on one of the three, we would only take that. I always lost my nuts.

The same Seder took place on the second night. However the additional soul was somewhat diminished, it did not tolerate repetition...

Between the Festivals...

Seven weeks, would be counted from Passover until Shavuot. This was known as the counting of the Omer. Weddings did not take place throughout the entire time, other than on the day of Lag B'Omer. All of our festivals, with the exception of Rosh Hashanah and Yom Kippur, were connected to historical events.

The Shavuot festival in the month of Sivan is the festival of the Giving of the Torah. The gates of heaven open at midnight. After we ate, we returned to the houses of worship and continued with prayer, supplication, and the recitation of Psalms. I raised my eyes toward the heavens. My soul desired to see the wonders, but I feel asleep. I saw the wonders in a dream...

There is a special charm to the recitation of *Akdamus*. It has its own rhythm. There is praise to G–d with sublime excitement, imparting pleasure to the heart and soul.

At this point, the season was particularly enchanting. The harsh, Polish winter had been forgotten. We enjoyed the heat of the sun and the aroma of the grass and fields. There were pleasant trees filled with green leaves in the forest. It was as if the place sang a song to the life that had awakened.

The only fruit orchard owned by the priest was leased to Yissachar the tailor as it was every year. We would go to the garden with Nachman Tikulsker to eat of the fruit. We quieted the noisy dog with *"Czycho Burek."* He listened to the command and went away. We had a ten [money bill] and we were able to eat of the apples, brown, sweet pears, and plums until we got a stomach ache... When we did not go to the orchard, we would buy the fruit from the women sitting in the market. They had *"milters"* and *"angres"* that were sold by weight, as well as stems that were given for a kopeck. They had cherries, and sometimes also berries.

On days when it did not rain, we would go to swim in the river. Behind the wooden bridge, we would turn right through the fields next to the forest, and reach the "Small Reide." On Friday, we would go to the "Large Reide," a bit far away, behind the slaughterhouse. We would swim to the other side of the river. We would try to wait

[Page 45]

for the two champions who made motions with their hands (Hirsch Dan and Avraham Sher). Who could compare to them? They were older, and they had long arms and legs.

We returned to get dressed. We stood naked between heaven and earth. There was no shame and no modesty. We were children of nature and the world for a few moments..

The Nine Days [prior to Tisha B'Av] arrived. We did not eat meat. We purchased butter, sour cream, hard cheese, and eggs from a Jewish villager who came to the market twice a week with his wagon.

The *shochtim* rested. Father went to expiate his sin in a cottage for seven days, for the sin of slaughtering a small animal outside the slaughterhouse. There was an immediate need for meat when a large animal was declared *treifa*[24]... He took his samovar, the Gemara, and pillows, and set them up in a comfortable fashion. We brought him food from the house. Relatives came to visit him in the cottage. They would come and go as they pleased. The door would only be closed at night.

The Days of Awe

As time goes on, the month of *Elul* arrived. The Days of Awe were approaching.

Father rehearsed with the singers every night as the holy days approached. If they sang incorrectly, he would shout, *"Treif, treif."*

The High Holy Days instilled fear upon all the townsfolk. They would awaken themselves to repentance, for there is no person who does not sin, some on purpose, and others by accident – and not merely with an impure thought.

During the month of *Elul* one would visit the graves of their forebears, to supplicate and awaken regret in the heart. Unhealed wounds would be reopened. Heartbreaking weeping would be heard.

Father, who regularly woke up at 5:00 to study his daily page of Talmud, did not rest during these days. He could be found in the cemetery early in the morning, memorializing the departed with the *Kel Maleh Rachamim*[25] prayer for anyone who requested such. Mourners would not visit the cemetery during the first year. When I would visit my mother's grave and whisper silently, it was if she heard my conversation, "My mother, my mother, why did you leave me. You were so young, and we were still children..."

Pirkei Avot[26] would be recited each Sabbath starting from the beginning of *Elul*. On the Saturday night prior to Rosh Hashanah, after midnight, *Selichot* would be recited[27]. The gaze in the eyes would become more serious, the body would thin out as if a heavy load was hovering over it. The fear of the Day of Judgment could be felt. Only one hope encouraged people, that prayer and repentance would avert the harsh decree.

For the book was open, and the hand was writing in the book of memories. We went to worship on the night of Rosh Hashanah with a feeling of fear and oppression. The prayers and supplications continued for both days of the festival. After the *Shacharit* service, Rabbi Rozenstrauch ascended the *bima* with Yisraelke the shofar blower, and they recited a silent prayer. Everyone was enwrapped in their *tallises*, quaking like trees in the wind . The congregation waited, as if streams of water had been streaming, and were now quiet.

[Page 46]

The waiting could be felt. Suddenly a frightful, loud voice could be heard, the voice of the shofar blower reciting, "From the depths I call out to God!"

The Satan was frightened. The *tekiah*, *teruah*, and *shevarim* sounds came out clearly. Father recited aloud to the nation and the community, "Happy is the nation that knows the *teruah* sound"[28] and began the *Musaf* service. After the *Shmonei Esrei*, the *kohanim* ascended to recite the Priestly Blessing. Prior to that they removed their shoes and washed their hands, for they would be standing next to the Holy Ark. The congregation did not have to look at them when they recited the blessing. Rather, they lowered their *tallises* over their faces.

In the afternoon, we walked through the fields to the river for *Tashlich*[29]. We stood next to the river and recited the special prayers. We shook out our clothes, thereby casting off our sins, and we returned with song and hymns.

The days between Rosh Hashanah and Yom Kippur are called the Ten Days of Repentance.

On the night of the eve of Yom Kippur, we fulfilled the custom of waving *kapores*[30]. Two or three children would hold the legs of the chicken and recite the prayer *"Benei Adam"*. When they reached the section "this is my atonement, this is my replacement" they would swing the chicken above their heads, as the chicken spread out its wings to fly and made all sorts of sounds. We finally tossed it under the table. We would eat it the upcoming day at the concluding meal before the fast.

The *gabbai* [synagogue trustee] would sit next to the table in the synagogue anteroom on the afternoon of the eve of Yom Kippur. There were three plates on the table, with a note in each plate indicating to which charity one is donating.

A person would then lie down on the threshold of the synagogue and somebody else would administer 39 lashes with a whip. This was a busy day. Even the women went to the *mikva* that day, and the men went afterward. They did not use the bathtubs that day. Everyone immersed, and everyone was in a rush. Toward the end of the day, people would partake of the final meal. Then the fast began, from evening until evening, an entire day.

Large tallow and wax candles would be brought to the synagogue, which would burn for 24 hours. They would be placed in the sandbox that stood empty all year, for it was designated for this purpose.

They would remove their shoes. They would be wearing white socks. Dry grass would be placed under their feet to make it easier to stand. They would stand when the Ark was open. It would be opened many times.

The cantor began with his private supplication in which he asked permission to pray for his congregation as its representative. He began *"Hineni Heani Mimaas"*[31]. His voice grew stronger from stanza to stanza. Then *Kol Nidre* would be recited. It was accepted that this was the echo of the auto–de–fe[32], the echo of a person suffering for his faith, the voice that passes from one edge of the earth to the other. On Yom Kippur, there are several prayers that touch the heart of the worshipper, especially *Unetane Tokef*, where it says "it is true that You are the judge." Some people burst out in weeping. The sounds of weeping emanated in particular from the women's gallery.

[Page 47]

Father's assistants (the singers) stood next to him on the stairs that went up to the Holy Ark. Father did not use a tuning fork. It is forbidden, and furthermore, he did not own one.

The son of the Blind David would sing his solo, "Is not Ephraim my darling son"[33] with such a clear voice, it sounded as if it was coming from the violin. His *"Li, Li, Li, Li"* is etched in my mind to this day, to the point that I cannot forget it even if I tried.

Yizkor was also recited on Yom Kippur. Great weariness was already felt at the *Neila* Service. Some people suffered greatly from the fast and got headaches.

Yom Kippur finished. It was the longest day of the year. We went home. Along the way, we stopped and recited the blessing of the Sanctification of the Moon, as a mitzvah counted toward the new year. After we ate a bit, we went out to the yard to drive in the first stake of the sukkah.

At the Sukkot Festival

The sukkah is a temporary hut, with a window and a door, covered with *schach*, which is tree branches through which the stars cannot be seen[34]. Then it was kosher in the best way possible. The Etrog, lulav, and four species played an important role on Sukkot. The splendor of the Etrog is its beauty. A small blemish on the *pitam* [stamen] will render it unfit.

The Etrog was kept in a box, and one was very careful with it. The service [with the lulav and Etrog] began with the *Hallel* prayer. The Etrog would be held in one hand and the four species in the other. The four species would be waved in the four direction and up and down at the recitation of *"Ana Hashem Hoshia Na"*[35]. The lulav and Etrog would be brought home so that the women could also recite the blessing on them; however, they satisfied themselves with a quick shake. After sukkot, the Etrog would be given over to a woman who wishes to have a child. She would bite off the *pitam* as a *segula*[36].

On Hoshana Rabba, they would hold the *"shanna"* [Hoshana bundle] and beat it until most of its leaves fell off.

On the last day of Sukkot, Simchas Torah, they would conduct *hakafos* [processions with the Torah], in which young and old, rich and poor, would participate. The children accompanied the *hakafos* with flags on sticks, upon which was placed an apple and a lit candle.

In Summary...

The nights got colder. The winter was approaching. The cold penetrated the bones. We again filled the windowsill with sand, place in it cups of "vitrol"[37], and sealed the double windows. The heater, which stood unused all summer, was lit. We now appeased it, and caressed it with our backs and hands.

Snow fell all night, and the world was white before us. Snow covered every living thing. People who rose early would leave their footprints in the snow. Others would walk in their footprints, broadening the steps and a

[Page 47]

path would slowly be created. The children waited for the puddles in which they could skate. If the adults were not careful, they would walk on them, and slip and fall. We began to wear our jackets, furs, shawls, and galoshes.

The farmers who came to town would exchange their wagons for sleds. They would tie a bell on the neck of the horse to sound a warning not to trample. The sled drew near to all the householders from the *briz*. The girls would sit there with their friends, covered in warm clothes, and their gentile would whip the horse, pass through the market and the Bridge Street until the route to the forest. The girls would enjoy this pleasure, whereas I did not.

*

The days of Chanukah approached. In memory of the miracle, candles would be lit for eight days, and a blessing would be recited. The neighbors would come to visit and we would play with the *"ternishke."*[38] Everyone would put a groszy in the plate and receive a pad. Each person, in turn, would declare the numbers, made out of wood, that would be removed without looking from the sack. He, like everyone, would cover the number (if he had it) on the pad. Whomever succeeded in covering all the numbers in one line received the money.

We also played cards. The game was 66 or Oko. Those who did not play cards permitted themselves to play *"kvittlech."* Father did not play at all.

*

Father and Yosef Leizer would take turns in teaching the *Chevra Mishnayes* [Mishna study group] after the *Maariv* service in the large *Beis Midrash*. When the portion of "turning after the majority"[39] was read, father immediately told his listeners about the dispute between the sages and Eliezar the son of Hyrcanus reading the *Bat Kol* [Heavenly voice] that supported him. Even so, they followed the majority. Then Pavel–Bunim got heated up and said, "Wonder of wonders!" Father continued and said, "Pshh, this is indeed a wonder of wonders, pssh." He raised his hand and shook it vigorously[40].

My father was very pious and a great believer. He was an optimist by nature and distanced himself from all worries. He only worried about the poor of the town. He would buy wood for them in the summer from Yosel–Meir Leib's and prepare the wood for the winter. Reb Yosel's habit was to review several pages of Talmud every morning. He would host a large celebration [*siyum*] each time he concluded the Talmud. I remember the 13th *siyum*.

Father was perplexed by our townsfolk who did not understand his tunes. It was primarily tradesmen who worshipped in the synagogue in which he served as cantor, for the wealthier householders worshipped in the *Beis Midrash* or *shtibels*. Reb Yakov–Pesach and Mr. Botchko (the son of the rabbi with whom I studied) were among those who understood music. The former would walk through the streets and hum to himself, and he would stand next to the windows of the Blind David to hear the singing of his daughters coming from inside.

[Page 49]

I felt a sense of respect for Rabbi Shlomo–Hirsch, who always spoke calmly, with understanding and appreciation for everybody. He spoke to the youth as a man speaking to his friend, in a quiet voice that penetrated the depths of the heart. He did not preach, but rather explained that we should not distance ourselves from the traditions of our fathers.

This was the era of "marching toward the nation" and escape from the norms. I was strongly attracted to these ideas. I would gather workers in the forests, speak to them about Socialism and read the brochures to them in Yiddish, as well as sections from the popular literature of those days. On account of this, I was not considered "completely kosher" by our townsfolk. This was also due to the fact that I talked to girls openly and even walked along the market in their company. Somebody even tried to malign me in the eyes of my father, telling him that I was smoking on the Sabbath. My father did not believe this, and curtly stated, "A lie and a libel…"

*

I felt great love toward my brother Avraham–Michel, who was attracted to the *Haskalah* [enlightenment]. Even though our world outlook was different, I was influenced by him in my way of life. He concerned himself with my studies and education. He became involved in business and frequented the Aleksander *shtibel*. He also concerned himself with the needs of those far away who were in need of economic and social aid and assistance. He was a refined soul with a heart that tended naturally to appreciation of his fellow. He inherited these traits from our father, even though he did not inherit the enthusiasm for cantorial singing from him. Nevertheless, Avraham–Michel excelled in his understanding and knowledge of popular songs, and he would sing many songs of this nature at home, in Yiddish and Hebrew, with a thin, pleasant voice. On the other hand, my brother Aharon had a powerful voice. He was interested in cantorial singing, and we hoped that he would continue the tradition of cantors in our family.

An elegy to my brother:

My brother,	enchanting to me was	God!
My heart is to you	Your good heart	How was it
An eternal light	and the purity of your soul	that You did not have mercy upon him
For	And I loved you.	And upon me...

*

Our family were *misnagdim* [non Hassidim]. On Sabbaths, I would go for a stroll with my friend Yehuda "Di Grajevke's" – today Mr. Wilson in Canada, who stemmed from a Hassidic family. He walked in a silk *kapote* with a crease and a velvet hat, whereas I was dressed as a *misnaged*. His father worshipped in the Kocker *shtibel*.

The *shtibel* was not considered by us to be a holy place, for it was not the same level as the *Beis Midrash*, where people would worship and also study. A Hassidic youth who wanted to learn would come to the *Beis Midrash*.

[Page 50]

The main activity in the *shtibel* was on Friday night and on Saturday. The tunes that burst forth from the *shtibel* on the Sabbath were those brought back from visits to the Rebbe. There were tunes that were appropriate for various prayers, and tunes that were sung without words "Ri, ri, reir," etc.

On the Sabbath eve, the melody received its soul, its warmth, and enthusiasm from the person who led the congregation in the service of Welcoming of the Sabbath and from the congregation that joined in with him. This was a communal song, albeit undirected. Everyone sang alone, and then suddenly, everyone together. With Hassidim, the voice was not important, but rather the manner, and the manner was the person.

It took some brazenness for a non–Hassid to go to worship together with the Hassidim, especially on the Sabbath. I once went to the Aleksander *shtibel* for the Friday night service, and all eyes were upon me. I was a stranger who did not belong to this community, and I found a place in the second room, as if I was hiding...

A prayer leader with a hoarse voice led the services. This was strange to me, and I asked about it. I was given the answer aloud, "This is the Heizeriker." Nobody had to explain how honorable the man was, and that his honorableness covered for his lack of a voice. I learned a principle of Hassidism from this.

Once, the Trisker Rebbe came to visit his Hassidim in our town. He conducted his *tish* [table celebration] in the *Beis Midrash* with 12 *challos*, in accordance of the number of loaves of the shewbread. He recited his Torah discourse in two voices, one for questions, and the second for answers.

*

I brought a book home and connected to it. My father was curious to know why I was looking into this book with so much diligence. He took the book from me to look at it for a bit. He began to read. He sat down and read it for several hours until he finished it. He said, "What type of a black thing might have they with this..." The name of the book was "Memories from the House of David." At times, father read the newspaper. I found Hamagid in the attic – a complete package of newspapers spanning several years.

*

Purim arrived. It was a secular holiday, the festival of giving of food gifts to friends, as is written in the Book of Esther. Plays about the Binding of Isaac and the Sale of Joseph were performed. Young people put on masks, visited houses and sang, "Today is Purim, tomorrow is not, so give me a groszy and throw me out."

*

Preachers came to visit throughout the year. An announcement would be posted on the door of the *Beis Midrash*: "Tonight after the *Maariv* service, so–and–so the well–known preacher will deliver a sermon. It will be pleasant for the listener."

The preacher ascended to the *bima* and waited. The *Maariv* service ended. The *shamash* knocked twice on the table, and the congregation turned their attention toward the preacher. The preacher was enwrapped in his *tallis*. The preacher presented three lectures, on three evenings. He began with a traditional melody, as follows, "It

[Page 51]

says in Midrash Rabba." He continued to draw his material from sources that were unknown to the large audience. The audience listened. They were finally listening to words of Torah, and it did not matter from what source they were. This is Torah and this is it reward. The preacher concluded his lecture. He then hastened to the door with a plate, and a candle in his hand, to collect his reward.

A preacher came who only had one lecture. He began with "Rabbi Bar Chana." This was not the first time that he had appeared before us. He began to sing "The Rabbi Bar Chana" as he repeated it, "Rabbi Bar Bar Chana said as follows; oy, he said as follows! I saw a bird with its head reaching the heavens. Oy, oy, until the sky."[41] He repeated it, repeated it again, continued, got confused, and finished... The congregation laughed in enjoyment. They had mercy and were generous with him.

A book seller would also come to town. He set out his wares on crates next to the door of the *Beis Midrash*. He sold *Gemaras*, *Chumashes* , *Machzors*, books of moral teaching, *tzitzit*, *mezuzos*, and *tefillin*.

*

The streets of the town had names: Brik Gasse [Bridge Street], Tifle Gasse [Church Street], Patshet Gasse [Gossip Street], Shil Gasse [Synagogue Street], Stadele Gasse [Stable Street].

There were also smaller lanes that were called by the names of the important residents who lived on them.

There was only one house on the market that had a balcony. Shlomo–Asher's house was called the Brick House. The streets in the market were paved with stones. The mud began on Shiel Gasse – the street where the *polkovnik* [colonel] lived, and continued until the border with East Prussia. The mud filled this area during the winter and the summer. The wagons would plough through this route and the grooves would fill up with puddles.

The market was on the incline at the side of Brik Gasse, and one had to go up steps to get to the shops there. The highest ones were next to the store of Itshe–Meir Richter at the corner of the street.

*

During their free time, the women of the town would sit next to their windows and doors, looking at everything passing by, following them with their curious eyes. Women did not go out to stroll, as it was not befitting for them. The husband did not walk along with his wife. He would walk in front and she behind if they were going to a celebration or a visit. When she reached the destination, she would be greeted warmly, "The kitten has arrived." The conversation was always flowing, revolving on the topics of children and diseases. If the topic was not polite, they would say, "permission."

*

One day a year made me afraid. This was the Green Thursday. The shops did not open. The gentiles put up images in two places in the market, next to the pork butcher and the tavern. The images were full of icons with the *Matka Boska* [mother of god] as well as images and statues with the crucified Jesus.

There were no Jews in the street that day. There was an unpleasant sensation of waiting. This situation

[Page 52]

continued until 12:00 noon, when the church bells sounded. I was always filled with fear. The fear on Green Thursday increased from hour to hour. When the procession began, I looked at it through a hole in the door.

The front marcher, a youth, carried a large cross with the crucified Jesus upon it. Two other youths wearing white cloaks covering their black clothing marched behind them, with incense vessels in their hands. The priest with his assistants marched behind them, followed by the men and women. All of them carried a plethora of icons. A large crowd of villagers (*korpiankes*) came. The *korpiankes* wore blue kerchiefs doubled over their forehead and tied behind their head. They all sang together, and the priest proclaimed in his thick voice, "*Gospidi, Gospidi, Ba–aa*"[42]. When they reached the hut, they would bow down on their knees. From there, they would return to the church with all the icons. A wonderful sight would then ensue. All the Jewish shops suddenly opened. All the fear left my heart…

*

There was an empty lot in front of the synagogue. There were always planks of wood there. Once, I was watching when they cut them into boards, the plank was placed on large poles. Stepan was above, and Antek below. All day, one pulled the saw from above, and the other from below. The one on top planned his steps very carefully so he would not slip. I was standing and staring, perhaps he might slip!

Once, I had the duty of collecting money for purchases and fixing of books for the *Beis Midrash*. The names of the people who were obligated for such were listed in a notebook. They paid their donations weekly. When I entered the house of the wealthy Feivel Szer, he took the pencil from me and himself drew the circle around "three kopecks" to indicate that the payment had been made. I got to know many people up close from visiting all the houses in the town for this purpose.

That is how I met all the family members of the "Briz." That is how I got to know refined young girls who got married very soon after. That is how I entered the home of Gwiazda, from whom I was given the opportunity to read the book "At the Crossroads."

At *cheder*, the rebbe taught us the story of Rachel weeping for her children[43] as follows:

And I
I am troubling you
With my burial
Even though for your mother Rachel
I did not do such.
When I came

[Page 53]

From Paddan Aram
Rachel died before me.
And I buried her in Bethlehem in Judea.
This was according to the Divine word.
For when Nebuzaradan would drive
The Jews into exile
They would pass by
Mother Rachel's grave
And she would begin to weep and shout out.
Then a Heavenly voice
Will come from above
And would say:
Refrain your voice from weeping,
For the children will return to their borders.
And the Jews
Will come back
To the land of Israel!

*

Today my home is in Israel with my family.

The cycles of life in the town of Chorzele have ceased. It is empty of its Jews. Strangers inherited our inheritance. The only thing left is the memory of the days of your youth. Our parents' home turned into a small plot of land where the bones of our parents are buried, without protection and without supervision.

What still remains? Only a legend. That is our inheritance that we can transmit to our children. Legend tells that there was once a Jewish town called Chorzele. However, for us and our children, only a legend remains, the legend of Chorzele.

Very few things move the heart of man as such a legend…

Translator's Footnotes

1. Note, this is also in observance of the biblical commandment, see Leviticus 17:13.

2. The Yiddish diminutive for "head", here meaning spaces for little heads.

3. Literally "damager." I translated it as "pest" but in the connotation it is slightly more endearing than "pest."

4. See http://www.yivoencyclopedia.org/article.aspx/Lachower_Yeruham_Fishel

5. See https://en.wikipedia.org/wiki/Peretz_Smolenskin

6. See https://en.wikipedia.org/wiki/Pirkei_Avot

7. A former name of Volgograd.

8. The Hebrew word here is "matza" – 'to find' (not the food). I believe that the innuendo here is from the adage, "One who finds a wife has found good."

9. The hymn welcoming the groom to the *chupa*. See http://www.zemirotdatabase.org/view_song.php?id=149

10. *Drashe Geshank* is a gift announcement. The way the words are written, they stress the fancy melodic elongation of the words.

11. Songs of Ascents, Psalms 120–134.

12. Most of this description is typical of any Bris ceremony. See https://en.wikipedia.org/wiki/Brit_milah for a definition of the terms: *sandek, kvater, metzitzah.*

13. Ezekiel 16:6

14. See https://en.wikipedia.org/wiki/Abraham_Goldfaden

15. See https://en.wikipedia.org/wiki/Malbim

16. "Blessed is He Who has freed me from the punishment of this one." Recited by the father of the Bar Mitzvah boy in recognition of the child's assumption of responsibility for his own actions.

17. Russian wild tobacco.

18. See http://www.zemirotdatabase.org/view_song.php?id=83

19. This is a departure from common custom, where the Levite does not receive a double *aliya* in the absence of a Kohen, but rather a Kohen receives a double *aliya* in the absence of the Levite. I suspect that the author may have made an error here.

20. The spelling here is *kigel* rather than kugel, reflecting a Hassidic style Polish accent.

21. See https://en.wikipedia.org/wiki/Tseno_Ureno

22. See http://yiddishwordoftheweek.tumblr.com/post/6083494792/got–fun–avrohom–%D7%92%D7%90%D7%98–%D7%A4%D7%95%D7%9F–%D7%90%D7%91%D7%A8%D7%94%D7%9D–god–of–abraham

23. A mushroom.

24. An already slaughtered animal was discovered to have an internal injury that rendered it non–kosher. This is the technical term *treifa*, although that word has colloquially been used for any non–kosher meat.

25. The Jewish prayer for the dead. See http://www.shiva.com/learning–center/prayers/kel–maleh–rachamim/ It would be pronounced and spelled in the original without the leading 'K' sound. However, out of sensitivity of spelling out a transliterated name of God, the leading 'K' is added.

26. See https://en.wikipedia.org/wiki/Pirkei_Avot

27. See https://en.wikipedia.org/wiki/*Selichot*

28. Psalms 89:16, recited immediately following the blowing of the shofar.

29. See https://en.wikipedia.org/wiki/Tashlikh

30. See https://en.wikipedia.org/wiki/Kapparot

31. "Here I am, poor in worthy deeds" This is the cantor's supplication prior to the *Musaf* service on Rosh Hashanah and Yom Kippur, so it is unclear why it would be recited prior to *Kol Nidre*. I suspect the author made an error here, and was referring to the "*Biyeshiva Shel Maala*" supplication prior to *Kol Nidre*.

32. See https://en.wikipedia.org/wiki/Auto–da–f%C3%A9 Indeed, the concept of *Kol Nidre* is believed to have stemmed as an absolution from the oath taken upon forced conversion to Christianity.

33. Jeremiah 31:20, included as part of the *Musaf* service on Rosh Hashanah.

34. He may have made an error here, as typically stars can be seen through the *schach*.

35. Psalm 118:28.

36. A portent or a charm. See https://en.wikipedia.org/wiki/Segula_(Kabbalah)

37. Likely vitriol – i.e. sulfuric acid.

38. Unclear what this term means, but it sounds like bingo.

39. Exodus 23:2 in the Torah portion of *Mishpatim*.

40. A Talmudic story from Tractae *Bava Metzia* 59b regarding whether halachic decisions can be made based on hearing a divine voice. The ruling is that one does not rely on a divine voice.

41. Tractate *Bava Batra*, 73b.

42. *Gospidi* is a term of address to respected people, such as Mister or Sir.

43. The verse if from Genesis 48:7 and the mention of Rachel weeping for her children is from Jeremiah 31. See *Rashi*'s commentary on the verses in Genesis, which matches the way the story was taught.

[Page 54]

Events and Images that are Engraved in my Memory
by Yosef Nesher (Adler)
Translated by Jerrold Landau

A. During the first twenty years of the 20ᵗʰ century
Rabbis, Persons, and Characters

When I was four years old, I entered the *cheder* of the rebbe Avraham Leib, the teacher of young children, like most of the children of my age. He was short, broad boned, with two *koncziks*. One had a wooden handle and four thongs, which he used to whip the child's legs under the table. The second *konczik* was a broad, thick strap made of strong, flexible leather. The rebbe would use it to whip the bare behinds of the child.

Yidel the teacher was the complete opposite of the rebbe Avraham–Leib. He did not maintain a *cheder*, but rather a school for reading and writing in Yiddish and a bit of Russian for boys and girls together. This was already the roots of a modern *cheder*, in a large building with rooms filled with light. The children played in the large playroom with joy and pleasure. The student became absorbed willingly and with contentment. Song came to me as naturally as Yiddish and Hebrew in my parents' house. I even merited to be appointed as the assistant of the rebbe Yidel in the study of Hebrew even when I was his student. It is perhaps because of this that my fine dream was to become a Hebrew teacher – a dream that was realized only in a small fashion.

The school of the rebbe Yidel was affiliated with the *cheder* in which *chumash* and *Rashi*, as well as introductory Gemara was taught. Reb Feivish, thin and slightly blind, was my Gemara teacher. It was solely due to his pedagogical abilities that he was able to take control of the wild class, whose entire purpose (according to the rebbe) was to play tricks. Indeed, there was no end to our mischievous plans – the weariness of the rebbe, his physical weakness, and nearsightedness helped us with this. Nevertheless, he served as an example to me regarding how to bear tribulations and pressure – never to complain to the Creator, but rather to bear and make peace with the difficulties with deep faith and acceptance of the decree.

Another wonderful personality of sublime culture and love of one's fellowman was the rebbe Moshe, the son of Kalman Ajzenstat. He had few students, but they were choice students, whose parents were able to appreciate Hebrew culture. He was nicknamed Moshe Kalman's. He brought to life for us the *Tanach* [Bible], the *Megillot*, Jewish History, Josephus, the past greatness of Israel, and its status throughout all eras. He instilled in us the desire to study, know, and become educated. He planted within us the sense of honor of being Jewish, and the virtues of honesty and self–respect, which Moshe Kalman's displayed in a wondrous manner.

There was another rebbe in Chorzele – Yechiel, who was old and lame. He taught Gemara and *Tosafos* at a high level. Contrary to the usual custom, students would go to him on Sabbath afternoons to read *Pirkei Avot*, or to have him read to use the legends and stories of Alfas, or other such things. He taught us to understand the deep, penetrating life wisdom of the authors of *Pirkei Avot* who set the paths for future generations, defining all their great volume of experience in short, clear, sentences that were straight to the point. Every tittle was a sea of thought and wisdom for grasping life.

[Page 55]

I recall another wonderful couple from the period prior to the First World War: Shlomka Tovia's and Rashka. They were childless, but their entire essence was light. He would walk in the street with a good, modest smile on his face. His eyes would light up at the site of any child. He would caress the cheek gently and give the child a candy.

I recall the personality of Shlomo the Shammas. Shlomo, the son of the rabbi, only attained the status of *Shammas* [beadle], and was considered in town to be an example of "rights from the fathers" that backfired. He had a pleasant appearance. His body was shapely and powerful. His beard flowed over his chest, imparting to him the appearance of a person ideal for a biblical portrait, like Moses who broke the tablets in his great anger. However, Shlomo the *shamash* was always angry, in complete contrast to Shlomo Tovia's...

Another personality: Yaakov–Pesach. He had a handsome face, a fine body, and was calm on the outside and internally. Nevertheless, he was full of thoughts that were foreign to his surroundings. He was very much into esthetics. His environment did not understand this, and he also did not know about this. He had a vibrant soul, and he loved and understood music. He literally pined for it, and was always humming. Who knows what type of supernal worlds opened before him when he hid and listened to "the immodest voice of women," when the daughters of the Blind David sang their wonderful songs.

Along with the aforementioned personalities, there were people who grew up and lived in the environment of the town, and added to its color during the course of their lives. There were also personalities who themselves created the communal picture – with their talent, dedication and deep trustworthiness for the good of the community. They could have taken their place and filled roles in large cities as well, but they ended up here, lived here, and fulfilled their duty here.

One of them was Reb Moshe–Aharon Gwyadza, who came to our town as the son–in–law of a wealthy merchant of the town, who worked in exporting fish from Astrakhan, Russia, but to everyone's surprise lived with his family in Chorzele. Moshe–Aharon was enlightened, infused with worldly culture, with a deep love for the culture of his people as well as the members of his people. He gave of his abilities to the entire city, and was a revered leader there.

The second was his friend and comrade, my brother Avraham–Michael. Since he was my brother, I can only describe him as a brother looks upon a dear, beloved brother. I left Chorzele at the beginning of 1919, and from what others told me later, he became even more refined than the image that was stored in my memory. My brother was a noble person, with sublime dedication and a heart full of love for every individual. The powers of tradition and wisdom blended together with him, and he dedicated everything to the welfare of the public.

[Page 56]

Three Occurrences

I recall three special occurrences from my childhood. The first – the appearance of Halley's comet[1], when people were talking about the end of the world, among us as throughout the world. The Jews of Chorzele reacted to the fear of the gentiles with mockery, for did not God promise in the book of Genesis that he would never bring another flood to the world – and the term flood includes all other calamities... Nevertheless, there was an elderly couple in Chorzele (who earned their livelihood in a covert manner: they wandered throughout the earth and collected money in an unknown fashion) whose faith was weak. Therefore, they spent all of their money to purchase all sorts of delicacies, and had a gluttony fest in their home, prior to the destruction of the world... News spread quickly throughout the town, and everyone went to the home of this strange couple, from where drunken voices of laugher and song were emanating.

The second occurrence: Weiser – a student wearing the customary gown (pelerine) that made a great impression in those days. He was summoned to serve as a teacher of the children of one of the wealthy families, and also conducted evening courses in Hebrew and Russian for the youth in general. At first, he earned the type of great admiration that such a personality could be given among the youth of a small town. However, with time, this admiration diminished. Finally, he assimilated among the gentiles of the town, and this aroused a storm against him. He became ill and died while residing in the home of a certain Christian family. The gentiles admitted that he had converted to Christianity prior to his death. The Jews claimed that this was a transgression "for the benefit of the cross and Christian love." The gentiles of the city conducted his funeral as a sign of the "sacrifice of the apostate." High level clergy from outside the town and crowds of people from the region participated in the funeral. This was a day of mourning and shame for the Jews. The stores were closed, and the Jewish residents closed themselves into their houses out of a feeling of both fear and anger.

The third event: the *aliya* to the Land of Israel of three of our townsfolk: Mordechai Ajzenstat of blessed memory, and, may they live, Eliezer Mar–Chaim (lives in Jerusalem), and my brother Simcha Adler (lives in Haifa). This occasion of *aliya* to the land of Israel became an event that aroused a great deal of discussion, the echoes of which continued when the letters and bottles of Carmel wine for Passover arrived to their families.

During the First World War

I was 12 years old when the First World War broke out. A Russian colonel, who was an officer of the border patrol, appeared in the marketplace in the evening. He summoned the townsfolk to come to assist him in loading up his belongings and government property on the wagons that he had prepared. Early the next morning, my brother Avraham–Michael returned from Warsaw with the intention of crossing the border to Germany to save himself from being drafted into the army for the war that was about to break out. My brother Aharon, a few friends, and I accompanied him to the German border. He entered Germany using the normal border pass that the residents of the border district on both sides possessed.

When the war broke out, a strange, worrisome quiet pervaded in town, for all government authorities disappeared suddenly. The elite "dragons" with their horses disappeared, as did the captains. The orders for meat for the battalion ceased along with their disappearance. Customers disappeared from the shops. Opportunities for the tradesmen to work disappeared. Commerce quieted. Unemployment pervaded, and border smuggling ceased. The wealthy people were the first to start wandering, followed by the shopkeepers with their stocks of merchandise. This was followed by a wave of general wandering, all the way to the poor people of the town. Only few remained, stubborn people who did not want to leave their nest. These were lone lads, whose families had left. There were two grandmothers from the wealthy Sirota family, and it seems me also the Mar–Chaim family. My family also remained, for we had nowhere to go. What place in the·world could absorb a cantor-*shochet* without a Jewish community? We fed ourselves from the produce of the field, and the abandoned gardens. We hunted fowl and small cattle who were wandering the streets without owners. In truth, we lived without worry. For us youths, this life was pleasant enough – until we too left the town.

[Page 57]

At first, we were a virtually closed area from a military perspective. At times, Russian scouts appeared, and within a few days, German scouts appeared. This repeated itself. However, this tense calm was shaken up when a brigade of about 200 Russian riders appeared one Friday in the marketplace. They performed guard duties along the border road, which ended next to the house of Tanchum Kowel. The Christian cemetery, which was located half way to the border, was at such a height that could see the entire area from there. About 30 Germans moved in their daily fashion toward from the border road to the town, and apparently did not know about the Russians. When the Germans reached the house of Tanchum Kowel, the Russians broke out in calls of "Hurrah" and attacked them with drawn swords. The Germans began to flee to the large field next to Tanchum's house, which bordered the synagogue. They indeed succeeded in this. This battle experience evidently shook up both sides: the Russians left immediately and were not seen again, and the Germans also did not appear for three days. However, for the remaining Jews of the town, this event caused fear and apprehension. The wave of departure increased, to the point where the city was virtually empty.

Rows of Russian pedestrians began to stream en masse toward the German side, and it seemed that they would strangle Germany with their hats. Four Poles (Nijewski, Narski, Sopieski, and Pakorski) passed through our town, followed by cannons with heavy ammunition. Innumerable supply wagons followed them, with many Jews serving as the suppliers. The conquest of the border district of Eastern Prussia was accompanied by the pillage and plunder of the German civilian population. The far–off, faint thunder of the cannons told about what was happening on the front. However, suddenly on Thursday evening, the reverse escape began, and continued throughout Friday. Calm pervaded on Saturday, interrupted from time to time by Cossacks fleeing on their small, nimble horses. Isolated soldiers, tired and desperate, gathered in the marketplace in the afternoon. They were forlorn escapees from a powerful, confident force. This was a sign of the famous victory of Hindenburg in the Masurian Lakes[2].

Following this, there were several more battles between Russian and German units, who engaged with each other within the bounds of the town and the region. The situation became more difficult day by day. We decided to leave the town, but only the Polish farmers had wagons, and they did not want to travel. It was decided that I, being 12 years old, would go to the villagers in the region to seek a wagon. I wandered from village to village for several days. The farmers related to me with mercy, fed me from the little bit that they had, and let me sleep in their houses. In the meantime, my family began to worry about me, since they had not heard from me. Then my older brother Aharon went out to search for me. We met under a frightening situation: as he was being held in the hands of two Cossacks, beating him and shouting that he was a German spy. I jumped toward him but was tossed to the side. Suddenly, a Polish shopkeeper from our town appeared. He knew us, and began to intercede in a very serious manner in favor of my brother. This intercession saved his life, but he had to give up his fur coat and all his cash.

[Page 58]

Not far from Chorzele, there was a sawmill for trees of the forest, owned by a Jew. It was next to the village of Duczymin. The manager of the sawmill made sure that there was a *minyan* there for approaching High Holidays and festivals. He invited my father to his home and sent a wagon to fetch him.

On the Threshold of Renewed Life

Whereas 300–400 Jewish families left Chorzele before the First World War, only about 200 families returned to the town after the war. Nevertheless, the youth began to develop cultural and communal activities, to collect books to found a library – of course in secrecy out of fear of the adults. The youth were so enthusiastic that, despite the extreme restrictions, they rented a spacious premises with three rooms and established a library. In essence, this was a cultural center. They gathered there to hear lectures and participate in discussions that broadened their horizons in worldly knowledge. They would hold "Postcard Evenings." Throughout the week, written questions would be placed anonymously into a chest. A gathering would be held every Saturday night to give the responses. Hebrew courses and even a choir were also organized. The evening gatherings in our cultural center forged the social life and saved the youth from the dangers of boredom and despair that were liable to take hold of the residents in a small, remote town, which had almost been destroyed and was also struggling from an economic perspective.

The Jewish shops once again provided sources of livelihood for the townsfolk, and enabled them to continue their lives of spiritual values, via the reestablishment of the religious, social, benevolent, and charitable institutions. Everyone, from young to old, was involved with these institutions. I remember an unforgettable incident when David Richter and I were serving as night guardians for a sick girl, having been send by the Linat Tzedek Society (we youths were the primary active force in this organization). The sick girl was the granddaughter of the rabbinical teacher of holy blessed memory, and her illness was severe. Her mother, the daughter of the rabbinical teacher, who was tired and without energy, lay down to rest a bit. After about an hour, the woman jumped up from her sleep and shouted out joyously, "The late father of the girl appeared to me in a dream, and told me that the girl will live!" This was indeed a critical night for the girl's illness, and she arose from her bed a few days later.

With time, the number of residents increased, and the owners of the burnt buildings began to rebuild their homes anew, larger and nicer than previously. An itinerant dramatic troupe, most of whose members originated from Łódz, all young, pleasant, and talented, appeared in town at that time. From them, we learnt what was possible to do on such a constricted stage as ours. The visiting troupe left Chorzele, but its leader, Ber, remained. He was a man of culture, with a great deal of knowledge. He gave classes in German, and set up a troupe from among the townsfolk, exposing valuable dramatic forces from within ourselves. We put on many performances, all of which breathed a breath of life into the town, even though the Orthodox circles were opposed to this.

[Page 59]

Another event broadened the cultural horizons of the town. The Germans drafted workers from the Polish–Russian border, and five young Jewish work foremen arrived in town. All of them came from the area of Baranovici, and had experience in communal service. They would spend their day off, Saturday, in Chorzele. They conducted public debates in parliamentary style in the cultural center, for there were Zionists and Bundists among them. Both sides presented their thoughts in a calm and logical fashion, preserving mutual respect and order. From them, we learned that heartfelt and warm relations can exist even where there are differences of opinion.

At that time, the youth in our town were for the most part non–partisan, and everyone worked together for cultural matters. One day, a youth named Hendler arrived from Maków as a partner in the iron utensil shop of his brother–in–law Naftali Ajzenstat. He approached me, as the Hebrew teacher in the town, and recommended that I found a Zionist organization. Such a thing was liable to endanger the social cohesion of our cultural center, but the idea enchanted me, because the need for Zionist activity had been sensed for some time already. I took my sister Hagar and my brother–in–law Shlomo Herzog,

Libe and Sheina Leah Scher, and others into confidence. When we reached 15 individuals, we convened a top–secret meeting in the forest, and this is how the first Zionist organization was founded in Chorzele. The founding of this organization aroused the opposition of several of our members who were already out in the world at large and were numbered among the supporters of the Bund. They claimed that this would create a schism amongst the youth and destroy the existence of the cultural center. This internecine battle grew stronger and led to the rental of a different premises for the Zionist organization. The dispute quieted after some time. Both institutions existed in fine fashion, each functioning within its confines. The Zionists were the active force in the entire town as well as in the cultural center.

The war continued in the battlefields, but Chorzele was quiet. The youths were lacking in activity, so they became active in matters of culture and the organization of the Zionist movement. The connection with the headquarters in Warsaw was strong. Chorzele sent the writer of these lines as a delegate to the regional convention in Mława. Hebrew courses for adults and youth were opened, and a special library for the youth was created. The students of the courses chose a committee to conduct their affairs. I was their counsellor and teacher.

We organized performances, plays, and evenings of culture and song in which the students participated. The organized excursion of the youth on Lag B'Omer had a great impact. We imbued a great deal of energy and effort into preparing for it: the children learned to march in formation, we learned Hebrew and Yiddish songs as well as games. On the morning of Lag B'Omer, all the youth as well as many adults gathered at the Zionist organization building. The parade was organized. The counsellors and onlookers surrounded everyone, and we prepared to set out. Several Poles who were unable to make peace with the joy of the Jews came in wagons to break up the rows, but they encountered a strong, unmovable stand. They were force to back off. This event raised our profile amongst both the Jews and the gentiles.

[Page 60]

The shops in the town were closed. When the parade set out onto the streets of the town, it was accompanied by young and old, and tears of national pride welled up in the eyes of many. The parade arrived at the Rembelianek Forest in peace, and we spent the entire day singing and playing games.

One winter afternoon, a young Pole arrived in the market and asked about the leadership of the firefighters. He gathered together Jews and gentiles and informed them that the Germans had lost the war, and the Poles have decided to take the government into their hands. An independent Poland was established. The Polish youth immediately began to gather in the streets and take the weapons from the Germans. The Jewish youth understood the danger that was liable to threaten the Jewish population during the inter–government period, when the Polish youth organized themselves within one hour to remove weapons from the Germans (most of whom would have preferred to give the weapons to us rather than to the Poles). In the evening, we organized a self–defense organization to protect us from our new "overseers." We had weapons and the knowledge of how to use them. The Germans left the city at night, and nothing happened over the following days.

*

Renewed Poland began its first steps in oppressing its Jewish residents, but there were Polish leaders who understood that they must impose order. They decided to conduct democratic elections for the local government institutions, and a directive came to Chorzele as well to elect the leadership of the town. In the evening, the gentiles entered the town school to elect the leadership, without thinking at all about the Jewish population. However, we organized ourselves and sent 70 youths to the school for the election meeting. Moshe Czwirkowski of blessed memory explained to those present, including agents of the central government, that the Jews of the town demand proportional representation in the leadership of the city and its institutions. At first, the gentiles were astonished about the brazenness of the Jews. Later, a debate ensued, and we stood our ground in an uncompromising fashion regarding our demand. Finally, we attained what we demanded. The gentiles understood that they had no idea about town economics, and hoped that the Jewish minds would organize everything. Indeed, the administrator Avraham–Michael Adler served as the representative of the Jews in the town council until the Second World War, and the Polish mayor did not move to the right or left without his advice.

*

I left Chorzele in 1919, when the town reached its pinnacle even though the poverty was great. The Jewish community and the youth were active at that time in a full social and cultural life – it was a vibrant life. Today, the town certainly continues to exist, and perhaps even to develop, but its Jews are no longer there. May their souls be bound in the bonds of eternal life.

[Page 61]

B. The People Who Served as Prayer Leaders...

With holy trepidation, I present this

Forgive me for the dearth of my ability

The Prayer Leader

He was tall, broad shouldered, with great strength. He had straight stature – he stood upright in front of everybody, except for his God. His broad beard flowed down, decorating his so good, good face. His large eyes, slightly weary, would peer at you with a strong, penetrating, and understanding gaze, as a smile settles upon his face.

He was the prayer leader, and he lived his calling, both as a position, as well as in all its details.

The *shochet* [ritual slaughterer]

The *shochet's* primary responsibility was toward the community of consumers. Kashruth was a cornerstone of the tableau of Jewish eating, and the *shochet* was willing to make any sacrifice and suffer anything for the maintenance of kashruth. The butcher and his family were living people, and any event of an animal being rendered *treifa*[3] would cause them a serious loss. If they had the poor luck of having several incidents of *treifa* happing consecutively, their livelihood was liable to dwindle down to the point of lacking a loaf of bread.

The most difficult situation was a case of uncertainty, when the lungs or liver were presented for inspection at the behest of the city rabbi, the rabbinical teachers, and the *shochtim*. The butcher would repeatedly blow up the lungs with his mouth, as the inspectors watched the inflated lungs. Fear and trepidation were in the hearts of everyone: the fear of feeding non–kosher meat to Jews on the one hand, and the fear of causing serious damage to a Jewish person on the other hand.

I am sure that the feelings of my father blended with those of all those involved in the judgment, but before my eyes, my father stands with a broken heart, for the animal was rendered a *treifa*.

The Cantorial Position

It is impossible to describe the connection of our townsfolk to music and song, which was expressed in some many varied ways: in the performance halls, musical productions, radio, and other means.

Our townsfolk lived very centralized lives, albeit also honorable and difficult. One would hear about the world, the world would call to him, and he might even succeed at times to come into contact with it or peek at it. However, these were all small snippets, from which a dream image, with shining light, could be formed. The dismal reality of the Jewish person, who was afflicted with the shame of the exile and lack of power, with extreme lack of horizons, with disgrace, poverty, and lack of options: only one thing remained – the dream. The angel of imagination covered enveloped him with his charm, and he caused him to dream of the Messiah, utopia, and Old New Land[4]. In the interim, however, the heart was overflowing with oppression and disgrace, with no solution. Then there was song, melody, hymn, and prayer, which broadened the heart, relieved the agony, and lifted the spirits on the wings of hope...

[Page 62]

It was the month of *Tammuz*. The heat caused weariness and dryness. The 17th of that month was a day of fasting and mourning, opening the flask of tears. Then the stream began, the month of Av – the month of destruction and mourning, the nine days of hopeless anticipation, culminating with the commemoration of the destruction on Tisha B'Av. The agony of "How has sat in desolation"[5] was barely assuaged, when the month of *Elul* had already arrived: a month in which the eyes were afraid and the heart trembled like a fish in the waters... with the accounting of the soul... and the Day of Judgment...

Cantor Moshe–Shimon Adler

There was something natural about it as well. The autumn turned things yellow, and evoked sadness. Weariness pervaded, and rain poured down. A grey pall fell upon the world, and the heart contracted and shed tears... it was night. The city was dark. Isolated lights flickered in isolation and loneliness... deepening the darkness... and suddenly – song!... In the home of the cantor, Rabbi Moshe–Shimon, the rehearsals for the High Holy Days had begun!

The cantor sat at the head of the table and smiled. One of his sons, the director, organized the outlines and prepared for his first lesson with the seriousness of a teacher. In the meantime, the singers assuaged their inquisitive tension by singing songs of mutual vexation, which were closed to all the people of earth, and only understandable by people of that class. Then the cantor banged on the table: everyone got quiet and the rehearsal began. Verses of song emanated from the mouth of the conductor. The singers repeated them over again until they merged together into a complete melody. The singers — experienced and with a quick grasp – caught on and joined in. The townsfolk gathered around the house, eager to listen. They enjoyed the "again," and "once again," that helped them grasp the melodies. As befits "experts,"

[Page 63]

the pointers from the cantor and the conductor deepened their understanding and improved the outcome...

All strands of sadness disappeared. Joy fell upon the town.

The Singers

I knew three types of singers from my father's house.

    a. The sons of cantors, who came to study voice development, the forms of prayers, verbal recitation, and the cantorial methodology in general, in preparation for the day when they would take over from their fathers.

    b. The children without homes, for whom song provided the content of their life, and they regarded this in the present (not thinking about the future at all). All of them formed a joyous group of youths without worries, who lived on "blessed is each day", and the meaning of "each day" was: to eat one day in one house, and another day in another house throughout the entire week. Eating "days" was an institution in the diaspora in those days[6].

    c. The residents of the city, who began to sing with the cantor as youths and only finished when they were old, with their children and grandchildren continuing along with them and after them. I recall the pleasant and phenomenal singer, Hershel the son of the Blind David. His soprano was imbued with the light of the sun, and rang out with unusual joy and beauty. His voice was heavy with color, and each light movement was like a ray of light. No high note was heavy for him. There were other excellent voices among the youths, but he was in a class of his own.

The son of Pesach Beker still lives among us. He is a policeman in Jaffa, a good singer, who participates in the opera. He enthusiastically sings the songs he remembers as a child from my father, from whom he studied and in whose choir he sang.

The cantor was the father who worried about everyone, and the home of the cantor was their home. Indeed, the space was tight, but not too cramped for any of them.

The Cantor

When the time came, he approached the prayer podium with fear and trembling, to serve as the messenger of his congregation before the All Powerful. Around him were his choir, and the congregants of the full synagogue – the holy congregation of the City of Chorzele.

He was expert and accustomed to leading prayers. He enunciated each word in accordance with its meaning and its role in the mighty service: the prayer that had had been sung for generations, in accordance with the style and melody that was transmitted from generation to generation. He would instill his own style, in the manner of someone "standing to entreat with prayer and pleas on behalf of the House of Israel," with his heart moved and his soul infused with fear on account of the gravity of the task imposed upon him. Every word is a world, and every expression is fateful. Every melody was a one–time creation, that would never return. With his great, deep, rich voice (he was a bass baritone, with his voice broad and soft as velvet) he would arouse his congregation to prayer, draw the hearts near, blending with the entreaties of his mission to merit forgiveness and pardon, and a good year from the Father, our Father in Heaven...

The Day of Judgment

The Torah Scrolls from the morning service were placed back in the Holy Ark. There was tension and quiet in the room...

[Page 64]

The cantor stood silently in the center, wearing his white *kittel* and enwrapped in his *tallis*, with his eyes closed, stripping himself of the "current reality" and waiting for the wave to come, the wave that would carry his prayers to the Above...

A groan... and silence, as thin as a Heavenly Voice, without words, lifted his melody of supplication throughout the building. It descended, and ascended, reaching all places. The rhythm was repeated, strengthening and weakening... the congregation and its representative entered a sublime state. Their soul opens up like a flower before God... And then, the words flutter up in lamentation and subordination, like a bird with weak wings: "Here I am, poor in worthy deeds"[7], and suddenly, cry of pain, "I am trembling and frightened...", and then, without energy, "From the fear of He Who is seated upon the praises of Israel"...

The seven–year–old child tucked his head into the door of the lectern – moved, trembling, and frightened. The congregation, imbued with fear, stood enchanted, given over to the mercies of the Lord.

Unetaneh Tokef[8]

Like the flow of a thousand streams, the voices of the worshippers pour out in a unified prayer. The group of frightened children wander about so as to find support in unity. Slowly, everyone quiets down. A groan still comes up from the heart, and stifled weeping can be heard from the women's gallery. This also stopped...

From the depths, the voice sounds out, quietly, stifled in its fear, and in acceptance of Divine justice, "It is true, it is true, that You are the judge, the judge, the judge the judge — — — and the one who proves, the one who knows, and the witness." Every word is frightening. Every word instills fear. One by one, the recognition of the dangers awaiting man in his sin and judgment are declared, as he stands without protection, without assistance (the Satan accuses, and the sins are the weapons in his accursed mouth...) He calls to God to help him out of despair... withered to the point of the nullification of the soul.

Then, a crack appeared in the iron firmament, and the splendor of heaven penetrated their hearts as an elixir of life with comfort and a promise... The prayers were taking hold in the firmament as talons grasping for salvation, reaching toward the Throne of Glory... Life returned to the soul. There is a solution. There is hope for man. The shout of encouragement broke out from all the worshippers: And repentance, prayer, and charity avert the harsh decree! The prayer leader comforted, graced and aroused his congregation to return in repentance with a full, upright heart, to prayer with all the powers of the soul, to open their hearts to charitable deeds that they would perform, so that they would benefit from His charity. Hope increased, and faith for a good verdict encouraged the hearts of the worshippers, as the choir broke out in, "There is no end to Your days..."

... Astonishment On the Day of Judgment

Our Father in heaven! On one Day of Judgment, the iron of your firmament hardened. Your glory did not shine upon your children. The prayers of Israel were caught up in the taloned fingers of emptiness, and did not reach Your throne. Destruction fell upon your nation, with none surviving.

... And Your rainbow sung out a promise from the cloud, that another flood should not come upon the world for its sin.

Only Your children were wiped out in the flood of blood – their own blood. The pure prayers were like souls wandering and lost

[Page 65]

in perplexity. The astonishment penetrated with thunder, but without a voice: "How could such a thing happen, Master of the Universe?" Father, Daddy, Why?!!!!

My Father

When my father became old, and no longer had the energy to serve as prayer leader, he took a staff in his hands, and went from house to house, knocking on the doors and the hearts of those who still had a loaf of bread in their basket – on behalf of those who had only hunger in their homes.

Silently in the evening, a hesitating hand knocked on my father's door. Faces pale with want and shame appeared at the door, with eyes of despair... but when the person left, his hand was encouraged, and his heart was a bit lighter. The pain was shared by both of them – the communal emissary and the child of his community...

The Prayer

My Father in Heaven! Open my heart, broaden my hand, and those of the generation to follow. And with this, the splendor of the soul of my father and rabbi, Moshe Shimon Adler of blessed memory, the cantor and *shochet* of the holy community of Chorzele, shall shine in splendor.

Translator's Footnotes

1. This would have been in April or May 1910.

2. See https://en.wikipedia.org/wiki/First_Battle_of_the_Masurian_Lakes

3. A *treifa* refers to an animal rendered non–kosher through an error in slaughter, such as using knife with nicks, using improper cutting motions in the slaughter, etc.

4. See https://en.wikipedia.org/wiki/The_Old_New_Land

5. The opening verse of the Book of Lamentations (*Eicha*), read on Tisha B'Av.

6. This refers to yeshiva students from out of town who were generally hosted in different homes for their meals on a rotation basis.

7. The opening phrase of the cantor's supplication prior to the *Musaf* service on the High Holy Days.

8. See https://en.wikipedia.org/wiki/Unetanneh_Tokef

[Page 65]

How Beautiful is our Heritage
by Aharon–Wolf Nafcha (Kowal)
Translated by Jerrold Landau

B"H

In memory of those from Chorzele who have no survivors to remember
them.

Remove the shoes from your feet	Your muscles will weaken,
For the Holocaust that was in your day	Upon your motherland
And over the destruction of your sanctuaries	For the survivors of your nation
And over the loss of your parents,	And for the peace in your world
And over the murder of your children,	We will cry out! We will shout! We will scream!
And over the uprooting of your daughters	We will flash like lightning
And over the tearing up of your children	Over the image that was erased
And over the disgrace of your God	And over the house that was broken
And over the honor that was melted	And over the child that was strangled
And over the blood that was spilled	That such things shall never happen again.

[Page 66]

And in memory of my revered mother, Miriam–Zelda the daughter of
Yisrael–Chaim the Kohen Anish; my sisters; my revered father Tona the son of
Aharon–Wolf Kowal of holy blessed memory; of clean hands and pure heart,
their soul was never taken with vanity, and they never swore falsely (Psalms
24).

From the Mouth of my Father

"May their eyes be dimmed so they cannot see, and may their loins
constantly slip" (Psalms 69:24)

It was in the year 1900. Because of its unique geographical location, the
residents of our town, especially the Jews, earned their livelihoods from
smuggling. My father, like many others, would transport, with his wagon
hitched to horses: a mixture of fruits (from Russia to Germany), and sacks of
coal (from Germany to Russia). There were secret crevices in the corners of his

wagons in which silver ingots were hidden. From this, our livelihood was bountiful in those days.

One Thursday, when my mother went to purchase fish for the Sabbath, the fisherman said to her that he was prepared to exchange his proceeds from selling fish for six months for one act of smuggling carried out by my father. Since these words were spoken in public, my father decided to go to ask a religious scholar about this – the Rebbe of Novominsk, of holy blessed memory. The Rebbe answered him, "There is no merit from the holy Psalms regarding what you say, that their eyes should be dimmed so they cannot see. For Your nation Israel requires sustenance." My father returned, encouraged in in faith in the holiness of Psalms and in the wisdom of the Rebbe, and continued on with his livelihood...

One evening, on his way back from Germany with a load of coal in his wagon, the captain in charge of duties stopped him and said, "A complaint has reached us that you are engaged in smuggling. Therefore, we will conduct a search of your wagon." A group of soldiers was summoned. They took down the sacks of coal, poured out their contents, dismantled the walls of the wagon and threw them to the ground with force, so that they could determine from the echo whether they were hollow. While the soldiers were still searching for smuggled objects, a piece of silver fell out from one of the secret corners. It glittered like stars at night among the piles of coal, as if it was winking and calling out the frightful words, "Here is the stolen object!"

My father was startled, but placed his trust in God and in the promises of the holy Rebbe. He did not stop reciting the verse, "Their eyes should be dimmed so they cannot see." Suddenly, my father heard the Russian captain saying, "My friends, who hate toil, the lowly libel was false, oh you people without conscience. The libel against this man who works hard to support his family was false." Turning to the soldiers, he said, "Help the man reassemble his wagon, and load the sacks upon it." Finally he turned to my father, clasped his hand, and said, "You are free! Please forgive me."

"Onward horsies... homeward..." my father prodded his horses. Indeed, the words of the Rebbe were fulfilled, "Their eyes were dimmed from seeing."...

[Page 67]

The Sound of Torah – a Fortress Against Cannon Fire

It was 1915. The world war was at its height. People were traveling by foot and by vehicle on difficult roads. It was a large crowd, especially of our fellow Jews with their young children and belongings, escaping in fear from the victorious armies. The roads of Poland, normally dark, were now lit up by the light of the flames of the burning villages and the thunder of the cannons. My father and his family of seven were among the many wanderers.

This took place in one of the camps of wanderers in the city of Prosienica in the month of Shvat. On an extraordinary Yom Kippur[1], on a wooden floor in an abandoned room in the home of a Jew named Goliborda, I entered the world, in hunger, want, and poverty... When I was 15 days old, my family was forced to continue its wandering toward the capital of Warsaw. When we arrived there one early morning, my father got off the wagon, looked here and there, as if he was asking, "Who knows us? Who do we know?" He turned his eyes heavenward and said, "My God, from where will my salvation come?" The echo responded to him...

Suddenly an angel in the form of a woman passer-by appeared, turned to my father and asked, "Uncle, whom are you looking for?" She approached the wagon, lifted up the tarpaulin, and said, "A curse!" Then, she turned to my father, and added, "Uncle, do not move from here, wait!" After some time, a group of people appeared headed by a nurse in a white cloak, and ordered my father, "Uncle, follow after us." Our wagon traveled to Gronica Street and stopped in front of a large house. We all got off, with our luggage. This was an institution for the homeless.

The great surprise took place in the afternoon. The director of the institution came to visit, and then, "Who did his eyes see, if not the resident that lives with us at home," the rabbi of Ciechanów, Rabbi Braunroth of holy blessed memory. The two of them, he and my father, fell upon each other's necks, and wept for a long time.

We remained in that institution for more than a year. My father also found some work for himself during that time. When the news arrived that quiet pervaded on the fronts and it was possible to return home, my father again consulted with the Rebbe of Novominsk of holy blessed memory. The Rebbe's advice was, "Return home in peace, for the sound of Torah once again echoes from its walls."

Throughout the years, rabbis, great in Torah and in fear of Heaven, lived in our house: Rabbi Koblaski of Włocławek of holy blessed memory, Rabbi Braunroth of Ciechanów of holy blessed memory, Rabbi Rosenstrauch of Olkusz of holy blessed memory, and after him, the holy Rabbi Mordechai-Chaim Sokolower of holy blessed memory – the father of Rabbi Ephraim Sokolower and of Avraham, Moshe, and Malka, who live with us in our country (may they live long). Indeed, when we returned home, we found that our house was still standing amongst the rest of the destroyed houses. (This fact was confirmed to me by the rabbi of Ciechanów, whom I had the honor of meeting in Israel a few years ago.)

[Page 68]

David Kowal and two of his grandchildren, Ita and Dvora

In later years, when Rabbi M. Ch. Sokolower was forced to leave our house as it was too small for his needs, a serious question arose with the heirs of the house after their father Aharon–Wolf Kowal. They were: my uncle David, my father Tona, and their sister Sara Jochet. The heirs were unsure how to ensure the continuation of the splendid tradition, so that the sound of Torah will not cease from this house, Heaven forbid. They offered the house to the holy Tzadik Rabbi–Yosef Shochet, who was known for his sublime traits as a fearer of Heaven. He lived in our house until the outbreak of the Second World War in 1939.

Our houses of splendor, the synagogue and the *Beis Midrash*, also remained as fortresses, despite the internal ruin caused by the horses who had been housed there during the First World War. Two holy, pure, working Jews, took upon themselves the burden of the huge job and effort to restore these sanctuaries of ours for prayer and supplication: Matityahu Sokolower, the glassblower (the father of Avraham, Simcha, Tova, Malka, Mirel, and David, all living in Israel), and my revered father Tona Kowal, the smith. Both were "beloved and pleasant in their lives, and were not separated in death"[2]. They both served as faithful trustees for the needs of the community for many years.

The Good in Contrast to the Bad

Our house was situated between two Christian neighbors – Gutart and Chagan. When our town was evacuated at the time of the First World War, the army turned the splendid synagogue into a horse stable. Gutart's oldest son Tadek did not suffice himself with that. He took an axe and burst into our house of glory, breaking everything, not leaving anything untouched. However, when he raised his axe to bang it into the Holy Ark, he missed his mark and the axe hit his foot. As a result of this miracle, he remained lame, and he limped for the rest of his life ("This is the sin and this is the punishment").

Entirely opposite was the opposition of the daughter of our neighbor Helena Chagan when the gangs of the infamous army of the anti–Semite Haller[3] looted, pillaged, and wreaked havoc in our town. Among their other sadistic acts, the Hallerists enjoyed capturing Jews to cut off their beards. At times, they would even tear off some of the skin of the chin along with the beard and *peyos*.

One day, several soldiers were running after Rabbi Sokolower of holy blessed memory to cut off his "locks of Samson" – his beloved, splendid beard that flowed over his cloak. As they were chasing pursuing him, Helena Chagan ran to greet them with a picture of Jesus in her hands, and burst out before them in hysterical screams, as she stood between them and the rabbi. She said, "I will not let you touch a man of God; go out to fight the wars of our homeland, and not against a defenseless person." Her screams chased away the gang, and the rabbi was saved from the hooligans. Later that day, the rabbi invited his neighbors, my uncle David and my father, along with the noble Chagan family, and he blessed Helena that she should merit happiness, wealth, contentment, and good health for her humane deed. The Good God apparently heeded the prayer of the righteous man, for Helena received her reward. She married a good, wealthy husband, gave birth to successful children, and remained beloved by her family and anyone who knew her throughout all the years.

[Page 69]

Love of the Nation and the Land

Our holy fathers, however, did not only live on miracles. Most of them were people of toil, who were blessed with skilled hands, as they synthesized Torah and labor in their day–to–day life. They also believed that work raises the man and purifies him. To this day, I remember our teacher and rabbi, the holy Moshe Ajzenstat, quiet and modest, who would hum the song that he loved so much, "Labor is our life, save us from every tribulation. Ya–chay–li–li– my toil is for me." We then sensed his devotion to Hassidism and to his fiery faith. I do not know the extent that he knew the ways of the world, but the ways of the heavens were certainly clear to him through this song... for an eternal flame of the vision of the return to Zion, the vision of the complete redemption, burned in his heart and the hearts of those like him.

Miriam Szar, the wife of Reb Avraham

I recall a Saturday night many years ago, when several tens of Jews gathered for the *Melave Malka* meal in the home of the holy Avraham Szar. This was the farewell party for Reb Meir–Yaakov Weingort and his family before they made *aliya* to the Land of Israel. I still recall the taste of the grits that we ate, prepared by the mistress of the house, the holy Miriam Szar. However, seven times more sweet to us were the words of Reb Avraham Michel Adler, who said, "My brother Jews, if the joy is so great that we have merited, after many generations, to witness the beginning of the redemption with our own eyes, as our land is redeemed, our sons become builders[4], and the exiles are returning to it; if the joy is great for every pioneer who makes *aliya*, for every additional chick in our Land – then for us, observant Jews, the joy is doubled and increased. After we were exiled from our Land and our Holy Temple was destroyed, the holy Divine presence implanted itself in the hearts of religious Jews who believe with perfect faith that the Holy One Blessed Be He, the Torah, Israel, and the Land of Israel are all one. Our dear friend Meir–Yaakov carries in his heart the Holy One Blessed Be He, the Torah and Israel along to the land of Israel, as he returns the Divine presence to its rightful place."

[Page 70]

I recall the illustrious teacher and educator, the overseer of the Jewish National Fund, the holy Reb Mordechai–Mendel Friedman (the father of Chaya Segal, may she live), and the dedication with which he worked for many years for the sake of the redemption of the land. More than once, on a rainy Sunday when the cold froze the limbs, he stood at the crossroads dressed in a fur coat with a high collar – for what purpose? To collect the pledge from a guest who had an *aliya* to the Torah on the Shabbat morning in the old *Beis Midrash* (of Mizrachi), and was leaving town on Sunday morning to take the train to Warsaw. In such cases, he would say, "With one action, the Holy One Blessed Be He allowed me to fulfill two mitzvos – the redemption of the Land, and saving a Jew from the sin of failing to pay his pledge."

How great a Jewish, popular, optimistic feeling, with heart and soul together, is embedded in the short poem that contains only two words, "*Lechayim* brothers," that was sung by Reb Michal Berent the holy butcher, at any opportunity when people were sitting together. (He was the father of Mordechai Berent who lives with us in Israel). How much meaning was embedded in these two words, and how do we remember them today.

Our fathers, mothers, brothers, and sisters, the holy ones of Chorzele, were blessed with love of Israel, Torah, toil, God, and man. How great is our lot in this, how great is our heritage.

May their souls be bound in the bonds of eternal life.

Translator's Footnotes

1. Yom Kippur is four months before Shvat, so I suspect that its usage here is not literal, but rather a term to express the hunger and want at the time of his birth.

2. II Samuel, 1:23.

3. See https://en.wikipedia.org/wiki/J%C3%B3zef_Haller

4. This is a play on Hebrew words: sons is *banim*, and builders are *bonim*.

The Branch of the Hechalutz Organization
by Yaakov Frenkel
Translated by Jerrold Landau

For all intents and purposes, Hechalutz was founded in Chorzele in 1929. However, around 1908, one of our townsfolk, Eliezer Mar–Chaim, was among the guards in the Land of Israel, and from then the atmosphere of Chorzele was fully directed toward the land of Israel. I recall that when I was 14 years old, I worked with a group of Jewish youths in straightening the Orzyc River during the time of the German occupation of the First World War. Our friend Yosef Nesher was among the workers, and we both felt at the time that we were preparing ourselves for *aliya* to the Land of Israel. The songs that we enthusiastically sang at the time were: "In the plow lies blessing and good luck"; "There where the cedar trees grow"; "I am a pioneer, a pioneer from Poland", and other such songs. Thus, in 1916, when all the routes were closed and the entire world was occupied with bloodshed, we worked, sang, and dreamed about the Land of Israel. Indeed, from the end of the war until the Holocaust era, *aliya* to the Land of Israel from Chorzele never ceased, and the strongest desire that pulsated in the hearts of the youth was – to make *aliya* to the Land.

[Page 71]

The factor that influenced the pioneering spirit of our townsfolk, that is, that led to the organization of a chapter of the Hechalutz Organization, was the riots of 5689 (1929) in the Land[1]. The riots left a deep impression on the town and aroused anger against the gangs of Arab murderers, and especially against the provocative stance of the Mandate government, headed at that time by the Jew, Herbert Samuel. We could not supress this matter, and we gathered in the Tarbut Hall for a protest meeting, with the participation of people from all the Zionist organizations of the town. I expressed the feelings of outrage that pulsated inside me at that time in the following words, which remain with me to this day as a manuscript.

"The human mouth is too weak. The thoughts are too obtuse, the heart is too soft to express even part of the feelings that each of us feels regarding the recent events in the Land of Israel. A gang of wild Arabs, driven by a fanatical dark clique, with the cold, sharp indifference of the Mandate authorities, fell upon the Jewish communities of the Land of Israel like wild beasts. However, the brave ones of Israel, our *chalutzim*, the most admired of the people of the world, the celebrated ones, those who, with their own sweat, made the soil that was vacant for 2,000 years waiting for the blessed hands fruitful once again, were now ripped away from their peaceful and blessed labor and took up the eternally despised sword. They also demonstrated their wonders. We say here that the forgotten blood of our martyrs in the Land of Israel, together with the solidarity of the entire Jewish people from all corners of the world, will arouse a strong force within us, a strong interest, so that the Land of Israel will certainly become the national home of the Jewish people." The powerful, very appropriate reaction to these events in the Land was *aliya*. I recall that two of our friends who were in a *hachsharah* kibbutz came to Chorzele at that time to prepare to make *aliya* to the Land. They were Davidson and Lanenter, who had gone to a *hachsharah* kibbutz even before the official Hechalutz was founded in Chorzele. The influence of the songs that they brought with them, and that were sung in the Tarbut chapter along with all our friends, will never be forgotten from my heart. One of the songs was:

From Klesowa until Shacharia, it is hard for you

I am preparing for *aliya*, and we laugh at you

Carrying blocks, hacking rocks, oh, it is hard for you

Gnashing our teeth, and we laugh at you.

This song expresses the anger toward the confirmed haters of Zion in Poland, and especially against those who were part of the Jewish nationalist movement, so to speak, but were prepared to sacrifice themselves for the Yiddish Language. It was especially during the disturbances of 5689 / 1929 that these haters of Zion found the opportunity to prove that their dark prophecies about Zionism were correct. It is worthwhile to note that well known Yiddish writers in America, including Avraham Reisen, H. Leivick, and Moshe Nadir spoke out against that stance. (The famous, humorous proclamation of Moshe Nadir is known from that time: Specifically if Rome is Rome, Moscow is Moscow, then Jerusalem – is Jerusalem...)[2].

[Page 72]

In addition to the two friends that I mention, the atmosphere of *aliya* and preparation for *aliya* prevailed in Chorzele at that time, and encompassed many of the members. Among them was Tova Eichelbaum. It was the custom in Chorzele that when a member was about to make *aliya*, people would write words of memory in their souvenir albums. One day, my sister Feiga, of blessed memory, surprised me when she brought the album of her friend Tova to ask me for advice as to what to write. I wrote the following words for her:

For health and happiness, be peaceful and joyous

For you are travelling to the land that belongs to us Jews.

The sad events should not impede your work and fortune,

Be cheerful, happy, do not worry, the future will be very good.

For in accomplishing your role in our place that we strive for

It is our greatest hope to be together with you there.

The Hechalutz chapter at the farewell party for Y. Frankel (in the center)

[Page 73]

These words express the general spirit that pervaded amongst the youth of Chorzele during the time of the disturbances of 5689 / 1929 in the Land. At that time, Avraham Bialopolski of blessed memory, from the Jewish National Fund headquarters in Poland, came to Chorzele. His speeches at the Tarbut Chapter and in the synagogue left a deep impression on all strata of the town. Through these speeches, he contributed greatly to the success of the founding of the Hechalutz Chapter in Chorzele.

The work in the Hechalutz Chapter in Chorzele covered many areas: first and foremost, the study of Hebrew, general and Jewish history, the history of the Zionist movement, and the history of the general and Land of Israel Workers movement. There were question and answer evenings for all the residents of the town once a week. In general, there was barely any Zionist event in which Hechalutz and Young Hechalutz (which was founded around the same time) did not participate, and were not involved with. It is interesting to mention the celebration of Nachum Sokolow's 70th birthday, organized in the town with the participation of all the Zionist factions. Among other things, I related at that celebration that when N. Sokolow visited Poland in 1923, a special booklet in his honor, called "Nachum Sokolow" was published. That booklet included the words of Yaakov Fichman, Shalom Asch, Nachman Meisel, and others, as well as the words of our dear fellow townsman, the famous writer Reb Fishel Lachower of blessed memory. In his "Agadat Sokolow" articles, F. L. tells how N. Sokolow was greeted at the border near our town and brought to the house with "the special porch." It is interesting to note the juxtaposition of the situation, stating that Nachum Sokolow was hosted exactly in the same house in which we were now gathered approximately a decade later to celebrate his 70th birthday in the Tarbut headquarters of the town. In that article, the various legends circulating in our town regarding N. Sokolow are mentioned, and a comparison is made between the legends of Napoleon and the legends of Sokolow, proving the great esteem with which he was held in our town.

Members of Hechalutz engaged in agricultural work

The primary objective of Hechalutz in all its activities was to send as many members as possible to *hachsharah* kibbutzim to educate them and prepare them for *aliya* to the Land. There was barely any evening during the week in which we did not gather as the group. In addition to our studies, we dealt with all realistic questions related to the land of Israel. It is worthwhile to mention the 20th of Tammuz, 1931, when the Zionist organization in Chorzele organized an assembly in memory of Herzl. The representatives of all the Zionist organizations of the city participated, including: Reb Avraham–Michael Adler of blessed memory, the head of Mizrachi and the head of the Jewish community of Chorzele.

[Page 74]

He was a man of many activities, in whom issues of the Land of Israel as well as local Jewish communal issues formed a synthesis. His dedication to any person was boundless.

Incidentally, I recall an event of 1920. during the Bolshevik occupation, when soldiers of the Red Arm camped in Chorzele, and it was cut off from the entire region. My father of blessed memory and I walked to Przasnysz, 32 kilometers from our town. As we entered Przasnysz, they arrested us, along with all those who wanted to enter that town that day. They brought us to the local prison. Incidentally, Avraham–Michael of blessed memory, the deputy of the Rabkom, was there that day. (When the Red Army conquered Chorzele, they chose a gentile and a Jew to direct all town matters. They were called Rabkom.) He did not rest until he freed us from prison.

Reb Mordechai–Mendel Friedman, of blessed memory, the sponsor of the Jewish National Fund in Chorzele for many years, also participated in that assembly. He was of fine stature, with a black beard, always combed and neat. His love of the Land of Israel knew no bounds. He would also say, "I am a Hassid of Otwock, and I heed the words of the Rebbe in all matters. However, regarding the Land of Israel, these are my affairs."

My brother Shepsl of blessed memory also participated in that assembly in his capacity of chairman of the Zionist organization of Chorzele. He was a man of many talents, with clear and pleasant logic, who possessed initiative and clear grasp in all areas, and knew how to easily find a solution to the most complex of issues. It was said of him that the gentiles in the city council (magistrate), where he was the Jewish representative, were full of wonder over his practical suggestions, in which he found a solution to every problem.

Hershel Grynberg, the secretary of the Zionist Council of Chorzele, also participated in that assembly. He was a lad with a great deal of energy and a constant desire to act and do. He was full of life and dedication for matters relating to the Land of Israel.

I too was among those who participated in the assembly as a representative of Hechalutz. I spoke there and concluded my remarks with the following words:

"Fifty years ago, Herzl stated: Zion will be redeemed through labor. I derive from this that labor has caused a holy transformation. Labor in the kibbutzim in the Land of Israel has created a new, pure, fair life (according to the writing from Herzl's pen), which does not allow us to be satisfied only with what they create in the Land of Israel, but also with we build here in avant garde fashion in the pioneering kibbutzim, in the quarries, in the forests, fields, in the sawmills – in which we Chorzelers play no small role. (There were seven comrades from Chorzele on *hachsharah* at that time.) In the name of everyone I declare that we will not be satisfied if we do not accomplish the colossal work of the 20th century, in accordance with the mottoes of the representatives of the Labour Party in the Shaw Commission (Harry Snell)[3] – the creation of a Jewish national home on firm foundations in the Land of Israel."

[Page 75]

Following the assembly, we organized an evening dedicated to T. Herzl in the Hechalutz chapter itself. I searched for material that would survey the connection between Herzl and pioneering. However, since I could not find any fitting material, I wrote the following poem myself and gave it over to the group of students to be read. The following is the poem:

The Young Hechalutz Organization

1.

How rare it is that we have such people as we have here
As we had previously,
That with your wonderful dreams of redemption
You have forged the path for an entire people.

2.

You have called, encouraged, aroused
To common cause, unity, work and good fortune;
To a healthy, natural, life of a people
That must never turn backward.

3.

And the call that has arrived
From the depths of your pure soul;
That has shaken itself off seeing the Jewish situation
And has demonstrated wonder after wonder.

4.

The people has straightened up and arisen,
To a life, not of servitude, but of might:
From the might that has charged, that has sparkled,
That will free you from the exile.

5.

And the best of the liberators
Charge through the pioneering camps like fire:
That flickers, that burns, and is never extinguished,
An end to the exile. We must leave it behind"…

[Page 76]

The Trumpeldor Group of Young Hechalutz

[Page 77]

Hebrew course of Hechalutz (1933)

In the Hechalutz chapter, we dealt with questions related to the land of Israel, *hachsharah* kibbutzim, and *aliya*, as well as with problems connected to the Hechalutz fund, and Workers of the Land of Israel Fund. We decided to go out to work in order to provide funds for the Hechalutz fund. The girls went out to bake matzos for Passover, and the boys went to chop wood.

We participated in all the activities of the Jewish National Fund, and contributed to general cultural activities. Many people certainly remember the general interest surrounding the cultural evenings that took place on Friday nights. Many would place their notes with questions into the chest during the week, and wait all week for the response. The debates that took place regarding every question on Friday nights were educational–cultural events of great value for the entire town.

There was a *hachsharah* kibbutz for Poalei Agudas Yisroel in Chorzele, the first and only one in Poland at that time. Before I made *aliya* to the Land, almost all the members of that kibbutz came to me to bid farewell, either because of my status in Hechalutz or because my father Shmuel, of blessed memory, was the chairman of Agudas Yisroel in Chorzele. From time to time, he also gave lessons in Talmud for the members of that kibbutz. In response to their blessings, I said that despite the differences of opinions between us, they would easily become absorbed in the fields of the Land of Israel. Then, Avraham–Michael of blessed memory, who was among those gathered around, said, "What an ideal I see here. The Hechalutz of Histadrut and the Chalutzim of Poalei Agudas Yisrael are sitting together..."[4]

[Page 78]

Hechalutz Organization in 1934

The Dror Group of Young Hechalutz

[Page 79]

Despite the differences of world outlook and Zionist ideology, all the residents of the town lived their lives together, as good Jews very dedicated to issues of the land of Israel and the mutual benefit organizations that existed in Chorzele. This was a variegated, vibrant life, full of the content of a Jewish town. Our hearts can find no comfort over their loss. It there is some sort of comfort, it is only from the fact that a large number of the brothers, sisters, children, and grandchildren of the martyrs of Chorzele merited in participating in the establishment of the State of Israel. Through this activity, the great aspirations of the people of the destroyed town, those dear people whom we never cease to think about until this day, were realized.

*

As I think about our town as it was during its life, and bring to memory its vibrant personalities and their activities, it is natural that, first and foremost, the sublime image of my revered father, Reb Shmuel Frankel, comes to mind, symbolizing the entire picture for me.

He was called "Shmuel the Rabbi" in town. Why was he called "the Rabbi"? My father was not a rabbi, nor a Rebbe, and did not use his scholarship as a means of earning a livelihood. He was a scholar and a Hassid. I still remember his gold watch with the gold change that he showed us as youngsters and told us that he received it as a prize for his lecture on Tractate Nedarim with the Ran commentary, which he gave by heart on the occasion of his Bar Mitzvah. From that time, throughout his entire life, he never deviated from his study. He would host celebratory feasts annually on the occasion of the completion of study of the entire Talmud. When his sight dimmed, and he could no longer study and review form the source, he would review the Talmud by heart, from his memory alone, as our sages of blessed memory did in the Yeshivas of the Land of Israel and Babylonia, before the oral words of Torah study committed to print.

My father was a Hassid. I will never forget the Hassidic stories that I heard from him, with the enthusiasm and devotion that could only be expressed by a true Hassid. The stories ranged from the early stories of the Baal Shem Tov[5] until the latter stories of *Tzadikim* and Rebbes – the Gerrer Rebbe who was his Rebbe, the Kocker Rebbe, the Ciecanów Rebbe, and many others. He could tell stories about them all with the same feelings of enthusiasm for truth.

He was a proud Jew, with faith and strength. Once, the Magid of Bialystock (Rappaport), who was famous throughout Poland in those days, came to our town. In Chorzele, it was forbidden to go out on the street after 10:00 pm. due to the proximity with the border. The Magid continued speaking, and the congregation stood around him listening open–mouthed to every word. The hours passed, and nobody sensed it. Suddenly, the police chief appeared along with policemen and began to scatter the gathering. Then my father arose from the congregation, approached the police chief (a tall, broad–shouldered man, with a strong manner of speaking, and who instilled fear in all hearts) and whispered something in his ear... After that, he turned to the crowd and called them to enter the synagogue again and to continue to listen to the words of the Magid.

[Page 80]

My father was a strong, wise scholar. Our house was always filled with people from all strata of the population. Some would come to seek his advice in various areas of life, and in matters of Torah and Jewish law.

This is how I saw my father, and this is how I still see him, hearing his quiet, strong voice, peering into his eyes that sparkled with enthusiasm and Hassidic devotion, hearing his unique melodies that he brought with him from the Rebbe, those melodies that he imparted to us and that penetrated our hearts...

Translator's Footnotes

1. See https://en.wikipedia.org/wiki/1929_Palestine_riots

2. See https://en.wikipedia.org/wiki/Moyshe_Nadir

3. See https://en.wikipedia.org/wiki/Shaw_Commission

4. Histadrut is the Labor Zionist organization. The secularist Labor Zionists and the Orthodox Zionists as represented by Poalei Agudas Yisroel (even more traditionally religious than Mizrachi) would have significant differences of opinion.

5. Rabbi Yisrael Baal Shem Tov, the founder of Hassidism.

[Page 80]

Rabbi Chaim–Mordechai Bronroth,
May the memory of the Righteous be a Blessing
by Shimon Rav Yerushalmi

Translated by Jerrold Landau

In the year 5712 (1952), on the 7th of Adar, the day on which our tradition states that Moses our Teacher, of blessed memory, was born, Rabbi Chaim Mordechai Bronroth, may the memory of the righteous be a blessing, died. He had served as the rabbi and head of the rabbinical court in the community of Tel Aviv–Jaffa until his last day.

He was born in the year 5641 (1881) in Ostrołęka (Łomża district) in Congress Poland to his father Rabbi Natan Tzvi of blessed memory, a scholarly Jew who earned his livelihood from the sale of holy books. When the lad grew up, they could not find teachers for him in the city to develop his talents and broaden his knowledge, so his father brought him to the famous Yeshiva of Sochaczew, headed by Rabbi Avraham Borenstein, may the memory of the righteous be a blessing, the author of the well–known books *Eglei Tal* and *Responsa Avnei Nezer*.

When he was still young, he was accepted and ordained to the rabbinate by three great men of Israel: Rabbi Malkiel Tzvi Tenenbaum, may the memory of the righteous be a blessing, the rabbi of Łomża; Rabbi Moshe Nachum Jerusalimski, may the memory of the righteous be a blessing, rabbi of Kielce; and Rabbi Shimon Dov Anolik, may the memory of the righteous be a blessing, rabbi of Siedlice.

His first rabbinical seat was in the town of Czerwin, district of Łomża, where he served from 5661 (1901) until 5666 (1906). Then he set his eyes upon the community of Chorzele, district of Płock. He was chosen as the rabbi and the head of the rabbinical committee of the committee. The previous rabbi served in this position until the outbreak of the First World War. Then Rabbi Bronroth moved to Warsaw along with his entire congregation. I also moved to Warsaw at that time, and I spent a great deal of time in his small home. I had the chance then to get to know Rabbi Bronroth from up close, and to see his fine character traits – the love of his fellow Jew that pulsated from within him, and his efforts to be supportive of any downtrodden person.

Rabbi Bronroth did not close himself off within his four walls as the chairman of the local committee to assist the refugees from his community. He was also elected as a member of the central committee. He dedicated himself with all the warmth of his Jewish heart, and attached himself to the broad-ranging salvation activities of that committee. He was engaged in that holy work for two years.

[Page 81]

During those times, he dedicated his best efforts to rebuild the ruined Jewish homes in Poland and to strengthen their communities. His own community of Chorzele, however, did not return to what it had been previously.

He was chosen as the rabbi of Ciechanów (district of Płock). He served in splendor on the rabbinical seat that had been occupied by Rabbi Avraham Landau of blessed memory, who was known as Reb Avrahamele of Ciechanów. Rabbi Bronroth served in that position until the destruction of Ciechanów in the year 5699 (1939) – the year of the beginning of the Holocaust and the destruction of Polish Jewry by the brigades of Hitler, may his name be blotted out.

It is appropriate to mention that Rabbi Bronroth, one of the founders of the Mizrachi in Poland, an organization that Agudas Yisroel fought against, did not refrain from supporting Poalei Agudas Yisroel when it set up Torah classes for its members. He strengthened them by delivering the Talmud class for that organization as well[1].

Rabbi Bronroth had a deep understanding of the spirit of the Hebrew youth and their cultural aspirations. He immediately recognized the new winds blowing in the camp of Israel, and girded himself to forge a path that would be especially appropriate for the development of the life of the nation. His fine speeches, delivered in modern style, woven with words of our sages, full of content and ideas, won over the hearts of the religious youths to Zionism. He also succeeded in influencing those circles of youths who had already distanced themselves from the observance of the practical commandments.

Rabbi Bronroth of blessed memory was a blend of an upright communal activist with a warm Jewish heart, and greatness of Torah. He merited to disseminate his Torah knowledge to the masses in his books *Otzar Chaim* (commentaries, and speeches, in two parts); *Omer VeDevarim* on the Torah, the first section of which (*Bereishit, Shemot*, and *Vayikra*) appeared in the year 5666 (1936); and *Setirat Zekeinim* (statements of our sages of blessed memory on Jewish law and lore) that was published in Tel Aviv in the year 5709 (1949). We must lament that many of his letters and Torah novella were lost in the depths of the sea on his journey from England to the Land of Israel, after he was summoned to serve as the rabbi and head of the rabbinical court of Tel Aviv. It is also unfortunate that the rest of his manuscripts on Jewish law and lore have not been published to this day.

We should note the pamphlet that he published on the laws of milking animals on the Sabbath. We should also note the refinement of his soul, his love of his fellow man, and his way of greeting everyone pleasantly.

Rabbi Bronroth was one of the select group of rabbis of Poland who were sufficiently daring and strong to establish the Mizrachi movement and to broaden its scope throughout the entire country. He and his friends even stormed the fortresses of the Aguda with the warmth of their heart and their deep faith. In those days, no community remained in Poland in which a Mizrachi chapter or Young Mizrachi had not been set up. The late rabbi was not only graced with his convincing power of speech, but also with his command of the written word and his publicist articles in various newspapers, that were always written with depth of thought, and at times also included pleasant humor of jokes.

In 1922, he was given the task, along with his like–minded friend Rabbi Yitzchak Trunk, may the memory of the righteous be a blessing, the rabbi of Kutna, to undertake an important communal mission to the United States. This kept him away from his home and community for two years. While he was in the United States, the heads of the Lubavitch Hassidim in Chicago looked toward him and asked him to accept the rabbinical seat of the Tomchei Temimim community in that city. However, he did not want to abandon his community, so he only agreed to serve in the rabbinate that was offered to him in a temporary fashion until he returned to Ciechanów.

[Page 82]

In 1939, approximately two months before the outbreak of the Second World War, he was asked to undertake an important communal mission to England. Then the war broke out, and he was prevented from returning to his home. His community of Ciechanów was destroyed.

He was appointed as rabbi of Tel Aviv – Jaffa in the year 5703 (1943). With this, his aspiration to be in the Land of Israel and work there was actualized. He dedicated all his time and the best of his energies to reinforcing the Yeshiva of Rabbi Amiel, founded by Rabbi Amiel, the chief rabbi of Tel Aviv, may the memory of the righteous be a blessing. After the passing of Rabbi Amiel, he was chosen as the chairman of the Yeshiva leadership. He concerned himself with all its needs, and with expanding it.

I feel that I am not fulfilling my obligation if I do not take this opportunity to express my pain and anguish that this dear soul, who dedicated his entire essence to Torah and who served his community with faithfulness and dedication, seemed to be forgotten from the hearts of the leaders, administrators, and communal activists of the city. The heart is anguished that a Torah institution has not yet been set up in honor of the departed, and a street in Tel Aviv, to which he was a father and patron to all its religious needs, has not yet been named in his memory. The mayor, members of the city council and religious council, and the national religious party should ensure that the memory of this illustrious great person never be forgotten.

(*Hatzofeh*, 6 Adar II, 5725 – 1965)

During the Polish national holiday of May 3, 1930.
In the center is Rabbi M. Ch. Sokolower, rabbi of the town.

Translator's Footnote

1. Mizrachi is the Orthodox Zionist organization. Agudas Yisroel is a non–Zionist Orthodox organization. Over the years, they were often at odds with each other, especially with regards to attitudes toward Zionism.

[Page 83]

The Town's Rabbi and his Community
by Avraham Sokolower of Tel Aviv
Translated by Jerrold Landau

Rabbi Mordechai–Chaim Sokolower and his son Avraham

RABIN

M. Ch. SOKOŁOWER
Chorzele
pow. Przasnysz.

ה ר ב
מרדכי חיים בר"י סוקולובר
אב"ד דק"ק חורזל
מחוז פרושניק.

ב"ה, יום .... לחודש .... ש"י יומי .... תרצ"

The letterhead of Rabbi Mordechai Chaim the son of Rabbi Y. Sokolower

At the time when the people of Chorzele turned to my father, may the memory of the righteous be a blessing, to accept the rabbinical post in their town, he was offered the rabbinical seat in two larger towns as well. Father chose Chorzele because it was noted for its scholarly Jews and its interpersonal relationships based on love. Indeed, all strata of the community stood with him during his entire tenure in the Chorzele rabbinate, and all the local Jews held him in esteem.

I remember an incident when my father served as the rabbi on his first Torah adjudication between Reb Tevel Pater and Reb Yosef Chaim Marchaim. The issue was as follows: Reb Tevel received benevolent loans from Reb Yosef Chaim. After some time, when Reb Tevel wished to repay the loan to Reb Yosef–Chaim, the latter did not want to accept the money, claiming that Reb Tevel had already repaid what was owed. When the matter came before the rabbi for adjudication, it was of course difficult for my father to issue a verdict, whether in favor or against, especially since there was no precedent for such in halachic literature. After weighing the matter, my father decided that Reb Tevel should repay half the loan to Reb Yosef Chaim, and that they should mutually forgive the other half.

The essence of that case, where the basis of the dispute demonstrates the uprightness, logic and pure conscience of two Chorzele natives, influenced my father greatly. He would often discuss this characteristic incident in rabbinical circles, throughout many years.

I will now mention a fact that demonstrates the esteem and respect of the people of Chorzele toward their rabbi.

On a Sabbath afternoon, as I was sitting next to the window and reading *Pirkei Avot*[1], the words of two *apikorsim* [heretics] of Chorzele reached my ears – Avraham-Yitzchak Glicksberg, the founder of the Bund; and Zelig Sniadower. The latter said that he was prepared to pass through the market place bareheaded, holding his hat in his hand (there was not yet an eruv in Chorzele, so it was forbidden to carry on the Sabbath)[2]. The former claimed that he would not dare to do this. Indeed, Z. Sniadower began to carry out his "brazen" act, but as he passed by our home, the home of the rabbi, he did not stand by the test, and he put his hat on his head…

[Page 84]

The love and dedication of the natives of Chorzele for their rabbi is demonstrated by the following two events:

The first one: the wedding of my sister Chana of blessed memory. There was a great deal of preparation in the city as the wedding approached. The women of Chorzele organized themselves in a spontaneous fashion and created a special committee to prepare for the wedding festivities. A few days before the wedding, four women, headed by the cook Chaya–Sarah, began to work voluntarily. Mottel Lichtensztajn and Berl Brener sent a sack of flour to the bakery that had been specially milled for the wedding. Natan Prznyczer and Shimon Sniadower, the fish merchants, brought special fish from Germany for the wedding. The butchers donated a cow and two calves. A sack of lentils was brought directly to the *Beis Midrash* from an estate owner in a village. People sat there and sifted through the lentils for entire days. In one word: the atmosphere of general joy enveloped all the Jews of the town, and its signs were very evident. Most of the residents took off work to prepare for the wedding. Meir–Yaakov even delayed his *aliya* to the Land of Israel, for he did not want to miss being present at the wedding of the daughter of the rabbi.

Ben–Zion

The second one: the illness and passing of the rabbi. When the rabbi became ill with a malignant illness, he traveled to Warsaw for medical attention. All the people of Chorzele were very afraid of his situation. A committee was founded, headed by the mayor. When the bitter news of his illness reached us from Warsaw, Zalman Szulcz, the son–in–law of Avraham Sirota, visited us with a delegation from the town council, and informed us that the community was willing to undertake anything necessary to save the rabbi.

When all hope of saving him disappeared, and they brought him back home, there was great worry. Members of the community set up a watch around his sickbed, day and night. Reb Yosef the *shochet* [ritual slaughterer] was disappointed that they did not include him in the watch around my father's sickbed because his age and weakness; whereas Avraham Sar, the town clown, had the good fortune of being part of the night watch at the bedside. Once again, the townsfolk neglected their personal affairs, and did not travel to Warsaw for shopping, lest the bitter day come and they would miss the funeral of the rabbi.

[Page 85]

Translator's Footnotes

1. See https://en.wikipedia.org/wiki/Pirkei_Avot
2. See https://en.wikipedia.org/wiki/Eruv for details on an eruv, and how its presence can allow carrying in public on the Sabbath.

The Gabbai of the Synagogue and his Dream
by Avraham Sokolower of Afula
Translated by Jerrold Landau

Chet – Grace and splendor are poured upon you[1]

Your streets were glorified by our dear ones in their splendor.

Vav – Your houses of study beamed with the radiance of their worshippers

Woe! How you turned from nobility to debasement.

Resh – The evil ones desecrated your honor, and you were given over to them

Your ground absorbed the blood of the martyrs, and you did not tremble.

Zayin – Your memory will be wiped out, and your name will not be mentioned

Only through an innuendo I will mention it, because of those resting in your dust

Lamed – The memory of the pure martyrs who ascended heavenward in a whirlwind

May their memories be bound in the bounds of life.

Father of blessed memory and Reb Tanchum Kowel of blessed memory served as the *gabbaim* [trustees] of the synagogue and *Beis Midrash* for many years, until they resigned for an unknown reason. The entreaties of Reb Avraham–Michel Adler of blessed memory, the head of the community, as well as various householders that they continue as *gabbaim* were to no avail. Only after a brief conversation with the rabbi of the town, the Rabbi and Gaon Mordechai–Chaim of blessed memory, did my father declare that he was continuing in his post of *gabbai* together with his friend Reb Tanchum Kowel. We did not know what influenced him until one day father told the secret when we were sitting in the *sukka* of Reb Tevel Pater of blessed memory on Sukkot. The following is father's story.

During the time of the Bolshevik war against young Poland (1920), the troops of General Haller[2] pillaged Jews throughout Poland. They also reached Chorzele. At that time, there were foreign Jews in Chorzele who moved from their places out of fear of war. Seven such Jews, mainly from Mława near Chorzele, were stopped by the army. The soldiers also wanted to remove

Father from the house. We children began to cry. A miracle took place, for the soldiers left him and disappeared. The army commander promised that nothing bad would happen to the imprisoned Jews. They would be sent to their hometowns, where they would be given over to civilian guard. To our great sorrow, we found out two days later that these Jews were murdered along the way.

The war ended, and life resumed its normal course. One night, Father saw in a dream the aforementioned murdered Jews, dancing enthusiastically in a circle. He stood and watched. One of them extended his hand and said, "Matityahu, come along, and we will dance together..." Father refused to approach, but when the person tried to pull him into the circle by force, one of the group of those dancing shouted to him, "Leave him, do you not know that Matityahu *gabbai*..." Then he woke up.

[Page 86]

He did not tell this dream to anyone other than the aforementioned rabbi. In the ceremony to ameliorate the dream[3], the rabbi told him, "You were given a great opportunity, for you occupy yourself faithfully with communal needs, and this good deed will protect you."

When he resigned from his position as *gabbai*, the rabbi reminded him of his dream. He then agreed to rescind his resignation.

Translator's Footnotes

1. This poem forms the acrostic Chorzele with the first letter of each pair of lines.

2. See https://en.wikipedia.org/wiki/J%C3%B3zef_Haller

3. See http://www.dailyhalacha.com/m/halacha.aspx?id=254 for a note on the *Hatavat Chalom* ceremony.

My Brother Fishel
by Dvora Lachower
Translated by Jerrold Landau

I will not reminisce about the childhood of my brother Fishel. Of course, in our family, they would always say that he was a very alert child, wild, joyous, and jocular. Therefore, all the members of the household loved him. His older sisters displayed special affection to him, and all spoiled him. Our mother used to say that when he would come home from *cheder* during the summer, he would take off his boots before he entered the house and toss them through the open window, as a sign that he was coming in. Garno, the "gentile" in our house, would say that "Fishek has come." The entire area was then full of bustle and noise.

I will reminisce about when he was an older lad, already studying with the prominent teachers in the city, who always praised him to his friends. Even with all this, there were times that he looked upon the childhood games with jealousy. I still remember how, overcome by the rage of a game, he once grabbed a rubber ball from my hands, and bounced it enthusiastically from the grass heap behind the thorn fence – straight into the fruit orchard of our neighbor the "Gentile". That person was known in town as the "witch" on account of her evil temperament. She instilled fear in young and old. And now, in the garden of the witch... The loss pained me deeply, and I cried bitterly.

He had a refined looking face, pale but not sickly. He was always thinking. He would pace back in the room for hours, to the point of dizziness. The look on his face stated that he was deliberating over something, for many thoughts eked at his mind. Our oldest brother, two years older than him, was also studying in *cheder*. The two youths were bond with a deep sense of love and friendship, even though they were different in spirit and character.

[Page 87]

The education of the children was primarily in the hands of our mother, since Father was employed in south Russia. He was away from home for most of the year. He would only come home for two months in the summer to rest a bit in the bosom of the family.

Our home, blessed with children, and considered one of the wealthy homes in the town, stood at the edge of the road. Large grassy meadows and fields extended out from there. The barns of the gentiles also stood there. The Orzyc River wound through it like a silver band, cutting through the areas of greenery dotted with flowers. At sunset during the summer, the two brothers would take long walks there, conversing animatedly. However, the older brother suddenly became very ill, and our mother went abroad with him for medical purposes. The illness lasted for years, and separated the beloved brothers for a prolonged period. The lad would then go into seclusion, and immerse himself even more in his studies, which were devoted half to religious studies and half to secular studies. He was now studying with the rabbinical judge of the city, a great scholar in Torah. He then studied with the rabbi, a progressive, enlightened man who enjoyed his "*maskil*" student very much. He also studied with the lads of the city in the *Beis Midrash*. On winter nights, they would engage in stormy debates on matters of religion and *haskalah*. The debates would often become very sharp.

Fishel Lachower during his youth in Chorzele (1900)

Fishel was the primary speaker, and on occasion, he would be reproved by his Orthodox friends for his heretical viewpoints. He would be especially reproved by the "silken men"[1] who came from afar, were supported at the tables of their wealthy in–laws, and were studying Torah for its own sake.

Our town of Chorzele was situated on the border of Eastern Prussia (only two kilometers away). Various business connections bound the two sides of the border together. The sons would also often become involved in this business with the Germans. On the other hand, the business of several of the prominent businessmen, such as our father, was in Russia. Thus, the town burst forth from its narrow, provincial confines, and became involved in international commerce.

[Page 88]

These business dealings with the broad world were one of the factors why the lads would not only diligently study religious studies, but also the German and Russian languages. Of course, this was without the aid of teachers, for there were no teachers of this sort in our town. There was only one "intelligentsia" family in town. It was a bit of a mystery how they came to this remote place with their expensive, shiny utensils, their fine mannerisms, and their European politeness. The townsfolk would mention their name with special awe: the sons wore "short" garments and the girls were finely bedecked, even on weekdays. All of them were sent to study in gymnaszjas in Warsaw. The young Nachum Sokolow[2] was apparently once a guest in this home, as is told, when he was passing through our town on route to Berlin. There was a Hebrew–German library there, where the few *maskilim* of our town quenched their thirst for enlightenment. There was another, larger library in our town, mainly Hebrew, owned by a neighbor and friend of our family, who had no children. (Like our father, he was a merchant in south Russia). He displayed a special love to my two brothers. This man was also known as "an outsider". He dressed in finery, and his small, shiny, nice house stood at the edge of the city, surrounded by fruit orchards and flower gardens. Bright pathways, decorated with grass, led to the lovely entrance and the clean, cool rooms. The library in that house was the first stop on Fishel's path to Hebrew education.

As mentioned, our father came home for a few months during the summer. He was not completely satisfied with his son, who dedicated himself more and more to *haskalah*. Father's desire was that his son dedicate himself primarily to Torah, and become a receptacle for it. He himself was a pious, learned Jew, but not zealous. During the summer, when he used to come to live with the family, he would read *Hatzefira* every day, and would especially enjoy *Haoreach Leshabat* and *Mamaranan Derabanan*. Later, he enjoyed the feuilleton of David Frischman in Hayom. He enjoyed publicity material. He read biographies of famous people, travel books, and the like with great interest. However, regarding words of *apikorsut* [heresy] or books about love, he literally trembled in anger, and took out his anger on his son, or even on us, his daughters. Due to his asthma, from which he always suffered, he would not attend daily services, but he would worship on Sabbaths and festivals in the new *Beis Midrash*, where the honorable *misnagdim* [Hassidic opponents] worshipped. Nevertheless, he would turn to the Rebbe of Amshinov (Mszczonów) for advice during times of difficulty. When Father was away from home, Mother would travel to the Rebbe in his stead. She would tell us with holy awe that it was the custom in our house for many years to light a candle on the yahrzeit of the elder Rebbe of Amshinov. Our father never failed to ask advice about how to imbue this spirit on his son the *apikorus* [heretic]. Once he asked the rabbi of the city to bring his student to the Rebbe of Gur. Fishel often liked to describe this journey – how he was brought before the Rebbe on a Sabbath afternoon, wearing a silk *kapote*, a *gartel* [ritual belt], and a *streimel* on his head.

[Page 89]

In the meantime, our oldest brother returned from Germany, where he had been convalescing from his severe illness for many years. He was diligent with his studies during his illness. He became fluent in the German language and its literature, and he greatly expanded his knowledge of the Hebrew language. The loving connection between the two brothers was renewed with greater strength. They would debate, and delve for many hours into literary matters. I remember how I listened excitedly to their words, praying in my heart that I would also be able to reach that level of understanding in my studies, and to understand the "language of innuendo" that the spoke.

Both brothers were immersed in their studies day and night – especially Fishel, who struggled greatly and attained new concepts in literature, history, geography, and the like on a daily basis.

Apparently, he began his literary attempts at the very young age of 14 or 15, but he kept the matter secret. However, when it seemed to him that he had succeeded in writing down that which was in his heart, it was difficult for him to stifle his spirit. "Behold, I have found a good word, but it is a word," he would declare enthusiastically. After deliberating, he declared a new "find," for in the meantime he found a "better" word than the first one. He continued to develop these "finds" and to forge and refine himself endlessly.

Our father was secretly proud of his successful son, but he would not admit such in public. He saw no "goal" for him in all of this. Out of concern for his future, he decided to direct him in the practical world. Therefore, he once took him to Rostov on Don in southern Russia where he ran a large–scale fish business, sending wagons of fish from the river abroad.

However, as could be imagined from the outset, Father's business did not attract the heart of the lad. On the other hand, he had his first opportunity to spend an extended period in a large city, to absorb the atmosphere of a metropolis, to visit libraries, and to meet with enlightened people. There he also met his good friend, a student of philosophy and a scholar of Hebrew literature, Vigdorov, with whom he exchanged correspondence for many years.

After some time, he returned to our town and to his studies. But our father did not despair of "turning him into a person." Not long passed before he made a match for him with a lovely girl, the daughter of a wealthy merchant from the nearby district city of Ciechanów. He bore the yoke of a family before he was twenty years old.

Then he endured difficult years of deliberation, for he was suddenly removed from the world of his dreams and placed in the world of reality. The home of his wealthy father–in–law, with its splendid fine goods shop in which all family members were involved on a practical basis, was not conducive to broadening his knowledge. The army duty that was imposed upon him sealed off his path of completion. Even later, when he was discharged, he was perplexed and confused, not knowing the path to take for himself. Father then made his final attempt to bring his son into his business, and summoned him to Rostov for that purpose. Father's command and the idea of meeting his beloved brother, whom Father had succeeded in attracting to his business even though his heart was far from it, influenced him, and he set out on the journey. Of course, he did not gain a hold in the business even that time, and he quickly returned home to his father–in–law. However, this time he had a reward for this journey. He went through Odessa on his way back, where he met Bialik and Ahad–Ha'am for the first time. This was a deep experience for him, and left an indelible mark on his soul.

[Page 90]

Now, his path was clearer. He did not waste the time in his father–in–law's home. He learned a great deal and broadened his knowledge. He produced the first of his literary attempts. When he was 20 years old, in the year 5664 (1904), he published his first article on Tchernichovsky[3] in the literary periodical of *Hatzefira*. Later his work on Bialik and short article on Ahad Ha'am were published in Brener's *Hameorer*. Finally, his article on Sholem Asch was published in *Haolam*. His articles, which did not go unnoticed in Hebrew literary criticism, strengthened his spirit, and further forged his path for the future. He left his city of residence, Ciechanów at the beginning of the year 5668 (1907) and moved to Warsaw. He then fully decided that his path was to be in literature.

In Warsaw, he stood on his own for the first time. He was liberated from the environment and atmosphere of the town. He thirsted for creativity and activity. He met the great writers – Peretz, Frischman, and Zeitlin[4], as well as the young writers of Warsaw, who gathered around the three great ones and formed a group of followers, as it were. On visits during Sabbaths and festivals, the homes of these three were filled with an enthusiastic crowd of admirers, who soaked up the words of their masters with thirst. There, they deliberated over matters of literatures, and conducted vibrant discussions, which were later disseminated by the young ones and served as topics of debate in the literary circles of Warsaw. Fishel, who already admired Frischman, would visit his home every Sabbath. His wife used to say, "He went to pray at Frischman." Indeed, it was a sort of prayer...

This connection with Frischman quickly led to a collaboration between them – in editing three anthologies of *Safrut* and later founding a library with that name. Together, they published the 50 booklets of *Reshafim*, — bi–weekly literary anthologies. As a sole editor, Fishel only published in the year 5673 (1913) in the *Netivot* anthology. In its time, it made a great impression on the literary circles. His plan was to publish *Netivot* as a monthly. The plan was abandoned because of the First World War, which broke out at that time.

The war quickly resulted in a cessation of all literary activity in Poland. Fishel who at the time was at the beginning of his path and in the spring of his life, with many dreams and plans in his mind, remained perplexed once again. He was also bearing the yoke of a large family. During the times of upheaval at the beginning of the war, he had no possibility in continuing his literary pursuits, so he started to work as one of the editors of the Merkaz publishing house. He edited several important books (in the public Achisefer Library of Warsaw–Berlin).

[Page 91]

These activities were insufficient for the livelihood of his family, so he was forced to take on the position of teacher of Hebrew literature in the well–known Gymnasja of Krinski. When Poland was conquered by the Germans, a pedagogic institution for teachers named for Sh. L. Gordon was opened in Warsaw, and Fishel was appointed as a teacher of Hebrew literature. (Hillel Zeitlin, with whom Fishel was very close, taught Talmud in that school.) The teaching job, which lasted for two years, and the preparations for it, which placed a heavy yoke upon Fishel at that time, later lead to the writing of his significant book "The Annals of New Hebrew History."

At the end of the war, when the publication of *Shtibel* transferred from Moscow to Warsaw, its leadership was given over to Fishel on the recommendation of Frischman. Anyone who saw him at that time, when the building of Hebrew Literature fluttered before the eyes of his spirit, saw the man in his boundless dedication. It was as if he found the blend of effort and actualization. Fishel dedicated himself fully to the publication of *Shtibel*. Even though running those matters occupied much of his time, he edited many more books of fundamental or translated literature, which were published by that publishing house. He also wrote the introduction to several important books of world literature. Then he published his book "Research and Experience (A)," his first anthology, which included all his articles on books of *Haskalah* and books of his generation.

When he was appointed as editor of *Hatekufa* along with Yaakov Cohen (later Yaakov Fichman also joined them for some time), Fishel participated in each book, with major articles, as well as in other articles in various publications. He immersed himself fully in editing and writing for eight years, as he faced the many constant obstacles and difficulties that are natural in such a major enterprise. However, he knew how to bear his suffering, for the benefit of literature was before his eyes constantly.

Throughout all his hard work in publishing Shtibel, Fishel had only one year of respite, and perhaps of great satisfaction, when he came to Berlin to spend time with his revered teacher M. Y. Berdichevsky, who agreed to publish his writings only under his own supervision. The almost daily contact with his great friend did wonders for his soul and spirit. It seemed as if many doubts that grew in his heart from way back and tormented his soul very much were resolved. This meeting, which yielded great results, was fateful in his life. Even during his most difficult days, and to his final days, he imagined Berdichevsky before him always.

He did not arrange its day of celebration, for *Shtibel's* business took a sudden turn for the worse, and he lost most of his money. The publication of books, which was a very broad endeavor, involved significant investment, and Fishel encountered difficulties. He made plans for naught, and sought advice which ended up not being legitimate. When things got very difficult, he hurried to Paris, then to London, and finally to America. Unlike his nature, he knocked on the doors of philanthropists and non–philanthropists – but the solution was not to be found. Disappointed and broken in body and spirit, he returned to Warsaw. Out of great despair, he invested his sole property, his wife's jewelry and expensive wedding gifts, in this bad business,

[Page 92]

with the hope of salvaging a small amount. However, fate did not allow him to see the strengthening of this fine structure, the desire of his soul, that was built with dedication of the soul and great love by two men.

He left Warsaw in 1927 with his family, and made *aliya* to the Land of Israel. Earlier, he had visited there briefly, on his way to America.

During the final years of his life, he continued in the writing of his large book "Bialik – His Life and Creations." At the same time, he busied himself with the translation of the Zohar[5] into Hebrew, together with his friends Sh. A. Horodsky and Y. Tishbi. In his quiet workroom, with the backdrop of books crowded on the bookshelves surrounding the walls, the man sat immersed in his work, introspective, and serious. His face exuded a shine, and his eyes sparkled. The tenderness that was constantly in his soul now shone forth more strongly to his family – to his children, small grandchildren, and his close surroundings. He was always concerned about his friends. At times, he would get up suddenly in the middle of his work to visit a sick friend.

On the last day of his life (1 Adar, 5707 / 1947), he felt well. He worked on *Mishnat Hazohar* along with Y. Tishbi of Jerusalem from morning until noon. He continued with this work in the evening, feeling in very good spirits. At the request of the members of his household, he set out before dinner on a brief walk to the nearby boulevard. (Fishel loved to take such walks on his own. In his own words, he was able to clarify for himself during those times things that he could not clarify as he sat at his table). Before he set out, he excused himself to the guests and said, "I will return home shortly. I am very tired. I will get a bit of fresh air, and return..."

What did he clarify for himself during his final flight of thought, before the light was suddenly extinguished, and darkness enveloped him?..."

(*Davar*, Tel Aviv, March 12, 1948).

Shlomo–Yehuda Lachower
(1846–1918)

Chana–Breina Lachower
(1858–1945)

Translator's Footnotes

1. A term for the wealthy young men who are supported by their in–laws and do not have to worry about the realities of life.
2. See https://en.wikipedia.org/wiki/Nahum_Sokolow
3. See https://en.wikipedia.org/wiki/Shaul_Tchernichovsky
4. See http://www.yivoencyclopedia.org/article.aspx/Frischman_David and https://en.wikipedia.org/wiki/Aaron_Zeitlin
5. The Zohar is the major book of Kabbalah.

[Page 93]

F. Lachower – Lines about his Life and Personality
by Yaakov Fichman
Translated by Jerrold Landau

F. Lachower

(18 Cheshvan 5644, 5 Adar 5707 1883–1947)

During his lifetime, he did not stand out, and he did not promote himself or his wide–branched activities. However, after he left us, the absence of this variegated writer, who served in many positions, and whose name is bound to many large literary anthologies, is felt. He was involved in valuable literary pursuits, that strengthened the creativity of the generation, and into which he devoted much of his talents, knowledge, and energy – much of his life. We feel that we lost a man of a clear pen and a clear intellect, for whom literature was not a diversion, who never treated his work lightly in any role that was placed upon him. He was a working man, diligent, trustworthy, a friend and partner in institutions of literature and writers – to whom he gave of his energy and time, and was also concerned about their honor, as he was concerned about the honor of literature. He was a man whom was always seen as stringent in his own work as a writer – a researcher, an editor – who literary gave his soul for these things.

[Page 94]

Such was the echo that he left behind after he left – an echo of clarity and dedication. His connection to the work was as important as the work itself.

a.

F. Lachower was born on the 18th of Cheshvan 5644 (1883) in Chorzele, a Polish town on the border with East Prussia. His father, Shlomo Yehuda, was a wealthy merchant, Orthodox in outlook, but not extremist — he would always read *Hatzefira*, and although he felt the Talmud and the religious legal decisions to be the main topics in the teaching of children, he also incidentally approved of the acquisition of secular knowledge. The writer displayed superior talents when he was still a lad, displayed a blend of expertise and sharpness. He tried his hand at the writer's craft when he was still a young man. Since most of his work was with works of research (one of the books which broadened his horizons in historical research of our literature was *Dor Vador Dorshav* by A. H. Weiss. According to his own words, he was also influenced by Shneur Zak's, whose works blended poetry and thought) – it is no wonder that his first efforts were in research. One of his attempts – regarding Hillel and Shamai – he sent to Dr. Sh. Bernfeld, with the understanding that this work would not embarrass him. Indeed, he received an encouraging response. However, he still did not see himself prepared for his great role as a writer, so he applied himself diligently to his studies. Through his reading at that time, he also gained vast knowledge in modern literature and world literature. By nature, he was diligent, and he loved learning for its own sake.

In 5664 (1904), he married Beila Krowiner, who was his faithful companion until his last day. He moved to Ciechanów, the city of his father–in–law, and lived there for about three years. During those years, he tried his hand at business, but did not succeed. He continued to study and to write.

In the year 5664 (1904), he published his first article in the literary supplement of *Hatzefira*. It was dedicated to the poetry of Tshernichovsky. He published his first articles on Ahad Ha'am and Bialik in *Hameorer*. The restricted confines of Ciechanów became too narrow for him. He set his intention on moving to Warsaw, with the hope and aspiration that literature or the publishing would be the source of his livelihood.

He moved to Warsaw in 5667 (1907). He became close with Frischman and began to publish the *Safrut* anthology, serving as co–editor. He also founded a publishing house by that name (the *Safrut* Library, and others). In 5669 (1909), he published the literary weekly Reshafim (in which he published the

Frischman's translation of Nietzsche's *Thus Spoke Zarathustra*, and Gnessin's best work, *Beterem*). As long as he was still a novice to literature and publishing, he quickly found people to be close with, and attracted them to his circles. The following names are prominent in the books he published: Berdichevsky, Brenner, Shufman, Gnessin – the forgers of modern Hebrew prose after Mendele. However, the Safrut publishing house could not maintain itself. He moved his entire printing press over to *Tushia* (*Central*) where he worked as an editor. He succeeded in that department, in which Sh. Y. Ish–Horowitz also worked as a publisher. With his help, he founded the *Sifria Hakelalit* (edited by Frischman) and he published on his own the large literary anthology *Netivot* – his first enterprise as an editor, in which he expressed his leanings to which he was faithful for his entire life. There, he published his large article on Berdichevsky, in which he expressed his soulful closeness – it is possible to say, rhythmic, to the wonderful poet of prose, full of flourishing resonance, with innuendos to expression better than the expression itself. He learnt the "anti–classic" style from him, the power of which lay in truncated lines on the threshold of expression – the power of anything that was truly modern. He also drew him closer to Shufman and Gnessin. In his introduction to Gnessin's letters (first edition), he was one of the first to capture the delicate charms of the author of *Beterem* and *Etzel*.

[Page 95]

These two articles, on Berdichevsky and Gnessin – were to some degree Lachower's first powers and strength, through which he acquired his place in literature. When he attained a certain status in his chosen profession, he began to wonder about his path, which seemed to light. This was during the time of the First World War, which for him were times of illness and great want. Nevertheless, they were times of study and preparation for the role of critic, in which he appreciated the significance of the works. As a teacher of literature in the Sh. L. Gordon institute, he stood up to the dilettantism that pervaded in the annals of history in general, and of the times of the *haskalah* in particular. Already at that time, as he would record his lessons in his notebook, he would turn his attention to the needs of the book, to light up the visions of modern literature for its era – without relying on hypotheses, but rather on an examination of the sources themselves. In *Hatzefira* (the seventh) during the war years, he published his articles on the era of the *haskalah* (on Ran'ak, Mapu, and others). The research strands of these articles were based upon the foundation of assessment. (Incidentally, in his articles on Mapu, there are several hypotheses – such as "At the time Mapu came to write *Ahavat Tzion*, his intention was to only create a type of literary allegory", etc. This was later confirmed by Mapu in one of his letters. In the year 5680 (1920, he published his article on Shalom HaKohen in *Hatefkufa*, in which he displayed signs of a literary historian, armed with vast knowledge. He constructed his research on the basis of material that he gathered from all corners of *haskalah* literature. He never presented a hypothesis without "breaking it on its back," without any struggle, but through enlightening the poet whose name had almost been forgotten, a sign of his new path – the transition of the path of the researcher. Or, as G. Kressel noted well, he forged the blend of the "law and lore" of the researcher, who did not forego the awakening of the heart, without which without which the words of poetry are only grasped from the outside.

[Page 96]

At the end of the war, he founded the *Arachim* stage, which had been cancelled in favor of *Hatekufa*, which moved to Warsaw. At that time, he was appointed as editor of the large Shtibel publishing house. Not only did he concern himself with its spiritual basis, but also, at the end, for its very existence when its time of crisis came. We cannot describe the energy that he imbued into the spiritual work, in terms of its content and variety. He became one of the editors of *Hatekufa*. He overcame and raised the status of that anthology. As would be done with any publication that tended toward fine literature, he also raised its scientific profile. As an editor and a publisher, he displayed the sense of a builder, whose attention was on the entire structure rather than solely on the isolated sections. His crowning achievement as editor of *Shtibel* can be seen in the organization of the writings of M. Y. Berdichevsky – an exemplary publication.

He continued with his personal work during this time of bustling activity. In 5685 (1925), he published his book "Studies and Experiments," the first anthology of his research. It was renewed and strengthened ten years later in "Early and Latter Ones" (published by *Dvir*) – one of the finest anthologies in our literature. When he made *aliya* in the year 5687 (1927), he finally approached his primary life's work – "Annals of New Hebrew Literature." The publishers of *Dvir* assisted the author while he was busy with that composition. It seems that everything that he had done until that point was only a preparation for that book, which served as an example, and to some degree a warning, for those that followed. In it, he presented a plan for an edifice of thoughts. The paths of the development of our new literature in all its facets are noted. With the legacy that pervades this profession, it was his duty to light up important and forgotten visions (especially in the areas of thought and science). He literally resurrected the dead. This was an effort that had some "novelty." Bialik, whom he praised in a great composition, was restricted in definition to a book. Heaven forbid, not a sharp survey, "deriving something from something" but rather the fruits of collection in the body of the sources – he taught and did not leave anything behind.

That collection, perhaps with the addition of depth and preparation, was displayed in his final composition on Ch. N. Bialik. What especially stood out was the dissection of the biographical section (particularly related to the circles from which he emanated, from the days in Volozhin, and other places) with an exacting examination that he dredged up from Bialik's archives. Before us is the most complete biography – a concentration of material that no future biographer of Bialik would be unable to make use of. He places before the reader all the sources that that the writer used in their full depth, so the researcher can study them. This is very important with Bialik's works, for he used such a massive number of sources. His diligent hands also added notes from his [Bialik's] autobiographic material. He especially dissected his [Bialik's] autobiographical letter to Klausner, in which the variances of text illustrate small nuances of the soul of the poet.

This monumental work, which he undertook after Bialik's death, and of which two volumes were published during the author's lifetime, was his chief accomplishment, and occupied him until his final days. He did not abandon this even during his serious illness. His great desire was to complete this life's work, into which he invested the love and dedication of ten consecutive years. To our sorrow, the third volume only included a third of what he had planned. (It has now been published by *Mossad Bialik* and *Dvir*.) Chapters of the history of literature, only reaching up to the first chapters of Bialik, were also included in it.

[Page 97]

In this addendum to his monumental book, he deals with one of the most interesting eras of our new literature – the era of the transition from *haskalah* [enlightenment] to revival. Here too, he leads us with a trustworthy hand through the fruitful web of the era of Chovevei Tzion, in which the first sprouts began to appear, a harbinger to the days of great fruitfulness that came with Tchernichovsky, Berdichevsky, Ahad Ha'am, and Bialik. He did not merit to record the new era, the era of actualization. Indeed, in "Early One and Latter Ones" he presented several of the great visionaries – from Ahad Ha'am and Berdichevsky to Brenner and Shufman, Agnon and Hazaz. In a small survey that was written twenty years ago, he outlines the main themes of Dvora Baron, the best female story teller in our literature.

While working as the editor of Knesset in memory of Bialik, in which he published several important compositions, including "In the Gates of the Tower" – he worked (along with Sh. A. Horodecki, and V. Tishbi) on the Hebrew translation of selections of the Zohar. His research during that time was especially dedicated to the mystical doctrine, especially in analyzing the Ramch'al from a Kabbalistic perspective. He struggled with enthusiasm and great zeal in exposing the mysteries of Luzzato's poetry. This was written during his last days, with great attentiveness. He was a small but powerful researcher in the Kabbalistic innuendoes in the Ramch'al's lyrics.

This enthusiasm for the Ramch'al, whom he regarded first and foremost as a great Kabbalist, demonstrates that those times in his youth that he spent with Hillel Zeitlin gave him a deep grasp of the world that only ripened in his latter days.

On his last day on earth, he sat for several hours with Y. Tishbi editing the translated chapters of the Zohar. When I went to visit him in the evening, his spirits were good, despite his weariness. It was evident that the work he was occupied with that day gave him great joy. Indeed, this was the final joy of his life.

When I entered his home, I found him in the corridor preparing to go for a short walk on the boulevard. I did not accompany him, for I did not want to get him involved in a conversation, since the doctors forbade such, especially at times when he was very tired.

He asked me to wait for him, saying:

"Sit down for a short while. I will return shortly..."

These were the final words that came from his mouth.

We, the entire family, sat together and waited for a long time. When his wife saw that he did not return, she got concerned and went to look for him. Before she returned, a representative from the Hadassah Hospital arrived, and we quickly found out that he suffered a stroke while he was walking. With a broken heart we saw the man, who was clear in his thinking throughout his entire illness and never lost any of his sharpness or even his sense of humor, now lying unconscious. The doctors did not conceal his desperate condition from us. His family members and friends, the veteran writers, stood guard by his bed day and night until he took his last breath.

[Page 98]

When news of his death spread, all his acquaintances fell into a deep mourning. A large group from Tel Aviv, Jerusalem, Haifa, and the settlements silently accompanied the writer, who maintained his position also during the days when the sharp knife was already resting on his neck. Everything that the man did was done with faithfulness.

Next to Beit Bialik, of which he was a dedicated member since the day of its founding, he was eulogized in his name and in the name of the Bialik Institute. He had imbued a great deal of his effort into that institute, and assisted in carrying out its construction. They presented the image of their member with penetrating and clear comments. I eulogized him to the extent that I could over his open grave. All the newspapers in Israel and the Diaspora dedicated words of appreciation to him, and noted his precious talents and the irreplaceable loss to our literature and our culture.

b.

His personality was more complex than his thinking. From the beginning he displayed a dual leaning, to scientific investigation as well as criticism of poetry. Even though he tended toward the research side in his latter days – he did not stop being a critic. This was evident when he developed his letters on Gnessin to true achievement, demonstrating his power of penetrating such veiled poetry.

This dual connection to criticism was the characteristic trait of his personality. This set him apart from most of the critics of his time. He was almost the only one like that. He was the first to demonstrate that poetry and science are not two opposites, but rather can be of a single essence when they both have true quality. He perhaps caught on to forgery in science more quickly than he caught on to forgery in poetry, but he was shocked with lies in either of them. He had a sense of true values in contrast to imaginary values. From this perspective, the students of Frischman and Berdichevsky were united; both learned to grasp the quality of dual creativity, and to expose its value in all its covers that it wore.

He delved into this great quality in all the many varied matters that were included in his life's work – he delved into the comprehensiveness of knowledge and the depth of understanding, and did not jump to a conclusion without a sevenfold investigation the foundations upon which it was based. An investigation of the sources preceded any conclusion. Nevertheless, even though he was a man of detail according to his education and tendencies, he was blessed with an appreciation and thirst for poetry, which was the essence and chief trait of any critic of stature.

At the outset of his work, before attaining fame, he involved himself in orderly research. However, the young man was attracted to poetry, and it was the poetry of Tshernichovsky that preceded that of Bialik. Berdichevsky preceded Ahad Ha'am. His roots were in Poland: Warsaw and not Odessa. Odessa, which was overly clear and overly linear, lacked the mystery. In the early days, he also expressed his opposition to this (in a booklet that was published against Ahad–Ha'am). Nevertheless, when he matured, he also understood the secret of the structure of the mighty ones of Odessa, and began to research Bialik, which was a synthesis of all varieties of new poetry.

Modern prose was close to his soul and his grasp. This led him to a different aspiration – poetry awakened an unexpected revelation, with an unexpected result. Therefore, his true teacher was not Frischman with his harmonic style, even though he served him throughout his early days; but rather Berdichevsky, whose pleasantness came specifically from the dissonance that accompanied him. It was not only the chapters of appreciation and memoirs that he wrote about Berdichevsky that demonstrated great sharpness and soulful closeness; but the style and forms of expression also demonstrated his strong connection to the man, to his poetry, to his struggles in style and struggles in thought. It was not easy to parse this, and he was not looking for ease. He did not become involved in anything in which he did not immerse his entire being.

[Page 99]

c.

When he came to figure out his prime role, and realized that his unique mission was in Hebrew criticism, and especially in an investigation of the sources and a collection of facts – he set his unique place in literature. This is what turned him into a literary historian, and led him to forge his path in this direction. All history is a control of the past. From Berdichevsky he learned the trait of investigating old vessels, and concentrating his gaze upon the values that his predecessors skipped over. Therefore, he studied, and studied again. He investigated and investigated again. He did not believe in anything that he did not conquer with his full investigation. From this perspective, he was a student of Rana'k, whose connection to this important way of thinking stemmed from the thought itself.

This precious trait of level–headedness – the trait of a scholar and person of refined traits, defined his unique place in literary criticism. He set a new relationship, a new essence in criticism, preceding all cultural paths. It was an uprising against nihilism, boorishness, and random ideas. He did not work with sharpness even though he specifically delved into the depths. Therefore, his teachings demand level–headed attention, getting accustomed to his methodologies and his means. Even his style, which is not always "smooth," is never populist. Anything he struggled with he raised up, and imbued with his essence as well as his charm.

This trait, which drew him close to the labor of literary criticism, made him into a fighter against all who are hasty to the pen, against all randomness and sophistics – even those who had talents.

His suspicious nature was always tense whenever anything required deep pondering, or about anything that was not nurtured from the ground of the sources. He skipped over criticism based solely on opinions, which signified the era of youth of new Hebrew criticism. He was one of the first who demanded a change of values, a change of path, and a change of means in the essence of the work. His book on new Hebrew literature was without doubt a turning port in literary science, making demands on those that followed him. He raised the bar of the profession.

The moral foundation of his work, and of his personality in general influenced, educated, and established a relationship of trust toward him. Even when we did not agree with him on the details, we trusted his rectitude, and we knew that he did not reach any conclusion without maximal knowledge and maximal gathering of information – after analyzing the matter from all sides.

From the introduction of Y. Fichman to "The Annals of New Hebrew Literature" (d), by F. Lachower, published by Dvir, Tel Aviv 5708.

[Page 100]

The Legendary Sokolow
by Fishel Lachower
Translated by Jerrold Landau

The name of Nachum Sokolow was the name of the first Hebrew writer I was exposed to, just like all the natives of Poland, during my youth – and he quickly became like a legend. I was eleven years old in those days and my self–control was not yet sufficiently calm; at that time, I stood on the crossroads. For some reason, the book "Foundations and Roots of Work" attracted me from one side, with its many directions, its simplicity, and straightforwardness, and with its subdued and controlled passion. From the other side, "apostasy" already attracted me. This apostasy was exposed to me in the form of the brief Russian geography of Zamnehof that I found in the home of my teacher, a teacher of young children who worked in the army during the war with Turkey, and whose handwriting was neat and wondrously fine. He taught us Jewish and Russian writing. Aside from these two books, there was the book "Times for Knowledge" by Yosef Ginzberg the son of Moshe Aharon of Cewice, which taught the foundations of technology based on the theories of Copernicus and the division of the house into 1080 units. I found this book in Father's house and served for me as a broad explanation of that brief geography. The image of Sokolow was revealed to me through his daily appearances in *Hatzefira*. Even though this image was not particularly simple, it seemed clear enough, but it was still like a legend to my eyes. Apparently, Sokolow dealt primarily with the day–to–day questions and needs – questions that were not my questions, and needs that were not my needs – but his way of presenting the matters enticed me to believe that when I would want – what would he not be able to do when I would want?...

Of course, during those days I got together with the *maskilim* of our city. There were two people who subscribed to *Hatzefira*, and a few others who read it. Of course, these were partial Hassidim, people who traveled once or twice a year to the Rebbe, like the rest of the Hassidim of the city – however, on their way back they entered and "subscribed." In the month of Elul, and more so during the ten days of penitence, they would not read *Hatzefira*, but only glanced at it. However, it was different on all other days of the year. At times, these half Hassidim were joined by actual Hassidim, mainly those who already peeked [at forbidden matters] during their youth, were not affected, but seceded later. They primarily came to benefit from *Divrei Hayamim*[1]. They would not withstand the test [of not looking] at this, so they violated "do not covet." There was a case where the rabbi of our city also stumbled in this matter. Once, a city administrator [*parnas*] entered his house and found a section of Hatzefira dropping down from his bosom. It was a miracle that the rabbi was returning from a journey at that time, and he had traveled together with the Rebbe, Rabbi Avrahamele himself, until the Nasielsk station. He explained immediately that the Rebbe's cheese had been wrapped in this section, and he had given it to him. They mentioned that Rabbi Shmuel, the son of Rabbi Avrahamele, was a subscriber who read it.

All these people did not read *Hatzefira* itself, but rather Sokolow. It once happened that Sokolow took a break from his articles for a long time, or that the "publisher went out on a journey," or simply went into his tent and did not go out from there to the community. The Children of Israel who were the readers of *Hatzefira* in Poland were then like people who prayed to the rain. The heavens closed their treasures to them, and dryness and desolation filled all eyes. There was no dew or rain to moisten the hearts a bit, which were hardened by the toil of life as well as the toil of the commandments. *Divrei Hayamim* also came in abundance at that time, but was not sufficient to satisfy the thirst. People called out to Sokolow, and at times he would send out one of his articles, Yacha'z or Weber, etc. Suddenly Sokolow heard the prayers of his people. There was a front–page article every day, signed by HN'S [Nachum Sokolow]. He gave, and promised more, a., b., and also c., etc. Suddenly "Is there Hebrew Charm?" with several continuations, and at times *Maranan Verabanan* with tens of continuations. He was a harsh critic, but nevertheless, his words were not like spurs. They were not humiliating. They penetrated the hearts and lives of the Jews of Poland, and placed something before the sun. He was far, but nevertheless close, close that became far. There was a sound of bustling within the camp. It seems that one more subscriber was added to the few subscribers of *Hatzefira*. Two or three of the readers subscribed in partnership. The subscribers would now go to the post office to get their newspaper with their own hands; or they would stand at the entrance to the store and wait for the letter carrier. When the newspaper reached their hands, they would not read it. They would only open it and see that "it is here." Then they would give the newspaper over to the hands of a subscriber who did not subscribe. They would then join together and read it with great diligence and concentration. In the evening, after the stores closed, the subscribers would gather in their meeting place and read with great concentration. They would read and enjoy...

[Page 101]

After this type of reading, some would gather together again to exchange impressions. Then, they would speak mainly about Sokolow and tell stories about him. In our town it was told that when Sokolow was supported at the table of his father–in–law in the nearby city of Maków, he would sit in the *Beis Midrash* all day studying intently, but his topic all day would be the laws of sanctification of the moon of the Rambam – a set of laws that no rabbi or scholar found resonance with any more[2]. It was said that among all the scholars of Poland, only Rabbi Yehoshuale, the great Gaon of Poland, the rabbi of Kutno, was expert in these laws. Sokolow occupied himself with them all day. According to the legend, he would be wearing a long cloak at that time, just like the long cloaks of the rest of the Jews of Poland. However, he had a cylinder hat on his head, and none of the young men of the city would say more than a few words to him.

It is told that even the Hassidim of the city took pride when he was once passing through our city. According to the legends of the city elders, among all the words of splendor of our city, either from in the city or nearby – Napoleon once passed through with his army on his way to Pułtusk. He [Sokolow] was then supported at the table of his father–in–law Rabbi Yosef Lewinstein, who later became a great rabbi in the city of Srock, so it also took on this glory: Once Sokolow passed through[3]. When he was living in the city of Maków, he was once summoned abroad. The situation was very urgent, and he came from Maków to our city, which was on the border of Prussia, to receive a "semi–certificate" to cross the border. He was then the guest at the "Ashkenazi"[4] of the city, the only Jew in the city to whom they added the surname when they mentioned his name; the only person who had stone steps leading up to his house and whose children had cut–off *peyos*. During this visit of Sokolow, several of the *maskilim* of the city entered the house of this "Ashkenazi" and saw Sokolow. Some boast that they even spoke to him.

[Page 102]

My heart is also proud that I saw Sokolow during my youth. This is how it happened. I once happened to be in Warsaw, and, of course, my first task was to go to Marianska street to "subscribe." When I reached the yard, I first looked for Sokolow. They showed me his house, which could be reached through the main staircase. I girded myself and intended to go up, but I noticed the level supports on the staircase, and immediately went back. I asked for the location of *Hatzefira*. I was shown another entrance, with completely different stairs. I went up, and subscribed. As I was subscribing, as I was saying the name of my city and place, the lad in charge of subscriptions told me that a telegram had reached them that morning stating that our city had completely gone up in flames. I swear to you that I paid more attention to the people entering and exiting the building than to this piece of news, for perhaps I might see Sokolow among them. Sokolow was then sitting in his private room, and I could not see him. — — However, when I went down the steps, with my heart saddened by the news and the fact that I had not seen him, it seems that I did see him at the gate of the house, going down the steps and the supports. I was then certain of this, and was very proud of this. It was a topic of conversation between me and my friends for many days. (One of my friends once endangered himself by entering one of the editorial rooms. However, the only person who came out to greet him was Michel Weber, who asked him in clear German, "Sir, what do you want?")

Of course, new times came later. I was a 17–year–old lad, and I received a letter from Sokolow as a response to the long poem that I had sent to the editors. I later also received a notice from him that my article would be published. It was indeed published in *Hatzefira*.

Thus began my literary journey. However, Sokolow's path at that time and onward was a legend.

Sokolow remains a sort of legend to this day...

From the anthology: "To Nachum Sokolow, a Jewish Guest from Vilna" (Warsaw, Shvat, 5723 – 1963, pages 10–11).

Translator's Footnotes

1. Literally "History," but from the context seemingly the title of one of Sokolow's columns in *Hatzefira*.

2. This section contains detailed mathematical principals of calculating the lunar cycle.

3. I believe that this means that a similar adage was used to describe Sokolow's connection with the city as was used for Napoleon.

4. In this context: German Jew.

[Page 103]

About Dvora Lachower
by Y. Maimoni, S. Or and A. Kalisz
Translated by Jerrold Landau

Dvora Lachower
(5651–5722 1891–1962)

Her death has left a void in all her many acquaintances, friends, and admirers in the Land. The group of friends from the beginnings of Young Zion in Poland is bereaved by the death of a dear member, who is irreplaceable.

She had a cultural and pioneering soul. She had great, boundless dedication to the values of the nation. I got to know her, and we quickly became friends, when we worked together during the First World War in communal affairs for benefit of the Jewish refugees who had been deported from the Polish–German border by the retreating Russian Army, and found refuge in the large city of Warsaw.

She was born in the small Jewish town of Chorzele, near the German border, into a house filled to the brim with culture and Hebrew tradition. She came to Warsaw to continue her studies. She finished the "High Pedagogical Hebrew courses" under the direction of the teacher, writer, and poet Sh. L. Gordon of blessed memory. She worked as a Hebrew and Bible teacher in high schools in Warsaw. This work did not keep her from being one of the first members of "The Center of Young Zionists" that was founded in Warsaw at that time, to teach courses in Hebrew and Bible at the Center. Later, she would one of the founders of Young Zion in Poland.

[Page 104]

She made *aliya* in 1920 with her friend the poet Y. L., however their paths separated after a brief time. She overcame her personal distress and began to dedicate herself to communal affairs with double energy. She translated books for youth and taught in schools. Later, she started to work for the Jewish National Fund, and served as an emissary and organizer of activities in the cities and towns of Poland. She worked as a counsellor and teacher in WIZO girls' institutions, until she found her natural place among the community of workers. She was a Hebrew and Bible teacher in the institution run by Chana Chizik of blessed memory, and a supervisor in schools for working girls until her retirement in 1960. As in all the roles she played as a teacher, emissary, and disseminator of Hebrew education, she displayed her enthusiastic personality, broad erudition, great responsibility, and talents to endear herself to her many students.

Her life in the Land was not simple. The loneliness and concern for the next day affected her to no small degree and robbed her sense of calm. However, she did not complain, and she accepted her situation with understanding. How great was her joy when she was given the opportunity to set up her own place among friends in the residence of writers: for she had a deep connection to poetry and literature. Poets and writers who appreciated her good taste, her refined soul, and her broad knowledge of ancient and modern Hebrew literature, as well as world literature were among her friends. She was a faithful accomplice of her brother, the writer Fishel Lachower of blessed memory and her friend, the poet Y. Fichman of blessed memory, especially during his last years.

Her death was particularly difficult. She was afflicted by a cruel illness, and was bedridden for an extended period. She spent a long time in several hospitals, but her spirit was intact. She understood that her end was near, and that her energy was ebbing, but she did not stop reading books that were of some comfort to her. She died on Tuesday, 27 Nisan 5722 (1962). Her close friends will always mourn for the refined Devora, for the exemplary faithful friend.

Y. Maimoni

(Davar, 27 Iyar 5622, May 28, 1962)

[Page 105]

On "Dvora in Writing"

Dvora's traits were not like firebrands or blinding lightning. She exuded a soft, modest light, that drew her close to her fellow and warmed the hearts of those who were with her. Her stamp of good will remained with all her acquaintances for a long time.

Apparently, Dvora did not suffer from stormy struggles. She did not have to master the language, culture, way of life, and spiritual values. It was as if she was born in the cradle of Zionism, with a silver spoon of the Hebrew language and love of her nation and its homeland in her mouth. Knowledge and Torah were her climate of life from her earliest youth. The environment of her upbringing and all the experiences surrounded her apparently determined her straight path. In light of that influence, it was natural that she would wish to impart it to others, and that she would be a teacher and educator with her entire essence.

Indeed, Dvora had strong Hebrew–Jewish roots, but along with this, she was enveloped by something drawn from the wide world. There was not a trace of anything frozen in her entire perception. She knew how to approach things from a levelheaded viewpoint, by understanding the proper connections and appropriate proportions. We, her friends at work, felt this approach also when we saw Dvora in her daily life. She was so diligent in nurturing the level that she finally reached in her latter years. She was so proud of her appearance as the master of her home. She was even meticulous about fine clothing and her external appearance. She was able to do all this with a smiling gesture, with a touch of mischievous humor, peppered with the saying of our sages. With this, even the mundane aspects of life were enriched by her externals.

*

Here are a few words about "Dvora in Writing" as was surveyed on the pages of *Dvar Hapoelet*.

In her writing, Dvora was literally as she was in her life: open and simple, her internals like her externals, devoid of any special polished style. Everything about her was truth and culture, as she approached the clarity of her internal life.

Her first article was published at the end of 1946. It was dedicated to "Hours of Study" – to that cultural activity to which Dvora had already begun several years previously, between activities in the factories, and the various organizations. Even though her life conditions were very different from those of the members of those two strata – she displayed in this article a great understanding of their problems and needs, physical and especially spiritual.

With time, Dvora started to describe the Hebrew culture of the new female immigrants in their settlements. She especially examined what was new, wondered about the new conditions, and prayed with her full heart that these women would grow into a good and well–grounded future here.

Later, she wrote about Puah Rakovski when she turned 85. This article was a testimony to Dvora's talent of maintaining trust and enduring friendship. Anyone close to her at that time knew well how much love and attention she dedicated to maintaining this human contact with her elderly friend, as with her many other connections. She also wrote about her in her book "I was not Subdued" and eulogized her when she passed away.

[Page 106]

A few times, she gave expression to her articles and summaries of the work in the sewing trade schools, in which she served as a teacher and supervisor. In this area, she did not restrict herself to direct supervision, but also dealt with the general problems. All this was close to her – the girls and their fate, the teachers and their problems, even concerns about budget and professional questions regarding sewing.

There were also different articles, dedicated to matters of the spirit which were her prime interest – about the 18th century Hebrew poetess Rachel Morpurgo[1], and the prayers and hymns of the High Holy Days.

With significant feeling, Dvora wrote down her impressions on a visit that she benefited from greatly – a visit to Nehora for the dedication of the local school named for David Shimony and the opening of the guest house in the name of Dvora Baron – two people who were very close and dear to her. That visit bound her to the Lachish District.

Fate had it that her final article, in 1958, was a farewell article for her close friend, the poet Yaakov Fichman, after his death. With deep closeness, we will bring down her words, written with full appreciation for his poetic soul. We will also repeat those bright lines of Fichman, which Dvora herself reminisced about there.

Indeed, someone went and did not return / and we will walk in his shadow. How painful is it / without him, the charm has darkened.

Shlomit Or

(Davar Hapoelet, Sivan 5722 – June 1962)

The secretariat of the Workers' Organization decided to establish a monument for Dvora Lachower:

A library in her name in the Iron agricultural school of Hadera

The Activist and Educator

Dvora had three wonderful traits that imparted appreciation of her personality: a wise heart, a refined soul, and pure character.

Her life was complex and rough. At times, someone would ask her to pour out her bitterness, difficulties, and sorrow, but to the end of her days, she knew how to guard her ideological line and independence with honor.

Dvora came to us from Poland, from a house of studiers of Torah and education. When she finished teachers' seminary (the Shla'g courses) she became a teacher in the Hebrew gymnasja of Warsaw. She was active in the Zionist youth movements and one of the first founders of Young Zion in Poland. She was alert to culture and literature during all the years of her work.

[Page 107]

She made *aliya* during the 1920s. From the day of her *aliya*, she became involved in forging souls for Hebrew, and in creating an atmosphere of the Hebrew spirit. Her first steps in the land involved teaching the living Hebrew language, and translating many books from other languages. Later, she became the editor of the Ha'isha [The Woman] monthly. She worked for the Jewish National Fund. In her latter years, she was a teacher for the active committee and a supervisor of the schools for working girls. She loved this task very much, and regarded it as her special mission. She related to the studies with awe and holiness, and she did everything with deep connection and responsibility. Therefore, she had the ability to impart her personality to all those with whom she came in contact. A good friend, a refined soul with overflowing feelings has been lost.

Ita Kalisz

(Davar, 28 Nisan, 5723 – April 22, 1963)

A certificate of donation of trees for the Jewish National Fund in the name of Dvora Lachower – Lichtenbaum, in the name of those who participated in the farewell party for her in Chorzele on February 17, 1934, when she visited the town

Translator's Footnote

1. See https://en.wikipedia.org/wiki/Rachel_Luzzatto_Morpurgo

[Page 108]

About one Association and Two Brothers
by Shmuel Lachower
Translated by Jerrold Landau

Agudat Zion in the Year 1900

After great searching, I succeeded in finding a single correspondence in *Hatzefira* in 1900[1] about the first Zionist delegates in Chorzele. The following is its text:

"Chorzele (Płock district). Agudat Zion was founded in our city, and more than 50 people donated their *shekels* to the fund. Thanks are given to the wonderful speaker Reb Yaakov Lisa of Kawle, who delivered his wonderful words before the community. His words left a great effect in the ears of the listeners. L. H. Lachower."

The speech of the orator in the synagogue and his visit to our city served as the opening for the work of the group.

According to my sister Elisheva Eizensztadt, the widow of Mordechai Eisenstadt of blessed memory, the following people stood at the head of the aforementioned Agudat Zion: Avraham–Yehoshua Bak, Fishel Lachower, Leib–Hirsch (Aryeh–Tzvi) Lachower, Fishel Mar–Chaim, Moshe Mottel (the son of Chaim Baruch the teacher), Zalman Adler, Aharon David Biszka, Avraham–Michel Adler, Avraham–Bunem (the son of Yisrael–Elia the teacher), Aharon David Nizkin, Binyamin Eizensztadt.

There is basis to say that the impetus for Zionism in Chorzele was due to the influence of Rabbi Yehuda–Leib Kowalski of blessed memory, one of the heads of Chovevei Zion and a founder of Mizrachi, who later served as rabbi of Chorzele from 1897–1898. He established a Yeshiva in Chorzele in which 2000 students, from near and far, studied. The city became a famous center of Torah. He also founded public institutions. Everyone revered him greatly. In the year 5659 (1899) he moved to Włocławek, and became known as the Rabbi of Włocławek.

Agudat Zion existed in Chorzele until the year 5654 (1904), during the time of the Russo–Japan War. Then, the group that maintained Agudat Zion broke up. Some immigrated overseas and other left the town and moved to other cities.

[Page 109]

Leib–Hirsch (Aryeh–Tzvi) Lachower

Leib–Hirsch Lachower
(1881–1942)

My eldest brother Leib–Hirsch the son of Shlomo–Yehuda and Chana–Breina Lachower of blessed memory was born in Chorzele in the month of Kislev 5642 (1881).

Our mother would say that his fame spread in town regarding his knowledge and greatness in Torah already in his youth. He was the student of the rabbi of Turek. Later, he was a student of the Yeshiva of the Rabbi of Włocławek. He had broad secular education that he obtained on his own. He was fluent in European languages, including Russian, German, French, English, and Italian. He also knew Latin and Greek. Of course, the he was fluent in the Hebrew language.

He was beloved by everyone due to his calmness and good heart. His words were always spoken calmly, as is the way of scholars. He was especially connected with bonds of love to his brother Fishel. This love never dissipated. When Fishel published his first book on Ahad Ha'am, he dedicated it to his brother (The preface states: Dedicated to my brother Aryeh–Tzvi).

He traveled with Father to Rostov on Don in the year 5664 (1904) to assist him in his business. He spent three years there. In 1907, he returned home, and married Chaya (Clara) the daughter of the ritual slaughterer (*shochet*) Yoel Zusman Hillelson of Konigsberg, the brother of Professor Herman (Tzvi) Shapira, the founder of the Jewish National Fund and a planner of the Hebrew University of Jerusalem.

Leib–Hirsh's daughter was named Zusa, after her grandfather Zusman. Leib–Hirsch lived in Rostov until the end of the 1920s. After the death of his wife, he moved with his daughter to Astrakhan on the Volga River. His horizons were too narrow there, and he moved to Moscow, where he headed a large government institution, thanks to his administrative talents.

After finishing university, his daughter married the son of Chava Nizkin, the grandson of Shmuel–Yaakov Nizkin of Chorzele.

Correspondence with Leib–Hirsch to our home continued until 1937. After the "Moscow Trials" and Stalinist purges, we knew nothing more of him.

He died in Moscow during the war, in 1942. May his soul be bound in the bonds of everlasting life.

[Page 110]

Moshe Lachower of blessed memory

Moshe Lachower in Chorzele in 1913
(1892–1943)

My brother Moshe of blessed memory, the son of Shlomo–Yehuda and Chana–Breina Lachower, was born in Chorzele (district of Płock) in the year 5652 (1892).

He studied religious studies in various *cheders*; and general studies with student teachers who came to our city during the summertime, as well as through self–study. He particularly excelled in mathematics. He completed a bookkeeping course given by Yaakov Mark of Libawa. Moshe was one of those active in the founding of the first public Hebrew library. He was a member of the library committee along with Moshe Nizkin, Mordechai Eizenstadt, Shmuel Mar–Chaim,

[Page 111]

Dvora Lachower, Leah Lichtensztajn. (The library was housed for a few years in the attic of the home of her father, Mottel Lichtensztajn.)

Moshe left Chorzele in 1912 and moved to Warsaw. There, he accepted a job as an accountant in a textile business, and later in the Central publishing house.

He went to Russia in 1915, and settled in the city of Kharkov, where he continued to work in his profession at private businesses. After the October Revolution, he worked as chief accountant in a government office of the Soviet Union.

He married his wife Manya in 1920, and they had two daughters: Shulamit and Lida. From letters that we received at certain times, it appears that they lived a fine and interesting family life.

With the outbreak of the Nazi war against the Soviet Union, after appeals of the government offices in Kharkov to their officials, Moshe, along with his wife and two daughters, moved to Kazakhstan, where he continued with his work. We learned from a Jewish refugee in Warsaw who worked together with him that his life was difficult, but he concerned himself with refugees and shared his meager bread with others.

He followed a straight path and had a straightforward heart, always doing good things.

He died in March 1943, during the war, in the village of Mikhaylovka near the city of Dzhambul, Kazakhstan.

May his memory be forever blessed.

Translator's Footnote

1. There is a text footnote here: *Hatzefira*, year 26, issue 289. Wednesday 5 Shvat 5660 – January 10, 1900.

My Husband Mordechai Eizenstadt
by Elisheva Eizenstadt (Lachower)
Translated by Jerrold Landau

My husband Mordechai was born in Chorzele in 1889 to his father Kalman Eizenstadt and his mother Chana–Rachel, the daughter of Yosef Monkarsz, known as Yosel–Meir Libe's. Mordechai lost his mother when he was five years old. A few years later, he left the home of his father and step–mother and moved to the home of his maternal grandfather, following his older brothers and sisters. He received his education from the teacher in the *cheder*, and from there, he went straight to the *Beis Midrash* at a young age to study *Gemara* on his own.

During that time, the *Beis Midrash* of our town was still bustling with lads who were studying Torah. It was customary in those days that the older lads would guide and teach Talmud to the younger ones. My brother Fishel Lachower was among those lads, and Mordechai, who was five years younger than he, was one of his students. Mordechai studied Torah from him. Mordechai was a diligent and attentive student, with a good head. People still remembered him in a positive light many years later.

[Page 112]

Mordechai Eizenstadt in Chorzele, 1913

Mordechai was an intelligent lad, who loved books. He studied secular subjects over and above his Jewish studies. He divided his time. He spent the days working in his grandfather's store, and the evenings and nights studying and reading books – on his own initiative, without the help of a teacher. He belonged to the group of progressive lads in our town, who concerned themselves not only with their own education, but also with the education of the nation.

He left Chorzele in 1911 and made *aliya* to the Land of Israel with two of his friends: Eliezer Mar–Chaim and Simcha Adler, who should both live long. Mordechai was accustomed to arduous work from an early age, first in his father's house (he was a lumber merchant), and later in his grandfather's house (who had an iron implements store). Nevertheless, he was not able to get used to the difficult agricultural work in the Land, and he returned home after about a year.

[Page 113]

He moved to Warsaw in 1914, when the First World War broke out. After the war, when branches of the Shtibel Publishing House moved to Warsaw from Moscow and Berlin, Mordechai began working there. He continued in this work for the entire time that publishing existing in Warsaw.

He made *aliya* to the Land of Israel once again in 1934, and settled in Tel Aviv with his family. When the state was founded, he began working in the Interior Ministry of the government. When the government offices moved to the capital, he moved to Jerusalem, and continued his work until the day of his death, on the eve of Tisha B'Av 1954.

May his memory be guarded by us forever.

The Family of Grandfather and Father
by Yechiel Nizkin
Translated by Jerrold Landau

My father Reuven–Tzvi (Hershel) Nizkin was born in Chorzele to his father Shmuel–Yaakov (Yankel) Nizkin and his mother Malka–Rivka. They had 12 children (eight sons and four daughters). Grandfather Shmuel–Yaakov was a wealthy man, a scholar, and one of the important householders of the town. His business was the export of all types of fish to far–off Russia.

Not one of the twelve children of Grandfather Shmuel–Yaakov survived. Most perished in the Holocaust along with their families. Only a few of the grandchildren remain.

My parents had five sons (Moshe was the eldest), and one daughter. We received a traditional Jewish education in Father's home, as was customary in our small town during this days. However, after we left he town and moved to Mława and then to Warsaw, we received general technical education. Some of us continued to higher education.

My brother Moshe belonged to the circle of young *maskilim* in Chorzele – the friends of Mordechai Eizenstadt and Moshe Lachower.

Three brothers survived from my father's household: Shmuel–Yaakov, Avraham–Meir, and Yechiel. Naomi, the only daughter of my brother Moshe, survived as well and lives today in Mexico.

My parents Reuven–Tzvi and Manya, my brother Moshe and his wife Adzia, my brother Mordechai, his wife and their son, my sister Freda, her husband Dov and their daughter Ruth, all perished in the Holocaust.

[Page 114]

My Dear Father Mordechai Biran (Przysusker)
by Naomi
Translated by Jerrold Landau

Mordechai Biran (Przysusker)

We stand mourning and with covered heads next to your pleasant grave. Only the rustling of the leaves disturbs the deathly silence on occasion. The white, marble monument only bears your name – Mordechai Biran of blessed memory.

You left us quietly and discreetly, without saying anything. To us, however, this was like thunder on a clear day, like a summer storm. A young tree, which was only beginning to bear fruit, was cut down. You left and did not return...

Your face, your warm smile, the caress of your hands, your footsteps, are guarded by us in silent grief. Your calming words sang through the atmosphere – however now you are no more. You — who helped all in need, who protected your fellow with your body, whose heart was open to every person and every tribulation. You – who dedicated all your free time, and even your non–free time, to your family and your children, whom you loved with all strands of your soul, whom you educated and walked with path after path, step by step.

You won the hearts of the masses with your charming personality. You conducted a large enterprise, into which you invest your best energy, initiative, and years. You built a house, the nest of my fortunate family, but you did not merit to harvest the fruit of your labors.

The pain is very great!

"There was a man – and we saw: he is no more;
This man died before his time,
And the song of his life stopped in the middle;
And it is too bad! He still had another hymn –
And that hymn is lost forever,
Lost forever!"

[Page 115]

My Grandfather's Image
by Dov Frenkel
Translated by Jerrold Landau

Regarding my grandfather Shlomo–Asher Rogen of blessed memory, it can be said with a full voice: he was a Jew who loved peace, pursued peace, and loved his fellow[1]. He greeted everyone with an effusive good–morning, asked about their wellbeing and the wellbeing of their family, took interest in the situation, and wished the person good.

He himself was satisfied with little. He would say, "The main thing is trust in the mercies of the Rock[2] who concerns Himself with His flock." Even when his economic situation weakened considerably he would also repeat, "Thank G–d for this."

He was an active member in almost all mutual benevolent and charitable institutions in the town, including *Bikur Cholim* [tending to the sick], *Linat Tzedek* [tending to wayfarers], *Lechem La'aniyim* [bread for the poor], etc. There was no joyous occasion in town (weddings, Bar Mitzvahs, etc.) in which he did not play an active role. In the event of an illness, he would visit the sick person daily. In the event of a death – he saw it as his duty to not only participate in the funeral, but also in the prayer quorum [minyan] organized at the house of the mourners during the period of Shiva. When someone left for some place abroad, he would accompany the traveler to the railway station and bid him farewell with an abundance of blessings.

When someone whose Orthodoxy was open to question immigrated overseas, he blessed him in the name of G–d several times and wholeheartedly wished him success and happiness. His acquaintances would ask him, "Reb Shlomo–Asher, he does not pray and does not observe the commandments, why this enthusiasm to bless him?" Grandfather would respond, "He is a Jew like all Jews, and a Jew even though he sins has a place in the World to Come."

His trait of forgiveness was only to humans, but his trait of mercy extended to other living beings. He would get up early to feed the cow, saying, "The cow does not know how to ask for its food, therefore humans must tend to it before they tend to themselves."

He loved people, and always looked for the good in a person, and sought to extend the benefit of the doubt. His patience was boundless. Nobody ever saw him angry in any situation. A faÃ§ade of joy was always upon his face, for he was always happy with his lot..."

Translator's Footnotes

1. Pirkei Avot 1:12.

2. A euphemism for the Divine.

[Page 116]

The Community and the Individual in the Circles of Life
by Matityahu Pater
Translated by Jerrold Landau

Rachel (Rachche) Pater

In this town...

Anyone who would arrive in Chorzele on the afternoon train would be astonished about the quiet and calm that pervaded the place. Already with the first meeting of the people of the town, one would feel that one arrived in a place with an abundance of culture. A Zionist emissary would find well–rooted Zionism in all its branches and factions. Even a businessman or ordinary guest would be received properly and with warmth.

This small town had a Tarbut center with a large library, many activities for the benefit of the Jewish National Fund (who does not remember the Blue and White parties), as well as an amateur drama club. This small town had a Beitar center – fine, well–organized, and cultural – that organized cultural and entertainment activities. This small town had a Young Agudas Yisroel center with a serious library, activities, and culture, especially focusing on the end of the Sabbath (*Seudat Shlishit* and *Melave Malka*). This small town had a Bund center named for Y. L. Peretz, with a large library and organized activities.

In the business realm, one would find a Jewish bank, well–developed and good, with financial connections to government circles.

An ordinary guest who came to town would find the *Hachnasat Orchim* communal hall, operating summer and winter, with hot tea and a bed to sleep, for no cost.

Rabbi Sokolower of blessed memory was famous in town for his warmth, pleasant mannerisms, and sermons in the synagogues. On the other hand, the Catholic priest was also well–known in a positive fashion, for he preached goodwill toward Jews every Sunday in church. He was loved by the Jewish community. The scholars Reb Yitzchak Meir Slowna, Reb Tevel Pater, Reb Shmuel Frenkel, Reb Mordechai–Mendel Farberowicz, were known in town. Other well–known individuals included Reb Menachem Kowel, Reb Mates Sokolower, Reb Michel Adler (the head of the Jewish community), and others.

[Page 117]

Reb Moshe Aharon

For a long time, it was not clear to me what preceded what: the Jewish National Fund to the Jewish Bank, or the Jewish Bank to the Jewish National Fund? This was because nobody could separate the two during the time that Reb Moshe–Aharon was the coordinator of both organizations.

Reb Moshe–Aharon, who was one of the prime initiators of both of those institutions, invested the best of his talents and his entire life into them. We regarded Reb Moshe–Aharon, the Jewish National Fund, and the Jewish Bank as one thing, for he lived his life to bring in more money to the Jewish National Fund and to develop the bank.

I remember when I came on Chanukah to purchase a Jewish National Fund stamp with the Chanukah *gelt* [monetary gift] that I had received: how he gave me over the stamp with such holiness and love, explaining the Israeli landscape that was illustrated on it. Reb Moshe–Aharon displayed the same holiness toward the bank: which he founded, in which he invested his money, concerned himself with its development, and set up financial connections to the wide world on its behalf. He succeeded in obtaining a government permit, giving the bank the name "The Cooperative Jewish Bank."

The History of Chorzele

The "History Book" of Chorzele would pass to different hands each year – to the first trustee of the *Chevra Kadisha* [Burial Society], who was the custodian of the communal ledger. It was a strict custom for generation after generation that each year on the 11th of Adar, the trustees of the *Chevra Kadisha* would be elected, and it was a general principle that the first trustee would be the custodian of the ledgers of the organization.

The living and the dead, the events that took place, in which institutions money was invested, and the like were all written in these ledgers. During the final twenty years before the Holocaust, Reb Tevel Pater held these books, with the appropriate assistance of Reb Yitzchak–Meir Slowna. Both would make their inscriptions with a sense of holiness, and sign every note in these ledgers with awe. The history of the Jews of Chorzele was written and sealed in these ledgers.

11ᵗʰ of Adar

There are history and legends connected with this date with respect to several events in Chorzele. It was said that the first Jew set foot on the soil of Chorzele and settled there on the 11ᵗʰ of Adar. The elders of Chorzele would further relate that there was a time when an edict of expulsion was issued against the Jews of Chorzele, but a miracle occurred on the 11ᵗʰ of Adar and the edict was repealed.

The last Jews left Chorzele on the 11th of Adar when they were deported to the Maków Ghetto.

The communal institutions held their elections on the 11ᵗʰ of Adar. The elections were democratic and inclusive. Everyone would gather for a meal at the home of Reb Tevel Pater, with Rabbi Sokolower at the head, and they would elect the head of the community, the head of the *Chevra Kadisha*, and the heads of all other communal institutions. During that meal, reports would be given about all the activities that had taken place, and plans for the future would be prepared.

[Page 118]

The meal itself was an important event. Mrs. Ruchchia Pater, with the help of the talented cook Mrs. Chaya–Sara, would serve homemade delicacies at the tables, with the taste of the Garden of Eden, made with the heart... When the Jews of Chorzele were goodhearted with wine, what did they do? Reb A. M. Adler would exchange clothes with Reb A. Shaar and they would dance on the table. Reb Yitzchak–Meir Slowna the scholar would compose words of didactics (a *pshetl*) on the spot in reverse logic. Then everything would conclude with a Hassidic dance.

The Final Moments

In memory: Our father Reb Tevel the son of Meir Pater; mother Mrs. Rachel the daughter of Shraga (Blum); brothers: Eli–Leib (with wife Tzlovka and children), Shalom (with wife Dina and children), and Hershel. Sisters: Leah (husband Moshe and children), and Mirel, may their souls rest in comfort.

Eli–Leib Pater and his wife

I experienced the last moments of our town. On Friday morning at 5:00 a.m., September 1, 1939, the German Army attacked Poland, starting the tragic Second World War. About two hours later, at 7:00 a.m., the Hitlerist soldiers stormed into our town.

Hands trembled, hearts were bloodied, and eyes were filled with tears. Pictures of our town Chorzele swim before me, pictures of my and your dear ones, of a piece of my and your life, a piece of our hearts.

On January 1, 1940, when the first wave of the war had passed, I visited Chorzele, returning from the Russian side. (Berl Ciechanowski brought me from Maków Mazowiecki.) To my wonder, I saw several tens of Jews in Chorzele who were managing even though commerce and work were forbidden.

[Page 119]

The synagogue and *Beis Midrash* were in ruins. A *shtibel* for worship was set up in the home of Reb Velvel Gutlezer. A Torah scroll, a rabbi, and a cantor were not lacking. All the benevolent organizations were functioning again: the *Hachnasat Orchim*, *Gemilut Chasadim*, and *Bikur Cholim*. People helped each other as in the good times. My father's house was open again, and Jews came to him, some to hear a page of *Gemara*, some for advice, some to discuss politics, and some just to spend time. My father was privileged to be the last person to leave Chorzele, and he helped with what he could until the last minute.

May the souls of all the martyrs of Chorzele be bound in the bonds of eternal life!

[Page 119]

From my Drawer of Personal Memories
by Meir Ben–Yosef Bachrach
Translated by Jerrold Landau

When I remember my town, Chorzele, in which I spent most of the years of my life, the Przytulanie Forest and the Orzyc River flutter before my eyes. I also see the two bridges (the large and the small), with the large tree next to the cross between them. The villagers from the area would put on their shoes next to this tree every Sunday on their way to church, and remove them on their way home. Motel Lichtensztajn's flourmill was next to the river in that area. During its operation, the rattle of its machinery could be heard throughout Chorzele and the region. I got used to this sound from my early childhood. I even went to sleep with its echo, and something seemed missing on the Sabbath when it didn't operate.

We would stroll through the Przytulanie Forest mainly during the summer. We would enjoy the pleasant aromas and songs of the birds. We would get up early during the spring and go to the Labylow Forest that was called "Mojowka." Nevertheless, we felt like strangers there despite the beauty of nature on those days.

Chorzele was close to the border district. Therefore, it was only permitted to travel around the city until midnight.

[Page 120]

It was forbidden to be seen on the streets after that time. All the lights were extinguished at midnight. A decisive darkness pervaded, and people would be afraid to go outside. This fear accompanied the residents of the town even during the daytime hours. The children were afraid of ghosts and spirits. Virtually everybody was afraid to pass near the church or the cemetery. If a child refused to wear the *tallis katan* [fringed undergarment], they would threaten that he would be snatched by the ghosts. In addition to these fears, the children were also afraid of the rebbe's *kontszyk* [leather strap].

*

I studied *chumash* and *Rashi* with the teacher Itche–Meir Nodel. When he would examine a student, he would sit very close to him, for if the student did not know the lesson, the rebbe would slap him with his thin fingers. This would hurt right through to the heart. The rebbe would barely use the *kontszyk*. However, the *kontszyk* of the teacher from Warsaw is etched in my mind. I cried because of it more than once.

Next to the gravestone of Avraham–Baruch Bachrach

The text on the gravestone is:

An excellent man, crowed with good traits.

An upright man,

a prominent Hassid,

fearing of Heaven,

Reb Avraham Baruch the son of Reb Moshe Chanoch,

died 23 Tammuz 5692.

May his soul be bound in the bonds of eternal life.

[Page 121]

Two of my classmates earned special merit with him – David Frenkel and Berl Fater. The rebbe had a special *kontszyk* for them, with a thick knot at its edge, for they never cried when they received beatings. This aroused the anger of the rebbe. Sometimes, he would grab the hand of a student and beat it on the table until it bled. We could not complain about the rebbe at home, because our parents would claim that we were surely deserving the beatings. In addition to the fear of the *cheder*, the street instilled fear, for when we went home at a late hour, we had to be careful lest we run into some *shegetz* [derogatory term for a gentile] who might beat us.

*

When winter arrived and the river froze, we would go to have fun, some with skates, and some with sleds. Even then, we would always choose a remote corner, so that the *shkotzim* [gentiles] would not see us. I remember an incident one winter when Moshe Zylberman (the son of Yankel Einbinder, who was an enthusiastic Bundist) came to me and recommended that I go to play on the ice. I refused, and said to him that there were many *shkotzim* on the snow at that time. He didn't listen to me, however, and said, "Am I not a human being like them?" Indeed, he went, and returned after some time with an injured face. I said to him, "Now you see that Socialism does not help you."

But we also had a "hero" during the winter time – Chaim David Kozycz, who would perform acrobatic tricks on the ice. The *shkotzim* honored him for this. Jewish lads hung around him, and the *shkotzim* would not hurt them. We also had a summertime "hero" – Yaakov Frenkel. When we would go bathe in the "*ryde*" he would appear before us, get undressed slowly, and then dive into the water for some time. When he dove, everyone would hold their breath until he came out of the water. Then we would cheer him.

*

I want to note here Reb Yosef Tyk, in whose store we used to purchase sweets from money that we "pilfered" from our fathers' drawers in their businesses or at home… Reb Yosef led the drama club, in which he invested all his energy and initiative. (I also participated in this club.) I remember that Reb Yosef once became very embarrassed when Yitzchak Gliksberg (the son of Hershel the rabbi) organized a play for the benefit of Linat Hatzedek. He wrote the lines himself and produced the performance with the dramatic group. Reb Yosef was embarrassed that he was not called upon to produce this play, and he decided to no longer organize performances.

The name of the performance was "The Consillium," and it portrayed the images of the "physicians of the idol" in our town: The Fat King (*der Grober Meilech*), Avrahamel *shochet* (*di Kishke*), the wife of the cantor (*di Chazante*), and others. It told libelous stories about the "consillium" [advice] that the "physicians" arranged when a doctor was called to a specific sick person. (I played the part of the Fat King.) I met "the Fat King" the day after the performance. He approached me and said, "You are the Grober Meiliech, may your name be blotted out. The next time they summon me to a sick person, I will send you…"

[Page 122]

We lived as a single family in our city. Everyone recognized each other. We did not consider pedigree or any such things. In business and economic matters, Aharon–Mottel Bekerman was friendly with Mottel Frum, Shmuel "the rebbe" would share secrets with Shmuel the wagon driver. All of them shared their bitter fate equally in the face of the enemy that brought destruction upon them.

Chorzele my town! Your soil will forever remain soaked with the blood of our dear ones. My heart will mourn until my last day over our dear ones who were slaughtered without any guilt on their hands.

The History of One Family
by Yosef Shafran
Translated by Jerrold Landau

My revered father, Mendel Shafran of blessed memory, was born in 1860 in the city of Nowy Dwór, Warsaw district. He moved to Chorzele in 1880, after he married my mother Hinda of blessed memory, the daughter of Reb Aharon Wallersztajn, one of the veteran residents of Chorzele, who was known in town by the name of "Aharon Grajewski" on account of his native town of Grajewo. During the early years, my father was supported at the table of his father-in-law, as was the custom in those days, until he opened his own grocery store. Later, he closed it and opened a manufacturing store. He was successful at his businesses, and eventually became known as one of the wealthy men of the town. He attained a high place in business circles, and had an important status among the residents of the town. Many would come to him to hear his advice on business matters. Shopkeepers and tradesmen regarded him as a trustworthy person, and left their weekly earnings with him from Friday afternoon until the end of the Sabbath.

In 1916, my father was appointed to the town council by the district city official, Wittenberg. The town council appointed my father to head the potato division, which Wittenberg obtained from the government for the starving, poor families. Every person received five kilograms of potatoes in return for a symbolic payment that went toward maintaining the fund for communal affairs. My father fulfilled this task honestly, without playing favorites. He guarded the collected money very carefully. After the rabbi and communal representatives decided to utilize the money for renovating the *mikva* [ritual bath], my father was appointed to arrange and oversee this work. He fulfilled that task as well efficiently and faithfully.

My revered mother was a pious and intelligent woman. She was goodhearted to every person, and would often read holy books as well as Yiddish books. At sunset on the Sabbath, she would gather her children around her and tell them about what took place during the week, about the B'esht [Baal Shem Tov] and *tzadikim*, about Dreyfus, Robinson Caruso, and other such things. She was a Zionist in spirit and aspiration, and dreamed of settling in the Land of Israel with her family.

[Page 123]

Mendel and Hinda Shafran

Their sons: Feibish of blessed memory with his daughter and wife; Yosef; and Yitzchak

[Page 124]

Indeed, her heart's desire was realized in 1927, when my parents arrived in the Land of Israel, after three of their children made *aliya* to the Land one after the other: Yitzchak in 1921, Feibish at the beginning of 1923, and the writer of these lines in the autumn of 1923. My parents' other children (Moshe–Leizer, Avraham, and Leah) did not merit making *aliya* to the Land of Israel. They died during their youth, and their bodies are buried in the soil of the Diaspora.

My revered father died in Tel Aviv in 1953, and my revered mother died in Tel Aviv in 1951.

Our oldest sister Sara was married to Moshe–Mendel Kahn, the son of Reb Yosef the *shochet* [ritual slaughterer]. My sister's family was also firmly based from an economic and social perspective. Two of her children, Efraim and Hirsch–Yitzchak, immigrated to the United States during the 1920s. The rest of her children, Yechiel, Aharon–Chaim, Ita–Tova, and Chana, perished along with our sister and her husband during the terrible Holocaust.

Our sister Beila, who was married to Chaim–Shlomo Wishinski, died in 1926.

Our brother Simcha–Yaakov was born in 1888, and was one of the leaders in town of the youth who turned toward the *Haskalah* [enlightenment] and Socialist ideas. He was a pleasant, thin lad. He studied Russian and English on his own, and even built a violin with his own hands, and became expert at playing it. He organized and directed a youth group for the children of the workers and tradesmen. He took risks in bringing in revolutionary books that were forbidden in town, and distributed them to the members of his circle. Under pressure from the townsfolk who were afraid that his deeds would create issues between their children and the authorities, our father sent him to the town of Woznowo to study watchmaking. He returned home after he learned this trade. My father gave him a room for work in our house, and hoped that his son would now return to the proper path. However, he continued in his ways, and dedicated himself to intellectual and educational work amongst the youth with full enthusiasm, until his time came to enlist to the army.

My father made efforts to free him from the army, but Simcha–Yaakov deliberately thwarted these efforts. When the draft notice arrived, my parents had no choice other than to permit him to immigrate to the United States – his longstanding desire. "The Land of the Free" in contrast to Czarist Russia made a deep impression on him. As proof of his appreciation, he volunteered for the American army in its war with Mexico (1912), and later, in 1915, on its war on the side of the "Entente" (Allies) in Europe. He excelled in battles in France and reached the rank of captain. He was killed in battle on October 3, 1918, a few weeks before the end of the First World War. He was decorated for bravery in a special notice from the Ministry of Defense of the United States.

Already from his youth, our brother, Feibish followed Zionist ideas. He disliked business, and became involved in trade. He studied watchmaking with the only watchmaker in town, Yudel the Watchmaker. Then, he spent about two years in Warsaw (1912–1914), and returned home at the outbreak of the First World War. He went through many experiences during the war. Here is a brief description.

At the outbreak of the war, the Jews of Chorzele escaped from the border. Our family settled in Przasnyce.

[Page 125]

When news arrived that the gentiles were pillaging the homes of the Jews who had left, a group of Chorzele natives, including my brother Feibish, was organized to return to town. This group guarded the abandoned property, but the gentiles slandered them to the local Russian commander, claiming that the Jews were spies on behalf of the Germans. The Jews were commanded to leave the town quickly. They went to the nearby village of Krszinobloga, when they remembered that they had left the Torah scrolls in the synagogue. My brother and one woman volunteered to return to the town to retrieve the Torah scrolls. However, they were captured by the Cossacks when they got there and hauled to the military command Michnicze. There, they informed my brother that he was accused of spying. They tied him to a horse and brought him to Zambrowo, from where he was taken from city to city for many months until he reached the city of Tyumen, District of Tobolsk, in Siberia. My father followed after him and made efforts along the way to free him, but he did not succeed. After several months of imprisonment in Tyumen, he was freed from jail but forbidden from leaving the city. He was drafted to the Russian Army in 1916 and sent to the Austrian front in Galicia, from where he was freed from the army at the outbreak of the Bolshevik Revolution in 1917. He remained in Kremenchug, where he married Rosa Schor. He had no way of informing his family of his salvation until 1921, because Poland was situated between two enemy armies. He and his wife arrived in Chorzele in 1922, and made *aliya* to the Land of Israel in 1923.

Feibish lived in Rishon Lezion for a brief period next to our brother Yitzchak, who preceded us in *aliya* to the Land of Israel. Later, Feibish joined the group of founders of Moshav Chitin near Tiberias, where he endured all the birth pangs of this group (removing rocks, uprooting stones, under conditions of hunger, thirst, and lack) until it disbanded. Feibish, his wife, and three daughters (Batya, Geula, and Arbella) moved to Tel Aviv, where his wife got a job in her profession (a nurse with Kupat Cholim), and he worked at whatever job came his way. At the outbreak of the Second World War in 1939, he started work in the military camp of Sarafand, but fate was cruel to him there as well. He was injured twice in automobile accidents while traveling from his work place to Tel Aviv. He recovered and returned to work the first time in 1945, but he never got up again from the second one in 1946. He was only 53 years ld.

Our sister Reitza was married to Velvel Gutleizer. They lived in Chorzele, where they established a large family – all of whom perished in the terrible Holocaust.

May their souls be bound in the bonds of eternal life.

[Page 126]

A Visit to the Town on the Brink of its Doom
by Reuven Raz (Korzenik)
Translated by Jerrold Landau

It took place on a summer day at the end of July in 1935. It was one of those dark, cold, mornings, with a mixture of mist and light heat, with the meadows carpeted by all type of grass. Grains and legume flowers could be seen from all sides. We set out on an uncharted path that morning, on a wagon strewn with straw, and partially covered by a thick, cloth tarpaulin. We traveled toward the town of Chorzele partly on a dirt path and partly on an unpaved stone path. We passed villages and churches. Wooden crosses stood on the side of roads at the entrance to villages, serving as guideposts for Christian believers of the region and travelers from time immemorial. Here and there, we encountered farmers and their families going out to work the fields. I was 21 years old at the time, and I had enough knowledge and experience to realize that primitivity still prevailed here in agriculture. I saw a scythe in the hands of the Polish farmer women, whereas we in the Land already had mechanized harvesters, tractors, combines, and bundling machines in almost every settlement. At that moment I thought of how great our Zionist pioneering energy was in conquering the desolation of agriculture where we were, in contrast to the situation in Poland, which had always been considered an agricultural country.

This how the journey continued until we arrived in my hometown, the cradle of my childhood – Chorzele. My desire then was to peer once into my past and remember my childhood and the town in which I was born – with its houses, Jews, realities, experiences, and communal life. As I was now passing through other towns in Poland, I did not see a great change in their way of life. However, here I was looking for homey, family warmth. I was immersed in thoughts until I reached the entrance to the city.

Before my eyes, I saw that "river" which was really a narrow stream, meandering in a hidden manner between the trees and grasses. Fat cows, laden with milk, grazed on both sides of the road. The horses lazily trotted up the hill across the wooden bridge – partly a bridge and partly a passageway. We were about to enter the town. Across the bridge, we once again encountered that traditional wooden cross, informing of the existence of a settlement at that place. Small wooden houses and even lone stone houses began to be seen before us. The scenery, the same Diaspora scenery that I had left when I was eight years old, remained in all its humbleness and modesty. There were simple wooden benches in front of the houses.

I searched for the home of "Yosel the Carpenter," as Yosef Korznik was called in earlier days. A holy awe enveloped me when the wagon stopped before one of the wooden houses and the wagon driver told me that this was the house in which Grandfather had lived, and now his two sisters live there with their families. At that moment I recalled that during my childhood, when I would visit the home of Grandfather and Grandmother with Father on holidays and festivals, a sense of calm and pleasantness pervaded these small rooms, the floors of which were made with wood covered with wax, painted red and creaking joyously... I also recall the large sawmill with gentile workers who toiled along with Grandfather. That sawmill would cut large boards into veneers. At that time, there were no machines in town. Everything was done by hand. I remember well how they would smooth out the odorous *"politora"* and the *"laka"* on the corners of wooden beds, closets, tables, and all kinds of chairs. There was the bustle of toil in that workshop on the long days and nights, especially before the fairs, whether in our town or in another town. "There were days which will not come back again," when this house was full of villagers on the fair days or on the eves of Christian holidays. These gentile Christians loved Grandfather and would be willing to sacrifice themselves for him...

[Page 127]

Grandmother Beila and their sons and daughters helped him in his work. However, time took its toll. The sons and daughters scattered in all directions, some to America, and some to the Land of Israel on pioneering *aliya*. Now I found a forlorn house. I found two families who lived their impoverished lives in this poor house. These were the families of my aunts Chana and Hinda. Both were old women (Aunt Hinda had several daughters, three of whom made it to the Land of Israel after the Holocaust.) My aunts received me with great warmth. After spending a few hours in that house, I continued on to visit other family members.

My first stop was at the family of Tzvi Jochet, the father of Menachem Jochet. It was also a hut made of wooden planks, but full of warmth and bustling with life. The father "sewed" shoes and the mother Rachel assisted him in all types of work with great energy. She would accept the orders and respond to all requests, while the two sons and the daughter were busy with the sewing machine. I will always remember the warm greeting that they extended to me, for this was an unforgettable experience. I remember how I urged these young people to liquidate everything and make *aliya* to the Land along with their parents. However... however, for this there is no response. They all suffered from the great inferno that destroyed six million Jews.

From there, I continued to the center of town – the small, square market place with its mold–eaten stalls. Sellers peered out from the counters. Here and there, at the side of the road, stood Polish farmers selling fruits, vegetables, wooden twigs for cooking and baking, and fodder and straw for animals. Here and there, large and small animals were sold next to the butcher shops. On the other hand, piglets were sold next to the Christian butcher shop. Along the way, on the side leading eastward, stood a sooty Jew who fixed the horseshoes of the farmers and wagon drivers who were passing through.

I continued to the family of Esther Bajszwajger. That wooden house was sustained by the mother, for the father had died during the First World War. The mother remained with two daughters and three sons, one of whom was completely handicapped. She bore complete responsibility for their livelihood for a long time. The oldest daughter was already in the Land, and the youngest son was in *hachsharah*. Nevertheless, the mother worked hard to sustain the two sons and the young daughter (who came to the Land after the Holocaust). I recall the large, wooden carriage with wide wheels upon which the wet laundry would be rolled by that elderly mother with her thin, veiny hands, so that she could sustain her family honorably. I held that woman in great esteem. She fought her battle for existence in the small town, and her only request was: would she merit to make *aliya* to the Land, and see her entire family there, along with her daughter who was already there? I parted from her with a heavy heart, and told her my answer: send the children first, and they will bring you. This is not what fate had in mind. Only some of the children reached the Land, but she herself – did not arrive...

[Page 128]

I continued on, passing the home of my grandfather's eldest brother, Mottel Korznik. He was already old and deaf, but was still full of life and wisdom. He complained to me that his children abandoned him in his old age, immigrating to South America with his two daughters. Only one request came from his mouth: would he merit to see them again? Hot tears streamed from his eyes. I could not encourage him when I advised: send you daughters to the Land...

I continued to the eastern side of the town, to peek for a moment into the old *Beis Midrash* and the splendid synagogue, the walls f which were filled with decorations and pictures from the Holy Land, the works of an artist. I found the same ceiling, slightly vaulted, and the splendid chandelier with the long chain. On Sabbath and festival eves, the branches of that chandelier lit up the building. At that time, several old men were sitting there learning Mishnah. They warmly greeted the visitor from the land of Israel.

I continued in the direction of the border, where I made a quick visit to the beer brewery. The brewery was owned by the Przysusker brothers, who also owned the brick kiln that was opposite the pine factory adjacent to the border. Nazi Germans were walking along the other side. As I stood next to the border with a passport in my hand, issued by the offices in the Land of Israel, the Germans and Poles looked at me from each side as a Jew who had come from the Jewish land – with more honor and understanding than they expressed toward local Jews...

This was 1935. Gloomy thoughts accompanied me after this two–day visit to my hometown. When I met with several of the youths, I infused them with a bit of faith about our future in the Land. I left the town on a horse–drawn wagon. I left it forever. At the time, I never thought I would have to describe that visit in this book, which is a monument to my town and its people who I saw alive at that time...

[Page 129]

The One and Only Who Survived Auschwitz
by David Fiszring
Translated by Jerrold Landau

Shalom Frenkeland his grandson David Friszring

I am the one and only person from our town who survived after going through Auschwitz.

The yellow patch of the Nazi occupation era was affixed to me in the Chorzele Ghetto. After that, I was in the Maków Ghetto, Auschwitz, Mauthausen, and Ebensee, from where I was liberated in May 1945 by the American Army.

I spent my childhood in Chorzele. Like all the children of the town, I began to go to *cheder* when I was five years old. I studied with the teacher Zalman–Meir, and then with Ben–Zion, as well as Lindenbaum and Ajzenstadt, who began to introduce more modern forms of study – meaning that he permitted us to go outside into the fresh air a bit, so we could see and sense nature. I also had to go to public school. In grade one, our teacher was Rabbi Nowicz, in the home of Feivel Kowel, where there was a Jewish class. In grade two, however, we were enrolled in the school that was next to the church. When I completed school (grade seven) in June 1939, I did not know what was about to take place within a few months.

I studied for two years in the new school building (on the road to Bagienice). This was a splendid building, with wooden floors. As we entered it, we had to exchange our shoes for slippers to protect the shiny floors. Everything was new inside, but the atmosphere was backward. Anti–Semitism pervaded all classes of the school. There were from five to ten Jewish students in every class, and we suffered greatly from the anti–Semitism of the Christian students.

At the end of the 1938/1939 school year, they distributed school graduation diplomas, and we prepared for the summer vacation. I had many plans for the future. I thought about continuing my studies in the trade gymnasja, which my parents were very pleased with, or perhaps to study some profession. I decided to make use of the summer vacation for something useful, so I traveled to the summer camp in ZduÅ„ska Wola organized by Gordonia. My friend in the movement, Yisrael Knott, also went to the camp with me and we spent several wonderful weeks there despite the difficult conditions that pervaded in the summer camp. We were fooled there during the time we stayed there. We got used to hunger and sleeping in uncomfortable conditions. Nevertheless, we went home happy and satisfied.

[Page 130]

At the beginning of August 1939, the atmosphere of war was already felt in our town. Anyone who had somewhere to go left Chorzele, for it was clear that the first front would be there. Jews rented wagons, upon which they loaded all the belongings that were possible, and travelled to other cities. Some remained in Prosienica, but others went as far as Ciechanów and Mława, and even to Warsaw. Only a few remained in our town on the day of the outbreak of the war on September 1, 1939. Those remaining included Esther–Liba and Shmuel Frenkel, Zalman–Meir the teacher, and two or three other families.

My family, consisting of my father Yechiel, my mother Miriam, me – David, and my two brothers, Shlomo born in 1930, and Leibel born in 1932, moved to my maternal aunt Malka's house in Ciechanów. My grandfather Shalom Frenkel, my grandmother Rachel, and aunt Sara, who left Chorzele before us, were all there. All of us crowded into my aunt's house.

[Page 131]

We somehow managed throughout the day, but the troubles began at nightfall, for not everyone had a place to sleep. Whomever could find a place to sleep elsewhere went to a different family. I too did so.

Rachel Frenkel, wife of Reb Shalom, and her daughters

The day after the conquest of the city of Ciechanów, the Germans began to pillage. They snatched for work anyone who crossed their path. They searched homes, and, with beatings and curses, took out the Jews to work at cleaning the bunkers and other institutions in the occupied city. One morning, they gathered all the Jews in the synagogue and informed them that anyone who wants could cross the border between the Germans and the Russians. However, the people themselves opposed this for several reasons: some said that this was a trap leading to disaster, and others thought that it was possible to organize things somehow so as not to be a wanderer.

The occupiers began to restrict our steps in a systematic manner. When we realized that the crowding of housing was increasing, and that there was no place to put our heads, and on the other hand, seeing that the general suffering was increasing, we concluded that it was worthwhile to endanger ourselves to return to Chorzele. Father and I returned to Chorzele to find out the situation with our own eyes. When we arrived there in the evening, we saw that our house on Ogrodowa Street 14 had been taken over by Polish residents, who had once lived on the Piaskes. We explained the situation to them and came to an agreement with them that they would free up our home for us in return for a dwelling in the second half of the house. It was clear that the situation in Chorzele was better than in Ciechanów not only from a housing perspective, but that it was also easier to obtain food. We returned to Ciechanów, obtained a wagon, loaded our belongings, and returned to Chorzele with our family.

At first, there were a few Jewish families there, but others slowly began to return, and a small Jewish community was formed there. The Jews were obligated to appear and register daily at the German command that was set up next to the Broiz of the Przysusker brothers. They began to enlist all the men for wood chopping and cleaning houses. The living conditions were generally comfortable. Everyone took up a dwelling where they found one, and we were scattered in all parts of the city. We gathered together daily for the *Mincha* and *Maariv* services, and on Sabbaths also for *Shacharit* and *Musaf*, until they canceled the rest day on the Sabbath. This was after the Sabbath when they confiscated all the gold and jewelry from the Jews. At that time, they also confiscated sewing machines, blankets, and pillows.

We carried out our work for free, without any payment. We earned our livelihoods by selling various items to the Polish residents. We worked at tearing down houses along Gornicna Street, starting from the home of Shlomo–Asher until the home of Polomski – along the entire street until the *mikva* [ritual bath]. We did not pass over the synagogue, *Beis Midrash*, or *mikva*. Everything was dismantled, and the wood was collected in the Breuer warehouses of the Przysusker brothers, where the city council warehouses were. The mayor was a Nazi who was one of the customers of Przenica. Our work supervisors were Volksdeutschen – one was Polish and named Kochel, and the other was Ukrainian, named Jakobowski.

One day, an edict was issued stating that Jews were forbidden from entering gentile shops. A sign was posted on every shop: "Entry by Jews is strictly forbidden." The portions of the Jews were given to one of us who opened a small shop in their house. We bought all our provisions there with coupons. The first command to wear a yellow patch (with a diameter of 10 centimeters) was also issued. Later, the command to wear the yellow Magen David with the inscription Jude was given – first to be worn on the left, and later the right.

[Page 132]

Bodnick was one of the anti–Semitic Volkdeutsche officials. He composed a song that, by edict of the mayor, we had to sing the entire way as we carried the wood to the warehouse. Moshe Fater, who was known for his sweet voice, paced along the "Dishel." He sang the stanzas, and we had to join in to the repeating chorus.

> *Przes 20 lat Żyd u Polaka kradł,*
> *jadał kury, raczki, kaczki;*
> *teraz niema na flaczki,*
> *aj waj, aj waj, aj waj...*[1]

After some time, they began to pave the wide street (Otostorada), and there was insufficient work force. The gentiles were given permission to enlist Jews as well for this work, but at a wage of 50% of the salary of the Christian workers. They brought us to the paving work area in gigantic transport trucks, gave the Jews the most difficult jobs, and supervised them more carefully. Nevertheless, I enlisted for this work, for I was the only one in the family who could earn a bit of money. I worked in paving the Otostorada for several months. Then I found more difficult work, but in the city – drilling a well next to the building of the Chorzele court. This work was difficult, for we had to do the drilling with our hands. Three of us carried it out: Berl Berger, myself, and Czechnowski from Myszniec who had gotten married in Chorzele.

Representatives of a filming company from Vienna, called Vienner Film, arrived in Chorzele one day, and started to make a film called "Haimker" – that is classifying the Volkdeutschen according to their birthplace. Then, the entire city became unrecognizable. They changed the facades of all the houses, as well as the appearance of the streets next to the railway station. The filming company set up workshops and offices on empty fields behind the ruins of the synagogue and the buildings that used to surround it.

When the filming finished, an edict was issued to make the area Judenrein, and to concentrate all the Jews into ghettos. One day, the ordered everyone to leave their homes, and placed wagons at the disposal of those leaving. The transfer to Maków via Przasnysz began. As we passed through Przasnysz, we were joined by local Jews who were being deported like us to the Maków Ghetto. Our family found itself in the synagogue that was divided into cubicles of several square meters – a cubicle for each family. The Judenrat and the Jewish police were comprised of the local Jews. Therefore, it was natural that the Jews who had arrived from outside suffered more. When a demand was issued to provide Jews from the labor camp in Nowa Wieś near Ostrołęka to clear stones from the road, we, the Jews of Chorzele, were the scapegoats. That is how I ended up in that work camp, which also contained Poles who had been convicted of crimes.

[Page 133]

In that camp, we were required to wake up very early and walk several kilometers to the place where the clearing of stones was taking place. Everyone received a quota of stones that had to be cleared within a day. Anyone who did not finish the quota would be liable to physical punishment, such as being forced to run in the snow, having their food rations lessened, etc. A typhus epidemic broke out in the camp, claiming many victims. As a result, an edict arrived to return us to the Maków Ghetto.

When that ghetto was liquidated, the survivors were transferred to the Mława Ghetto. However, we only remained there for five days. Members of the Jewish police of the ghetto broke into our house at midnight, and removed my father, my mother, and my younger brother Leibel. I, the eldest son, and my brother Shlomo (two years younger than me), were not taken in that aktion. Thus, we remained ripped apart from our families, who were sent to the crematoria of Treblinka. The next day, the men of the Jewish militia once again broke into our house, and gathered all those who remained. They permitted us to take whatever we could load into a sack, and brought us to the railway station. This was December 1942. The cold was very great, but we were still obligated to stand in the railway station for long hours until we received a command to board the train. They pushed us into the cars with beatings and curses, and sent us to the Auschwitz death camp. When we got off at the Auschwitz railway station, we were broken, hungry and thirsty, and we fell upon the puddles of slimy water to lick the slime.

Entrance to the Auschwitz death camp

[Page 134]

The famous selektion began: whom to the right and whom to the left! Nobody knew which was better – the right side or the left. Everyone had to announce their name and age out loud. I decided to add a few years to my true age, and I told my brother Shlomo to do them same when we approached the selektion table. However, the selector separated me from my brother. Soldiers with guns stood in the side. They separated us by force, and I never saw my brother again, because he was hauled straight to the crematoria of Auschwitz.

We were ordered to march several kilometers until we arrived at the Birkenau Camp. There, they took our sacks from us, stripped us naked, and dressed us in camp uniforms. Each of us was tattooed with a prisoner number on our left arm. This number served in place of a surname and a first name. I received the number 80388.

Ten prisoners had to sleep on an area of about 1.5 square meters. The conditions were intolerable. There was no water for washing. Everyone suffered from diarrhea. Illnesses spread in the camp, and tens of prisoners who had died through the night were removed every morning. For a certain period, I had to load such corpses on transport trucks to bring them to the crematoria.

One day at the end of December 1942, we were arranged in two rows of about a half kilometer long. S.S. men ordered us to fill our coats with sand or stones, and to run with the load, as they hit us with their sticks. Many victims fell that day, as became clear during the daily roll call the next day. The roll call took place every morning and evening, even though it was clear to everybody that one could not escape from there. The camp was surrounded by an electric barbed wire fence (double or triple), and watchmen guarded around us with projectors that were lit up throughout the night. One day during morning roll call, a command was given that all youths up to the age of 20 must present themselves before the camp commander. I was 17, and I decided that I had nothing to lose, for I was disgusted with life. It was not important whether I would be sent to the crematoria. However, fate was otherwise: I was chosen to be among those youths who were transferred to the Auschwitz camp, several kilometers away from Birkenau. These youths were placed in the building school in Auschwitz (block 7). We studied building in a theoretical and practical way. After gaining our knowledge, the graduates were sent to work outside the camp, where we built large buildings. The head of our block was a German with a green triangle on his chest – that is to say, he was a convicted criminal from Germany. He was very meticulous about insisting that we wash our feet and heads. We were all required to wash, without considering the 25° cold. He once conducted a nighttime hunt. He placed several tens of lads on the roof of the building where there was a fierce wind. He made us kneel on our knees for several long hours, and finally poured cold water on us.

I was one of those injured who was taken to the hospital (block 19). I lay there for several days with a high temperature, and was affected by an ear infection. There was an urgent need for surgery, and I was taken to block 28 where there was an operating room. I was operated on by a Polish doctor named Waszilowski. I must thank him for surviving at that time.

After the surgery, I lay immobile for several days, for I was forbidden from moving my head.

[Page 135]

However, the wound did not heal due to lack of vitamins. I managed somehow to remain in the hospital for a longer period, and they even helped me dress up as a nurse during the S.S. inspections of the hospitals, in which they removed the sick people and send them to the crematoria. The wound finally healed. I was permitted to leave the hospital, and I returned to the building school.

When the Russian Army neared the Auschwitz camp, the Germans decided to liquidate it. This was the famous march known as the "death march" from Auschwitz to other places. We marched by foot from Auschwitz to the railway station. Thousands of marchers met their deaths, whether from weakness or from the S.S. bullets that accompanied us. We arrived in the Mauthausen camp after much wandering, and were placed in bunks. I was later transferred to the Mielec camp, and then to Ebensee. Great hunger pervaded in that camp, to the point where the workers who were involved in digging tunnels in the mountains would eat the ground compost, which we would call "margarine." Many people died from eating this "margarine."

When the day of liberation arrived, the Germans wanted to place us in the mountain tunnels and detonate them. However, they failed in carrying out this plan. The American Army took control of the camp in a sudden wing operation. We found ourselves saved from the danger of death that had accompanied us day by day and hour by hour.

Translator's Footnote

1. This poem translates as follows on Google Translate:

   20 years a Jew from the Pole stole,

   Food chicken, handles, ducks;

   Now there is no tripe,

   Yeah, yeah, yeah, yeah ...

[Page 135]

My Home that was Destroyed Upon me
by Dov (Berele) Fater
Translated by Jerrold Landau

In memory of my father Reb Tevel Fater, my mother Ruchtza; my brothers Eliahu Leib (and his wife Tzlava and their children); Shalom (and his wife Dina and their children); the youngest Tzvi; my sisters: Leah (and her husband Moshe and their children); Mirl – who were all murdered by the Nazis and their assistants.

My large, prominent family was murdered by the murderers without leaving any remnant in the Diaspora. I will therefore permit myself to describe in detail the influence of the family of Reb Tevel Fater in the life of our town, as well as all branches of business and activities of my father, who excelled in his traits, with his warm home open to all in need. My mother Ruchtza, good hearted and merciful, with few like her, looked after the home.

The life of my family and the connections of love binding it to all groups in the town, without distinction, are still etched in my mind after being in the Land for 30 years. If there was a question about Jewish law, a Talmudic discussion, or some religious matter in the city, our honorable city rabbi, Rabbi Sokolower of blessed memory, would always confer with my father, who was a personality in our city as a scholar who was expert in Talmud and rabbinic decisions. Both would deliberate and debate until the matter became clear. If there was a problem in the town, such as a collection for the poor, economic assistance, the setting up of a bank, the construction of a communal building, or any other problem, almost all the city notables would come to our house. These included the head of the community Reb Avraham–Michel Adler, Reb Mordechai Mendel Farbowicz, Reb Bekerman, Reb Avraham Schorr, and many others. They would sit down for a light snack, and discuss all important issues of the world and the city. My father would always be among the first to give an honorable donation for the needs of the city, for my family was known as being well–based economically, and my father was considered to be among the wealthy men of the town.

[Page 136]

The Czwyrkowski brothers, owners of Remblink's estate

Issues of Zionism and the Land of Israel would always be deliberated in our house in the presence of my father, who was one of the founders of Mizrachi, and had been a member of it for many years. He was among those who excelled in love of the Land of Israel and the Torah of Israel. Even after he transferred to Agudas Yisroel in his latter years, issues of the Land of Israel continued to remain very close to his heart. When the *Hachsharah* of Poalei Agudas Yirsoel was set up on the land of Moshe Czwyrkowski, my father lovingly gave the best of his ability to ensure that the *Hachsharah* would succeed, as it certainly did. (It was through this *Hachsharah* that I made *aliya* to the Land.)

I will take this opportunity to mention my two brothers, Eli–Leib and Shalom, who were founders of Tarbut in our town. They were prominent Zionist activists for many years.

My parents' home also served as a center for assistance and support activities for those in need. My father, assisted by my goodhearted mother, was always ready to offer help. My father was always ready to even leave his business to help the needy. My father served as a member of the town council (ławnik) for many years. He would appear as a representative to the authorities in times of need, and would defend the town's Jewry with great faithfulness.

When one of the Jews of the town died, they would turn to Reb Tevel Fater, for father was also the chief *gabbai* [trustee] of the *Chevra Kadisha* [burial society] for many years. Natives of our town certainly remember the large feasts of the *Chevra Kadisha* that took place twice a year in our spacious home. Delicacies produced by my diligent mother Ruchtza were served. She concerned herself with anything needed in the city. My diligent sisters Leah and Mirl helped Mother in this activity with great dedication. We, the sons, also helped. My sister Mirl was also very active in the Beis Yaakov religious school.

[Page 137]

A *Hachsharah* group of Agudas Yisroel in Remblink (1934)

The tragedy that befell us with the loss of our family, of which it is possible to state that it possessed a blend of Torah and greatness together, merges with our general tragedy of the loss of all the Jews of Chorzele, precious, pure, and good hearted, who were prepared to help anyone in need, and who were occupied in issues of the nation and the Land of Israel.

My destroyed home was one of the typical homes in our town, to each of which the full sense of the word "home" applies. It was a home to the family members as well as a gathering place for communal affairs. Homes such as this in Chorzele, as in other towns in Poland during that era, forged the image of the town and stamped the town with its way of life.

Woe to those that are lost but will not be forgotten.

[Page 138]

Youth of Agudas Yisroel

A Beis Yaakov group of Agudas Yisroel

[Page 139]

The Blood Account of my Family
by Moshe–Chaim Rostoker
Translated by Jerrold Landau

Keila Rostoker

My entire family was tied to our town of Chorzele: my father Shmuel–Yechezkel, my mother Keila, my four sisters Golda (Zahava), Chaitsha (Chaya), Sara, and Feiga (Tzipora), and me, the youngest.

My father was an upright, good hearted, G–d fearing Jew, who distributed charity with an open hand. He died at the beginning of the First World War (21 Elul 5774, 1914), during the epidemic that broke out due to hunger and disease.

My mother remained a widow with her five young children. She toiled on their behalf for many years to raise and educate them appropriately. We moved to Warsaw in 1930 to improve our livelihood. My mother's great hope was to see her children make *aliya* to Zion. I indeed made *aliya* in 1933, and brought my mother to live in the Holy Land two years later. Here, my mother worked a great deal for the natives of our town and for various other communal institutions, especially *Yeshivas*, charitable funds, and *Hachnasat Kalah* (providing for poor brides). She died on 5 Tammuz, 5705 (1945), and was buried on the Mount of Olives in Jerusalem.

My sister, Golda, her husband Gavriel, their sons Yechezhel, Yisrael–Shalom, and Yosef, and their two daughters whose names I did not know, all perished in the Warsaw Ghetto. That fate in the Warsaw Ghetto also overtook my other sisters: Chaitsha (with her husband Tzadok and three children Yechezkel, Yitzchak, and Sara), Sara (with her husband), and Feiga.

I am the only surviving member of the entire aforementioned family.

[Page 140]

A group of religious youth

Agudas Yisroel youth

[Page 141]

Yizkor...

by Bella Tykulsker (Walzer)

Translated by Jerrold Landau

Perl Tykulsker

I will recall our holy community, with its splendid families from all strata, as well as the communal and political organizations that no longer exist.

I will recall our father Yitzchak Tykulsker, who dreamed his dream to return to our town already during the First World War, so that he could sell his property and make *aliya* to the Land of Israel.

I will recall our mother Perl, who succeeded in making *aliya* to the Land. She lived here for about 20 years, in the bosom of her sons, daughters, grandchildren, and great-grandchildren, and witnessed the establishment of the State of Israel.

I will recall our brother Nachman, in whose heart the vision of renaissance pulsated already from his youth. He prepared himself to make *aliya* with the first pioneers, and did his part in the building of the Land.

I will recall our eldest sister Chaya-Sara, who remained alone in the exile of Russia, without any connection to the family, and died there.

I will recall Uncle Chaim Tykulsker, who died during the First World War, as well as all his family who were murdered by the Nazi murderers during the Second World War: his wife Golda, and their daughters Liba-Roiza (with her family), Mindel, Dvora Rivka – the good and pleasant mother and daughters, of whom no survivor remains.

May their souls be bound in the bonds of life.

A Memorial Candle for my Revered Father
by Chaya Segal (Friedman)
Translated by Jerrold Landau

Esther and Mordechai–Mendel Frajdman, and their daughter Chana

My revered father Reb Mordechai–Mendel Frajdman was a scion of the family of Admorim [Hassidic masters] of Warka, where he was raised and educated, and where he absorbed the values of Hassidism. He was very pious during his youth, and was strict about every detail. However, he became more balanced with the passage of time, and even compromising to a certain degree. He was enthusiastic throughout his life, and everything in which he became involved had the imprint of an internal flame, in accordance with the verse "all my bones shall say"[1]. A fundamental sense of energy was imprinted in his soul. Nevertheless, success did not shine for him in his private affairs, for he believed too much in the honesty of the individual.

My father was the force behind the founding of *Kupat Malve* [loan fund] in 1922. Together with Avraham–Michel Adler (chairman of the fund) and Moshe–Aharon Gabiazda the treasurer, he gave of his energy and money to develop and establish the fund. My father was one of the founders of the benevolent fund in 1939. However, that time, he was not able to prove his energy in communal activism, for the world war broke out a few months later.

[Page 143]

My revered father also served as the representative of the Jewish National Fund for many years. He dedicated himself to this role as well with the full warmth of his heart, despite the complaints of my dear mother that he was neglecting his livelihood due to his communal work. He treated his efforts for the Zionist idea as holy. He encouraged *aliya* to the Land of Israel with full appreciation and satisfaction. He would say, "For any lad or young woman that we send to the Land of Israel, it is as if we have added a layer to the structure of the nation." These words of his and his dedicated activity on behalf of the Jewish National Fund provoked the wrath of the zealous Orthodox people who negated the value of *aliya* to the Land of Israel. These groups even called him "*apikorus*" [heretic], and damaged his source of livelihood.

In accordance with the advice of our friend and neighbor Yechezkel Segal, my revered father turned to teaching in his latter years. He displayed his full spirit in that endeavor as well. He regarded this profession, imparting Torah and wisdom to Jewish children, as a mission, from which he gained great satisfaction. This occupation was also agreeable to the spirit of my mother Esther, who dedicated her entire life to her husband and children, and toiled on their behalf until her last day.

I remain alone to weep over dear Father and Mother, and their children: my dear brother Yaakov, with his wife Rivka and their son Simcha–Bunim, who met their deaths among the martyrs of the Holocaust; my dear sister Chana, who fell victim to the enemy as she was on the threshold of marriage.

My heart mourns, and I have no comfort over the death of my family, as well as all the martyrs of our town.

Children with the Blue Box at an activity for the Jewish National Fund

[Page 144]

The family of Mendel Kac

The family of Hershel Jochet

Translator's Footnote

1. Psalms 35:10

[Page 145]

About the Holocaust of my Family
by Penina Biran
Translated by Jerrold Landau

Reb Yitzchak–Meir Richter and his granddaughter (daughter of Dvora)

My revered father Reb Yitzchak–Meir Richter of blessed memory was the youngest son of an honorable family of Ger Hassidim. He arrived in Chorzele as a young lad, as the son–in–law of Reb Feivel Lichtensztajn of blessed memory, a G–d fearing scholar, one of the city notables and leaders, who served as the head of the community for 30 consecutive years. My revered father quickly blended in to his new environment. He would attend the shtibel, was a regular studier of *Gemara*, and befriended the fine young men of the town, especially with the one who would in the future become the well–known Rabbi Graubard.

Father was only married to his first wife for a few years, until she died. (She died after childbirth, leaving behind two babies, the youngest ten days old.) After some time, he married my future mother Naomi, of the Przysusker family, a refined woman with a boundless good heart. My dear mother died in her prime, leaving my father alone to bear the yoke of raising and educating the children, in addition to the yoke of his many businesses.

My father prepared to make *aliya* to the Land of Israel in 1938, and even began the preparations. However, in the interim, the sky clouded over, the Second World War was about to begin, and all plans were thwarted. Father was forced to leave Chorzele in July 1939 along with his daughter Fruma and his granddaughter. When the war broke out, he brought the rest of his family out of Chorzele. However, this too was to no avail, for the hand of the enemy reached them even in the distant place, where they were all murdered.

The following people perished in the Holocaust along with Father: my intelligent brother Motel, and his wife of valor Yocheved; my beautiful, intelligent sister Dvora; my young, talented sister Fruma, who was always full of grace and joy of live. We, the family in Israel (David, Yehuda, Penina, Yeshayahu) and our families will always preserve their memories in our hearts.

May their souls be bound in the bonds of eternal life.

[Page 146]

The family of Aharon–Pinchas and Rachel Silbersztajn

The Berent family

[Page 147]

I Saw the Town in its Destruction
by Henry Adler
Translated by Jerrold Landau

This is what is left of the cemetery...

I am the son of Wolf Adler of Chorzele. My grandfather Reb Moshe–Shimon was the cantor and shochet [ritual slaughterer] in that town.

I was born in London, where I was raised and educated. However, I felt an internal impetus to travel to Poland after the Second World War, to see with my own eyes the town of my father and that of my mother (Miedzyrzec), in the hope that perhaps I would find some survivors of their families.

From Warsaw, I traveled first to Miedzyrzec, where I discovered a relative name Fiszbajn. He was one of the three Jews who I found at that time in the town, which had 1,400 Jews before the war. I traveled to Chorzele the next day.

When I arrived in the town, I immediately asked where it would be possible to find Jews. I was told, "There are no Jews here." I went to the cemetery, and found it completely destroyed. Nevertheless, I placed flowers on the site and recited *kaddish*. Then I went around the streets of the town, and, with weak knees, went to see the house in which my family had lived. I also approached the river to look at it, for my father told me that they would often go there to bathe...

The house in which my grandfather had lived was abandoned and desolate. I went up to the attic and began to search through the remains, for perhaps I might find something. Indeed, I found a piece of linen from a nightgown. I said in my heart, "Perhaps this is from one of my family members. I will take it as a souvenir." I guard the piece of linen and the photographs that I took during my visit as an eternal souvenir.

I saw the great destruction of Polish Jewry in the two towns in which my parents were born and raised. Since that time, my heart was further attracted to those two towns. Perhaps I will visit them again.

[Page 148]

The family of Yidel Eichler

The Lanenter family

[Page 149]

Two Meetings with Chorzele in Israel
by Moshe Baharab
Translated by Jerrold Landau

It seemed that all the residents of Chorzele were Jews. Even the few gentiles that I remembered there spoke Yiddish. I remember one gentile, a border guard named Wronski, who would come to my parents' store and speak fluent Yiddish. He came to the Land with the Polish Army during the Second World War and visited us in our home. I took him on a comprehensive tour of the Land. Tears came to the eyes of the "gentile" when he visited Kibbutz Yagur. He wept with actual tears even when he left the Land with the Polish Army. This man had a "Jewish heart," and when he expressed the name Chorzele, it seemed to me that he was referring solely to the Jews of Chorzele at that moment.

In November 1948, at the end of the attack, and before the storming of an Arab village in the Galilee[1], three of us Chorzele natives sat and discussed – about what? Of course, about Chorzele. I recalled one Simchat Torah evening in the town in the home of Moshe–Aharon Gabiazda (after he had married a very young woman). We recalled the songs of Zion that we sang in that house, and the discussions about Mizrachi and Zionism that took place in that house. We also talked about the members of Agudas Yisroel, who at that time were very active against Zionism and against the vision of the establishment of the State of Israel.

On the other hand, we recalled the speeches of M. M. Frajdman (my teacher in the *cheder*) who was the head of the Jewish National Fund in Chorzele. He spoke enthusiastically about the Land of Israel, and all his dreams were only about the Land of Israel. How much would this man had given to merit to see natives of Chorzele among the first ranks of the fighters for the Land of Israel.

The aforementioned discussion, which started with intimate silence, turned into a general conversation after half an hour. All the Yemenites and Sephardim in my brigade (of which I was a commander in the Israel Defense Forces) listened to it with great interest, and they could not pronounce the difficult name "Chorzele" under any circumstances. However, when we meet at times, they all remember the town in which I was born. They know its name, and know that our teachers and counselors were among those pure, faithful people in the towns of the Diaspora who dreamed throughout their entire lives of the establishment of the state, but did not merit to see it.

[Page 150]

The family of Mordechai Kaszeniak

The families of Meir Alter and Yechezkel Segal

[Page 151]

Deep pits, red clay –
I once had a home.

Spring – the orchards would bloom,
Autumn time – the birds would migrate,
Winter – snow would fall there,
Now – wind and pain blow there.

Year after year passes,
Those pits are full,
And the clay is even redder,
Every piece of clay is now my home.

There lie my brothers,
Those whose limbs were torn apart,
Those who were slaughtered in the home,
Those who were shot by the pit.

Deep pits, red clay –
I once had a home.

Sh. Halkin

Translator's Footnote

1. This would seem to reference battles during the War of Independence.

[Page 153]

Chapters From the Past
by Moyshe Koval
Translated by Miriam Leberstein

Chorzele Rabbis

In the 1890's, the town rabbi was "the Turker Rabbi," a great religious scholar. He was always dancing and singing and preached that one must serve God with joy and jubilation.

After him came Rabbi Kovalski from Vlotslavek [Wloclawek]. Some of the town's prominent men travelled to Prushnits [Przasnysz] to meet him, and others met him in Ritshik (6 kilometers from Chorzele) bearing torches. He entered the town in a carriage sent for his special use by Moyshe Yeshaye Pshisusker, who owned the village of Rembelinek.

Later, Rabbi Roznshtraf became the town rabbi. Chorzele was his first rabbinical post and there was controversy over his hiring. So his father–in–law came to town and offered to pay a thousand rubles if his son–in–law was hired. This caused a great stir and two sides were formed. Those opposed to the hiring complained: "How can this be! Such a young whippersnapper, and a graduate of a *gymnazie* [academic secular high school] to boot!" (He had completed *gymnazie* in Plotsk [Plock]). "After all the renowned rabbis Chorzele has had!"

But the thousand rubles received by some of leading townsmen outweighed these objections, and "The Rich Son–in–Law from Plotsk" (as the town called him at first) had the good fortune to become the rabbi. He arrived in town, a handsome, tall young man, with a trimmed beard. The *rebitsin* [rabbi's wife] was also an intelligent and pretty woman. (They had a little girl, Leyele.) Chorzele wasn't used to such a rabbi, so they didn't like him at first. But as time passed, they came to love him for his sermons and for the folksy tales he told, which everyone came to hear. In later years, he would become known as "The Great Rabbi," renowned all over Poland. But at this time, he left Chorzele and went to Elkish [Olkusz], for financial reasons. The rabbi had demanded a raise in salary from 17 to 20 rubles. The Jewish community after long debates agreed to his demand, but the rabbi was no longer willing and left.

[Page 154]

After him, Rabbi Broynrot came to Chorzele and served as rabbi until after the First World War. During the war, when the Jews were driven out of the border towns, Rabbi Broynrot went to Warsaw, where he was an active member of the committee for aid to refugees and became famous for this throughout Polish Jewry. When the war ended, he moved to Tshekhanov [Ciechanow] and then went to Tel Aviv, where he served until his death as head of the rabbinical court.

The last rabbi in Chorzele until the Holocaust in 1942 was Rabbi Sokolower.

The entire population, great and small, rich and poor, treated the rabbis with great respect. In those days the greatest honor for a Chorzele Jew was to be a regular guest at the rabbi's table. The rabbi's word was holy, and his rulings were carried out to the letter. There was a case where one of the more prosperous Chorzelers did not comply with the rabbi's ruling. Very soon after that, he died under mysterious circumstances. The whole town saw this as a sign from God and no one talked about it further.

The rabbis elicited respect by the manner in which they conducted themselves. The Elkisher rabbi, handsome and tall, always carried a cane with a silver handle and a silver monogram. The *shames* [sexton] Reb [respectful term of address] Hershele almost always followed him around, also holding a cane in his hand. Everyone looked at the rabbi proudly when he would take a stroll with the commandant of the border guard, Colonel Khabarow, or with the priest, Proboshtsh.

The Khevre–Kedushe [Burial Society]

I remember that when I was still a child, at the end of the 19th century, my father had the good fortune to become a member of the burial society. This was no small accomplishment. First, one had to submit a recommendation from two senior members of the society. Then there would be a meeting of the *gabes* [administrators] and finally a general meeting of the membership.

[Page 155]

For the first three years, each new member had to be a "*mlotsh,*" that is, they had to do all the dirty work and be ready to respond to each summons by the *gabe* in case of a funeral. (At the time the *gabe* was Reb Yisrolke Tik.) The tasks of the *mlotsh* included calling all the members to a meeting, preparing the *kiddush* [reception] for Shimini Atseret [8th day of Sukkot] and the yearly feast on the 7th day of Shvat.

On Shimini Atsteret the *khevre kedushe* would take over the synagogue for prayer. The *gabes* would take charge of giving out *aliyahs* [privilege of reading the Torah portion] among the members. After prayers, they would have a lavish *kiddush* and Simkhes Toyre in the evening after prayers they would gather at the *gabe*'s house and drink beer from barrels.

But the *kiddush* was nothing compared to the yearly feast on the 7th day of Shvat. Preparations would start many weeks in advance. Large cakes and rolls were baked by special baker women (Korte Platshke, and in later years Khaye Sore, Fishl Stolier's mother–in–law.) They ordered huge fish from the German lakes so everyone could have a large portion. For each person they prepared a quarter of a roast goose and the goose livers and gizzards were chopped and cooked in goose fat. They also prepared 95–proof liquor and to top it all off, a *tsimis* made from dried plums (not carrots). In the morning, the members prayed in a separate *minyen* [prayer group] and didn't say the *takhnen* prayer.

They would invite to the feast the prominent men of the town, with the rabbi in the place of honor. The event was very festive; no other group was capable of organizing such a splendid feast. Of course, the senior members of the *khevre kedushe* enjoyed themselves very much; they had a good time, ate their fill, and went home. But the *mlotsh* had to do all the preparations – buy fish and meat, slaughter the geese, and carry tables and chairs from the *besmedresh* [house of study/synagogue] to the *gabe*'s house and afterwards carry them back again.

I remember how hard my father worked for many days before the *kiddush* and the feast. But the most important thing for him was the merit he earned, the opportunity to perform a *mitsve*, which immeasurably outweighed the heavy labor or even the money spent.

He spent three years in this way as a *mlotsh* and after that became a regular member. But even in the later years he was always active and ready to carry out his duties. After the First World War, when the Poles marched in (in 1920) after driving away the Bolsheviks, and the famed anti–Semitic General [Jozef] Haller entered the town of Chorzele, my father almost lost his life while carrying out his duty as a member of the burial society.

[Page 156]

After the Poles took over the town, life began to return to normal. Peasants began to come to town and they reported that the corpses of many murdered Jews were lying about in the swamps of Great–Kushinuliga. My father, along with Kasrielke, obtained two wagons, and set off to these places. They retrieved the bodies of the 18 of the murder victims and brought them back to Chorzele in order to provide them with a Jewish burial.

As they were driving on Briker [Bridge] Street, where the Hallerites had their headquarters, the Hallerites stopped them and asked what they were carrying. Hearing that the cargo consisted of corpses, they asked my father if he had had a permit. My father replied that he didn't need a permit, because he was a member of the burial society and this was his job. They beat him so badly that he lay ill for weeks.

Biker Khoylim [aid to the sick] and Lines Hatsedek [housing for the poor]

My father was also a member, and in later years a *gabe*, in the organization *Biker Khoylim*, along with the *shoykhet* [ritual slaughterer] Reb Avraham. Every Friday two members of *Biker Khoylim* went door to door and collected money for this organization. In my youth, on Purim the collectors would make their collections dressed as Russian soldiers (in uniforms and military hats, with masks on their faces).

The organization had an arrangement with the doctors and pharmacists (in large part Christians) that whoever came to them with a voucher signed by the *gabes* would receive a discount of 50%. (There were cases where the organization paid 100% for the patients.) It often happened that people would call in a doctor from Tshekhanov or even Urtlsburg (East Prussia) and they would also send the sick to hospitals, all of which entailed quite large expenses. The organization would also lend out (upon posting of a pledge) thermometers, equipment for giving enemas and for cupping, and other such items. (The main *feldsher* [unlicensed medical practitioner] who did cupping was Melekh Tsitriniazh.)

The question arises: How did the organization obtain money for all these expenses? How did those small contributions cover everything? Once, when my father was *gabe*, he called in a doctor from Germany, who received 100 marks ($25 or 5 English pounds) for his visit at a time when a well–off resident of Chorzele earned that amount in a month. My father, in fact, would constantly complain: "I can't continue as *gabe*. There's never enough money in the treasury and every month we have to redeem the vouchers for the doctor and pharmacist. If they don't get paid they'll stop accepting patients and writing prescriptions." When my mother would hear that my father wanted to give up his position as *gabe* she was very upset that he might, God forbid, give up such a great *mitsve*.

[Page 159]

The organization *Lines Hatsedek* worked together with *Biker Khoylim* and was mainly a women's society. Its chairwoman was Sore Mashe Sniadever; the secretary was Penine (Perl) Rikhter; the treasurer Tova Koval. Their work was similar to that of *Biker Khoylim* but it consisted first of all of sending members to stay overnight with the sick, or sending a poor patient soup along with meat and fruit to revive the heart and refresh the soul

[Page 157]

The family of Tankhem Koval

Yitshak and Golde Kitnik

[Page 158]

Libe and Fayvl Koval and daughter Ita

Libe and Dovid Koval with their son Moyshe and his wife

Malke (Koval) and Khaim Shmuel Krishtol

My Teachers

When I turned four, my father wrapped me in a prayer shawl and carried me to *kheder* [religious school for young children]. At first I studied with Reb Aron–Yenkl who, in addition to teaching, had a side business chopping up fodder for horses and selling it to wagon drivers. On market days, Tuesday and Thursday, he would interrupt his teaching and go to the market to sell straw that he had chopped up. (He had his own fodder–making machine.)

My second teacher was Reb Fayvush Student. He was also an expert in driving away the evil eye, and people would come to him from near and far for this purpose.

The only *kheder* that felt like a real institution of learning was that of Reb Yudl Wengel. Reb Yudl had previously been a soldier and had fought in the Russo Turkish War. It's possible that this influenced him to organize the studies in *kheder* according to a specific and permanent schedule. In his *kheder* the children sat quietly at the table. Each one recited a verse of the Bible and each hour they studied a different subject. In short, it was a fine *kheder*. All the children of the Lakhower family studied there. (Fishl Lakhower was one of his students.)

[Page 160]

Trade with Germany

Chorzele, as is well known, was two kilometers from the border with East Prussia and was considered a good place to earn a living. Many Jews did business with Germany, some legally, others illegally. The legal business consisted of exporting bran (which the Christians would buy from the mills in Prushnits, Makov [Makow–Mazowiecki], Krasnoshelts, etc.), wood products, and vegetables (cucumbers, onions, carrots).

The illegal business consisted of exchanging German marks for Russian rubles, and transporting contraband, mainly via the thousands of workers who in the summer months would travel to Germany for work. Every resident of Chorzele would receive from the government an official permit that allowed him to pass freely into Flamberg, the first village on the German side.

The contraband consisted not only of merchandise, but also of people. After the revolution of 1905, when the Tsarist reactionaries began arresting Jewish youths, the border towns like Mishinets [Myszyniec], Prushnits and Chorzele became known as transfer points on the way to Germany and from there to America.

The merchandise smuggled though Chorzele consisted of saccharine from Russia, flax shawls from France, various gemstones from Czechoslovakia, lace from Germany, etc. This all provided a way for Chorzelers to make a living but there were still so many poor people, you count the rich on the fingers of your hands.

The Jews had to work very hard to make a living, and had to constantly protect themselves from losing it. My father, for example, dealt in eggs, butter, vegetables, dairy products and poultry. When the season for young geese and ducks arrived, before the holidays, he would send out thousands of geese and ducks to private customers all over Germany, who would pay higher prices. In our house we had a German stamp with the inscription: "Poultry suppliers, eggs and butter, Flamberg at Vilenberg, East Prussia." Every merchant who did business in Germany had a post office box in Flamberg and every day, at 10 o'clock in the morning, half of Chorzele would go to Flamberg to pick up their mail.

[Page 161]

Jewish Fishermen

Chorzele had Jewish fishermen who fished the German lakes. Of these I remember Naftali Zabludowski, who was called Koheyn HaGodl [the High Priest]; Heniekh Pshenitse; the Goldshteyn brothers; Elihu Beynish; and others. Every Sunday they would harness their horses to wagons and go to Germany where they would catch bream, tench and pike and on Thursday they would return to Chorzele with chests full of fish. In winter they would bring smelts, which the housewives would cook in a sweet–sour sauce. Each fisherman leased his own lakes.

As a child I once went with the fishers to the German lakes and I remember how they ate bream fried in butter with pancakes made from grated potatoes, and drank aquavit. (They didn't eat meat in Germany because of the need to keep kosher.)

There were Jews who would travel to Germany to catch fish and stay there an entire month. They would come to Chorzele to renew their permits. These were highly skilled experts who earned 6–8 rubles a week.

Reb Naftali "Koheyn HaGodl" would bring fish to Warsaw and back. He would travel either with a carriage or with the wagon drivers. Later, when he gave up fishing and began making kvass [a fermented drink] from bread, he revealed his secret. "When I earned a lot from fishing, I would travel with the wagon drivers, so my competitors would think I had done poorly. When I did poorly, I would travel in a carriage, so my competitors would be upset, thinking I had done well."

Tailors

In Chorzele there were many artisans who lived in poverty. Only a few made a living. Reb Fayvl Berl the tailor had a workshop with apprentices. He would exploit the beginner apprentices, who worked from the time of the first *minyen* [earliest communal morning prayers] to late into the night. (On Thursday into Friday as well as the nights before holidays they worked all through the night.)

[Page 162]

My uncle Dovid Hersh Yukht became a tailor. When he was 21, he was drafted into the Russian army and served in Siberia. He arrived at his posting at Passover, having travelled all winter. The entire four years of his service he did not eat the regular army food, because of his concern for keeping kosher, but made do with packaged foods.

After his military service he went to America, where he worked hard for four or five years and then returned home with a few hundred dollars. With that money he returned to Chorzele, bringing also an apprentice certificate, opened his own workshop and worked hard to make a living.

Signs of Poverty

Dr. Mietshenski was a good person. The first prescription he would write would be for two to four glasses of milk, in the morning and evening, and a good soup with meat to be eaten at each midday meal. A large portion of his Jewish patients were malnourished and he told them to eat a lot of vegetables. The Jews at that time didn't know about raw carrots (or tomatoes); they would eat a carrot *tsimes* [sweet stew], and that only on Friday night. I remember once a working man came to a wealthy man's house to demand payment of a debt, and found the man eating *tsimis* at his midday meal. He left shouting, "You tell me to wait until tomorrow for payment and you're eating *tsimis* on a weekday!"

In general, a well–off family ate twice a day, at breakfast after prayers and at supper after the nighttime prayer. A pound of meat cost 1 Â½ gulden and a pound of bread cost a "*firer*" (two kopeks.) Mostly people ate whole grain rye bread. People baked their own large breads, weighing 10–12 pounds each. In the well– off homes they ate bread made with finely sifted flour or half–black bread. Each morning, every child got a roll with which to make the *hamotsi* prayer. A roll cost a *tsveyer* (one kopek), three rolls a *finfer* (2 Â½ kopeks).

Between Jews and Christians

The relationships between Jews and Christians were very good; you could even say ideal for those times. I remember only one case of tension, in the year 1905–06, during the "Green Thursday" after Easter. There was talk that the Christians were preparing for a pogrom in the town. The town rabbi at the time was Rabbi Roznshtrakh, "the Elkisher rabbi," a great speaker and prodigy as well as an expert in European literature. The commandant of the border authority was then the Russian colonel Kharbarow, who was very friendly with the rabbi and would often drop in on him for a chat. The rabbi told the colonel about the Jews' fear of a pogrom and the colonel assured him that there would be no pogrom. He asked only that the Jews stay out of the streets during the procession. And in fact everything remained peaceful.

[Page 163]

In addition to the border authority, Chorzele also had a "chief" policeman as well as a regular policeman, a "chief" gendarme with an assistant, and a mayor who was elected every 3–4 years. But it was always the same person who was mayor – Kabilenski, who had an administrative office with a scribe.

Every month every Jewish resident had to go to the administrative office to obtain the pass to cross the border to Flamberg. Officially, the pass didn't cost anything but everyone paid the mayor a *tsvantsiker* (10 kopeks) and the scribe a *tsener* (5 kopeks.)

The chief policeman Koleshnikov was very friendly with the Jewish tradesmen. Every Friday he would receive *khale* bread from the bakers, meat from the butchers and additional items from the others.

A Paved Highway on the Map

I remember that engineers came to Chorzele and began to measure the roads in order to build a paved road to Prushnits. Until World War I Chorzele was situated in a kind of desert, surrounded by sands on all sides, and it was necessary to pass through the sands even to travel the two kilometers to the border. There was only one well–used path with two rutted tracks – a wide one for the German wagons and a narrow one for the Polish wagons.

In the beginning there was great rejoicing – how wonderful, they were going to build a highway to Chorzele. The peasants began to bring stones but gradually they stopped doing that and only the heaps of stones bore witness that a road had been planned.

[Page 164]

Many years later, at the beginning of the First World War, a big scandal occurred regarding the road. [General Alexander] Samsonow's [Russian] Army tried to invade East Prussia. When the army moved from Prushnits to Mikhova (a village three kilometers away) there was still a portion of paved road, but from Mikhova to Chorzele (a distance of 24 kilometers) there was only the difficult sand road. The heavy cannons, pulled by 4 or 6 horses, sank into the sand. The puzzled generals pulled out their maps and looked for the paved road from Prushnits to Chorzele, but it existed only on the map.

After General Samsonow's army was defeated in East Prussia part of the remaining forces returned to Chorzele and went on from there, leaving most of their ammunition behind in the sands.

The Jews of Chorzele ultimately had to pay for Samsonow's defeat. After he died, leadership of the army passed to the Tsar's brother Nikolai Nikoleyevitsh, who ordered the expulsion of all Jews living within 50 kilometers of the border. The Chorzele Jews were among the first to be driven out and their suffering is hard to describe. Many families never came back, dying homeless and hungry and sick in other places.

Personalities and Types

The respectable, prosperous members of the Lakhower, Nitske and Gviazde families conducted their fishing business as far as Rostov–on–Don. They would spend the whole year in Russia and returned to Chorzele only on Passover and the High Holy Days. The town boasted of its wealthy families, especially the Lakhowers who were among the first to bring culture to the town. During World War I the Lakhowers and Nitskes left.

[Page 165]

Moyshe–Zorekh – "The Dziedzits" [leaseholder of an estate]

Yankev Zilberman

Yosef Munkarsh

Aron–Motl Bekerman and Khatskl Segal

[Page 166]

Naftali Zabludowski

Khaye–Ester Zabludowski

Yisroel–Yoysef Beylovitsh

Melekh Tsitrinazh ("Der Royfer") [unlicensed medical practitioner]

[Page 167]

There were left only Reb Moyshe Aron Gviazde and his wife, who was called "The English Queen." Reb Moyshe Aron was among the first *maskilim* [followers of the Jewish enlightenment] in Chorzele. His home was the only one in town that had a fence around it and trees in front. He was the founder of the first Jewish cooperative treasury and until his final days was a member of the management and the treasurer. The management also included Mordkhe Baran, Aron–Motl Bekerman, Tevl Fater, Mordkhe–Mendl Ferberovitsh, Moyshe Koval and A.M. Adler.

*

Before World War I, there stood in the middle of the marketplace a two–story building belonging to Reb Yoysef Meyer Leyb. He was a short man with a fine beard and thick eyebrows, always serious. He owned a big hardware business, with a shop, as well as a residence that had several large rooms.

Reb Yoysef Meyer was an ardent Gerer Hasid and his wife was also very pious, always standing at the window holding a prayer book and waiting for Messiah. Their house was open to all. All the banquets and *kiddushes* of the burial society were held there. (On the second floor of the same house lived one of the Nitske family.) Although Reb Yosef Meyer's house was a "Hasidic" house, it nevertheless produced one of the first *maskilim* in town, Mordkhe Ayznshtof, who was also one of the first *khalutsim* [agricultural pioneers] in Eretz Yisroel.

*

Near Reb Yosef Meyer's house was that of Itshe Meyer Rikhter, with a large wholesale and grocery business. In the same building there was also a liquor store. There Jews would buy a bottle of 95% spirits for the Sabbath and the Christians would drink to drown their sorrows.

On the other side of Reb Itshe Meyer was the Grayevske family business, with a clientele mostly of border patrol personnel. The whole family emigrated to Canada and the son Yehuda was a well known philanthropist there and also donated a Torah scroll to the synagogue in Ra'anana, Israel.

[Page 168]

The chief letter writer who wrote in German was Reb Avrom Sher, who was trusted by the merchants. He had four daughters (Etsile, Malke, Ruzhke and Leye) and two sons (Yankev and Meyer), but unfortunately none of them survived.

Reb Avrom was an able young man, cheerful and full of humor, but he was not successful in business and struggled his whole life. Right after he got married, they took away his pass that allowed him to cross the border into Germany, which meant he couldn't make a living.

He was an ardent Zionist and agitated for emigration to Israel by any means. When there was a shortage of certificates permitting entry into Israel he actually could have gotten one by using his "pull" but he didn't want to exploit his pull, nor did he want to leave behind his entire family. So that entire family was killed, along with all the Chorzele Jews in the era of death.

[Page 168]

Last Traces of Life and Death
by Gershon Sniadower
Translated by Miriam Leberstein

September, 1939 – June, 1941

In August, 1939, before the outbreak of the Polish–German War, the mood, especially among the Jewish population, was very oppressive, because people sensed that the war was very near. When the war broke out the Polish regime ordered the entire population, Poles and Jews alike, to evacuate the strategic area where our town Chorzele was located (1 B= kilometers from the border with East Prussia).

The population fled to the surrounding area, wherever they saw fit, because the local administration had no evacuation plan. The Jews poured into these towns in particular: Krasnoshelsk, Makov–Mazovietsk [Makow–Mazowiecke], Prushnits [Przasnysz] and Mlave [Mlava]. It should be noted that the majority of the Jews from Chorzele were concentrated in Makow.

[Page 169]

Three days after the Germans took Chorzele the Poles returned to the town and immediately began collaborating with the Germans in the looting of the remaining Jewish property and in forming a local administration under the leadership of a mayor chosen by the Germans, Lorentz, a worker of German origin.

Several Jewish families that wound up in Makov, including the families of Avraham Sher and Segal, crossed over the Bug River to the area under Soviet power, settling in Bialystok and Slonim.

When the Germans entered Chorzele, there were no Jews there. The majority of Chorzele Jews later died after being taken from the Makov ghetto, via the Pultusk Road, 13 kilometers away, woods where some of them were shot after first having prepared their own graves. Others were taken in groups from Makov to the death camps Auschwitz and Treblinka. The Jews from Chorzele who had settled in Slonim were killed in the Slonim ghetto in 1942.

[Page 170]

I and my brother Yitshak left Warsaw a month after the war broke out and went in the direction of Semiatitsh [Siemiatycze] so we could smuggle ourselves across the Bug River and then reach Bialystok. After three days we managed to cross the Bug in a little boat and immediately fell into the hands of the Soviet patrol, which took us to their headquarters in Bialystok. There, after a brief questioning, they released us.

The Sniadower family 1938

From Bialystok we set out toward Lomzhe [Lomzha] to Kolne [Kolno], my mother's birthplace, where to our great surprise we found our entire family. After we had been living in Kolne for three months, the Soviet government instituted a registration of all Jewish refugees. Those who declared that they wanted to remain had to adopt Soviet citizenship under paragraph 11, according to which one had no right to live in a whole array of towns and had to settle a hundred kilometers from the Russian border, that is, to remain second class citizens. The alternative was to return to our former homes, to the Germans.

I and my family, except for my brother Yitshak, registered to remain with the Soviets. My brother Yitshak, who didn't take Soviet citizenship, was not sent back to Warsaw, but instead was shipped off, along with others who had registered to return to Poland, to labor camps in Siberia.

We had to leave Kolne and after a long time wandering settled in a small provincial town Shviente Volya, in the Pinsk region. We could not find work there because we were "bezhentses" [refugees] and we suffered hunger and poverty. After great effort I found work in a hospital as an assistant bookkeeper but my salary was not sufficient to feed my entire family. Through the influence of the Jewish Doctor Gitel, who was then the director of the health administration, they raised my salary and provided better living conditions.

In June, 1940, my brother Dovid was drafted into the Red Workers' Army from which he never returned, and to this day we don't know what happened to him.

I myself moved to a neighboring town, Lubashov [Lyubeshov], near Kamin–Kashirsk [Kamien Koszyrski]. There I obtained a government job in forestry work and quickly advanced to a position in charge of provisions and clothing for the workers. After a short time, I brought my family from Shviente Volya, so that there remained in that town only my sister Dvoyre and her husband Moyshe and Grandmother Sheyve (my father's mother).

[Page 171]

Death and Revenge

In June 1941, when war broke out between Germany and Russia, my father was killed, shot by Ukrainians along with 80 other Jews from the town. The corpses lay unburied on the field, where dogs and wild animals ravaged them and dragged them away. When we finally received official permission to bury them, there was nothing left to bury.

At the same time, my sister, her husband, and Grandmother Sheyve were killed in a pogrom in Shviente Volya. My mother Sore–Mashe and my wife Tsilie were killed in the Lubashov ghetto in 1942, in an operation involving 350 women and children who were stripped naked in a synagogue and driven through town to graves already dug near the cemetery, where they were shot with machine guns.

I was left the sole survivor of my family. During the last German operation in Lubashov ghetto in 1942 I managed to escape. I hid in a forest, then joined a Russian Partisan unit where for three years, night and day, I confronted the Germans face to face and fought like a lion, trying to kill as many Germans as I could. I acted with a clear conscience, lusting for revenge for my parents, sister and brothers and for all Jews.

At the end of March, 1943, I participated with a large group of partisans in a three–day battle against the Germans in Lubashov, where my family had died. We arrived in the town at 4 am and I immediately rushed to the two mass graves near the synagogue where several hundred Jews lay buried. The graves were still fresh, the earth had cracked and black blood spurted from it as from a fountain. I stood frozen, leaned my head against the barrel of my gun and with tears in my eyes quietly moved my lips and said *Kaddish* [prayer for the dead.]

[Page 172]

Then I went with my partisan group to seek out the criminals. In a small street near the church, we noticed the house of the Ukrainian military chief Isayev, the leader of the pogroms and the commander of the Ukrainian police. We entered and found him playing cards with his friends around a table. On the table stood bottles of whiskey and snacks. As long as I live, I will remember the satisfaction I felt when I ordered him at gunpoint to lie down on the floor. I stepped on him with my feet in the German manner and hit him over the head with my pistol. He recognized me, begged for mercy, but I grew even more enraged and finally threw him, half dead, through the window, firing off more shots. I felt a sense of calm, although a cold sweat flowed from my forehead. I felt like the luckiest person in the world, not because I had survived, but because I had been able to take revenge against the bandits and murderers who so horrifically killed the Jewish people.

In May, 1944, our partisan unit met up with the Red Army in the town Dumbrovitsa, near Sarny. I joined the army as a volunteer and fought on the front line on the third Baltic Front. I was wounded twice, the last time in Port Klaypeda (Memel) two weeks before the war ended. From the Riga hospital I went straight to Bialystok, arriving on the day the war ended, May 9, 1945.

My goal was to visit Chorzele, but the Jewish Committee in Warsaw held me back because Polish bands were still ranging, killing Jews. A year later, in September, 1946, I decided to go to my hometown, no matter what.

Chorzele After the War

I left from the Praga Bus Station (of the [state–run] P.K.S.) on the Warsaw–Nashelsk–Pultusk–Makow–Mazowiecki –Prushnits– Chorzele line. No one looked at me on the bus and it appeared that the bus was "Juden reyn" [free of Jews]. Christians from Warsaw province, with their bags and packages, sat on the benches eating bread and sausages. These were the "heirs" of the Jewish small shopkeepers on the Warsaw line who before the war bustled about struggling to live and make a living.

[Page 173]

I sat by the window and gazed with forlorn eyes at the green fields and villages where Jewish families once lived, where Jews who were violated and robbed, burned and annihilated from the face of the earth, shot and buried alive by the Nazi bands by the perpetrators of the greatest crime in world history, who ignited the terrible Holocaust of our epoch.

As in a dream I saw before me the raw reality, the fate shared by our beloved home town Chorzele, where I was now headed, as to a dead planet. Here I was already in Prushnits, in our district, where I had reported for the military draft. I looked about the marketplace and the streets, thinking I would soon encounter Shmilke the Wagon Driver with his two skinny old mares who dragged themselves for three hours from Chorzele to Prushnits (32 kilometers.) I think he was the most honorable wagon driver in the world, yet the Germans did not trust him and cut short his honorable, difficult life.

The bus drove past Little and Big Kshinavlage and arrived at Rembalin. On the left there should have been the farmyard of the Tsvirkovski family, the only Jewish *dzhedzhitz* [leaseholder of an estate] in Chorzele. The fields lay uncultivated; there was no sign of life in the house; the lovely glass greenhouses where tomatoes and strawberries got an early start under the warm sun were empty and abandoned.

Then I was at the crossroads at the edge of town, the meeting of the roads to Bzushesk, Rembalin, Pshantaline – the same roads and the same woods where Jewish families and young people from Chorzele used to spend time in summer. I stood there near Ilataska's red brick building, drew close to the cellar window where one of the Vina brothers used to sit, a madman who would always smile and spit. It was 3:00 o'clock in the afternoon. There wasn't a soul in sight. To the right, at the river, there could be seen traces of Likhtenshteyn's burnt out mill, where the mechanical tick–tock once sounded all day and night. It seemed to me that the two bridges over the river had suddenly gotten shorter, that the river was partly dried up and covered with wild plants.

[Page 174]

The entrance to town looked like an old abandoned cemetery. I didn't see the Head Boss of the town, Moyseyke, sitting on the steps. On Brik street there was no Yukl nor "Old Borek" with his pipe nor the Yukht, Katz or Bakhrakh families or the other Jewish families who used to bustle about from morning to night. Familiar Christian faces on the street looked at me as if I was a Negro among whites.

I entered the marketplace. There was no more "Kkoshtshushko's [Kosciusko's] Monument," no signs with Jewish names, no Jewish customers, no Jewish salespeople, even the paving stones seemed to me more sunken and covered with earth. Everything appeared smaller, shrunken. The roofs of houses were caved in and covered with moss, looking forlorn as if pining for their owners.

No Jewish complaint, no Jewish song was to be heard. Jewish children no longer ran or played games in the streets. Gershon the porter didn't sit yawning on Moyshe Hersh the baker's steps. Sholem Oser and other storekeepers weren't waiting for customers in their little stores. All you could see was a few drunken Christians showing no signs of life or humanity.

I stationed myself on the corner near Little Rikovski [street] and looked around to see if I could remember where Jewish families and storekeepers once lived. I saw as in a dream the Bekerman family and across the street the Gutleyzers, Kohens, Black Moyshele, Yenkl the bookbinder and many others.

I set off for my house. My feet wouldn't carry me, and I had to stop several times. On the roof only a few shingles were left; smoke rose from the chimney; some of the windows were boarded up. I was standing on the very ground on which my parents, sisters and brothers had for decades made a life. I saw myself as a child, playing around the house with other Jewish children, knocking out the neighbors' window panes, playing and singing with my several brothers outside on a bench until late at night. All was as in a dream...

I opened the door to the house. Four families of Christians from the Piaskes [lit. sands, an area of town] who were strangers to me were living there. They were very surprised when I said that I was the owner. The whole house was in ruins and I quickly left with tears in my eyes. Near my house I saw again as in a dream our neighbors: The families Berlinke, Lanienter, Zagatsker, Milshteyn, Glikowski, Shoyme the butcher, Tik, Gerlits, Kozitse, Anakhovitsh, Tsignbok, Bayshvayger, Sokolower, Mandelsteyn, Fater and Dziedzits.

[Page 175]

I returned to the marketplace and encountered the first Christian whom I knew, Fredek Polanski, the son of the former mayor. He was very glad to see me and told me various details about several Jewish families who were in Chorzele under the Nazis. He told me that Nutke Berent hid out with his boss, Hage. In the end, Christians informed on him and the Germans shot him.

At the grave of Menukhe Tsvirkovski (1928)

At the departure of Leyzer Tsvirkovski

[Page 176]

A group of young people during Purim (1936)

A Hebrew class at the Tarbut School

Polanski came with me to Yablonski's restaurant, drank a whiskey with me, and soon many familiar Christians rushed over. Each one had something to relate, as if they had all been friends to the Jews and not a one had Jewish blood on his hands.

I set off alone in the direction of the synagogue but I sought in vain for a trace of it or the *besmedresh* [house of study/synagogue]. Not even a stone remained; everything had been burnt and destroyed, along with the holy Torah scroll.

At a distance I could see some ruins of Pshisusker's brewery. Then I was in Hertzog's courtyard and saw stone gravestones with inscriptions lying about. As I walked toward the cemetery I could find no traces of it at all. Even if I had walked 10 kilometers, I wouldn't have seen a trace of it. It had been plowed over and destroyed. You couldn't even tell the place where the cemetery had been.

That was how I found my Jewish town after the Holocaust – a town that had been renowned in the entire region for its religious scholars – Hasidim and *misnagdim* [opponents of Hasidism]; a town with progressive young people, Zionist and Socialist movements; well–off burghers, tradesmen, merchants, workers and laborers, who earned their bit of bread with difficulty and with honor, and who were content with their lives.

In memory of all our town's martyrs, who were so brutally killed at the bestial hands of the Nazis, I will here eternalize several episodes and types that made a deep impression in my memory.

Desecration of the Sabbath by my Grandmother

At the beginning of spring, when the sun shone warmly by day although the nights were still a bit frosty, there was already a warm mood in the town, especially among the poor, because they would not be needing wood and coal for heating. The richer Jews would stockpile cords of chopped wood in summer, so they were not bothered by the winter. After Purim, people would start getting ready for Passover, remove double windows, clean and whitewash every corner.

[Page 178]

At our house there would always be a good bit of coal left in the storehouse to be used the next winter. One time, on a Friday at daybreak, we heard footsteps in the attic and thought it was a thief. My father went up to the attic where he found his mother, Grandma Sheyve, hauling large pieces of coal from the storehouse to the attic in her apron. He asked her why she was doing this, and she replied that it would be safer to store the coal in the attic. Grandma spent that entire Friday hauling coal. Then she celebrated the Sabbath in her own room. She prepared everything for herself separately, because she didn't trust us to follow kosher laws. After eating, she went to bed as usual and quickly fell into a deep sleep.

At one o'clock in the morning there was a lot of noise in the town, with people crying, "It's burning." I peeked out through a window and saw the sky red with fire. Shidve's windmill on the road to the village Bidek was in flames. There was a lot of noise and commotion and everyone ran to the windmill, but it had burnt and they all returned home. There they related all the details of the fire and didn't fall asleep until dawn.

Saturday Grandma stayed in bed all day and didn't eat or drink anything. They asked her if she was, God forbid, sick, but she said she wasn't. No one knew what had happened to her. When she did the same on Sunday, lying in bed more than walking, we knew something had happened. So we asked around and found out from Aron–Yitshak Gliksberg that Grandma had been to see his father with a query. She opened the door, stood with her shoulder turned toward Reb Hershl and weeping loudly related the sin she had committed. On Friday night when the windmill was on fire she woke up, very frightened and upset, forgot that it was Friday night and lit a candle, thus desecrating the Sabbath. She asked for a penalty that would atone for the sin.

Reb Hershl was a quiet unassuming man and a great religious scholar. He answered her calmly that it wasn't a sin, because she had not acted consciously, so she had not desecrated the Sabbath. But my grandmother didn't agree and fasted for three days and recited psalms day and night. Only then did she believe that God had forgiven the sin and felt relieved.

[Page 179]

The Porter

One hot summer day, as I was returning from the beach, Gershon the Porter detained me and told me about his job. His hat was pushed back on his neck, which flowed into his broad white back, on which he would unceasingly carry sacks of flour from Tevl Fater ("Kvashnik") to Dovid Hersh, the baker, then to the market place. His tired green cross–eyes watched me to see if I understood him. With his thick, kind, bluish lips he began to speak: "In a way I'm like a general medical doctor in a small town. In a big city there is an ear doctor, an eye doctor, a doctor for stomach aches, so that every illness has its own doctor. The same applies to porters. In Warsaw there are porters who carry coal, but not flour; porters who carry iron, but not textiles. Each porter has his specialty. But in a small town there's one doctor for everything and one porter for everything. So am I not like a doctor?"

He was called "Fonye" [diminutive of Ivan, used by Jews to refer to Russians] because he had served in the Tsar's army. Whoever had the time and patience could listen to him tell countless stories of his military service. He would spend more time sitting on the steps in the market place, yawning or sneezing, than he would working. You could hear his yawns and sneezes all across town. Almost every evening he would go fishing. He was a certain kind of small town porter who would always live in poverty.

Reb Wolf and His Pipe

There were quite a few Jews in town who smoked pipes: Motye–Leybe Karzeniak, Moyshe Zerekh (Dziezdzits), his son Shayele Bik, Mikhal Katsev, Black Moyshele and many others. Our neighbor Reb Wolf Tik had the longest and most beautiful pipe. He was a typical patriarchal Jew, tall, thin, always wearing a *shtrayml* [Hasidic hat] and a long, shiny silk caftan.

[Page 180]

He had a long sparse brown beard. In his mouth he always had a long, twisted pipe that looked like a saxophone, with a silver monogram, that dated from the distant past. As far back as I can remember, ever since childhood, this man with a pipe in his mouth was a familiar sight. When he was home he rarely sat down, because his whole life was spent sitting in the *besmedresh* and studying.

I attended the *kheder* [religious school for young children] of Rabbi Ben Tsion (who was called "the Warshaver") and we studied in the upstairs women's section of the *besmedresh*. One day when the teacher had gone off to eat, Shmulkele Maytes carried out a stunt and jumped down from the women's section to the *besmedresh* itself. Reb Wolf Tik happened to be sitting there studying, engrossed in a certain passage and he was so startled by the jump that his pipe fell out of his mouth and broke into pieces.

It's hard to convey what followed. He made such an outcry that Yenkl the Bath Attendant came running. Reb Wolf chased us all, yelling in his loud voice, "Get out of the *besmedresh*!" With trembling hands he held the broken pipe, lamenting to the shames [sexton] Yehiel–Dovid, that he had had the pipe for 20 some odd years and because of these rascals it had fallen out of his mouth. From that time on, none of us boys showed up in the *besmedresh* when Reb Wolf Tik was studying there.

The Water Carrier

At home we had a small soda water factory. Of course in summer it was vital to have water brought in, because there was no town water service, and so we had a regular water carrier. This was Avrom Flude, a man over 60, very nearsighted, who wore blue spectacles tied to his ears with two colorful ribbons and clumped around in big tall boots.

In the hottest weather he would carry with a yoke on his thin shoulders full buckets of water from Dziabek Milevske's well. He received 5 groshen for each "mol" of water. On a hot day he would bring 40–50 mol of water. To keep track of his accounts he would make chalk marks on the red door.

Once our maid, while washing the red door, erased all the chalk marks. Avrom got very angry and tried to hit the maid with the yoke. When he calmed down, my father wanted to pay him what he had paid the day before, because it had been just as hot, and they had sold almost the same amount of soda water. But Avrom rejected the offer and shouted that if there was no record, he didn't need the money.

[Page 181]

Avrom Yekl the water carrier   **"Old Man"**

[Page 183]

He was an example of a simple honest Jew. His son was a cobbler, one of the better craftsmen in town. His mother sold sauerkraut. In one family, many different trades and very little money.

Zalman "the Zarember"

Shimen Orke the Apostate

The family of Pinkhes Aykhlboym

The family of Shmuel Frenkl

The Feldsher [unlicensed medical practitioner]

In every town there were people who gave advice on matters of health, who detested doctors and their remedies. In our town there was "Der Grober [Fat] Meylekh" – that was what they called him. He was a very comical character; his unique physiognomy and clothing made you laugh. He was small, with a big, pointy belly, a big round head with a mall black Hasidic hat, round, grey eyes, short thick arms. On his feet he wore big unlaced shoes, a long American–style jacket with a vent at the bottom and wide long trousers. He had two chief medicines: leeches and enemas; the leeches he would sell and the enemas he would lend out.

Among our neighbors were the orphaned children of the Zagatsker family – two spinster sisters and two brothers. They lived modestly in poverty. Once, one of the brothers, Dovid the baker, became very sick. So they called in Fat Meylekh. Even before he knew what the illness was, he brought with him a jar holding several leeches and an enema. First, he said, they had to purge the patient's bowel with enema; that would ease the illness and the fever would go down. Then, as was the custom, they needed to bleed the patient a bit by placing a leech under his ear. These were two proven methods which couldn't hurt and he wouldn't die from them.

When these two remedies failed to affect a cure, they called in Dr. Poshet, who diagnosed pneumonia.

The currency dealer

He was called "Little Rabinovitsh." He was a friend of our family and would drop in for a glass of hot tea. He was a thin, short man with a round Hasidic hat perched on his narrow head; he had dark, half–closed eyes, sparse eyebrows, and a big pointy red nose that looked as if it had been borrowed from a Purim player. He had a mouthful of false gold teeth that intriguingly sparkled from behind his narrow lips when he talked. He wore a long greasy black caftan. His head was full of Jewish learning and wisdom, but he was socially conscious, knowledgeable in worldly matters and had read many works of modern literature and newspapers. In short, he was a man with whom you could carry on a good conversation. His wife, Leye, was much older than him and they didn't have any children.

[Page 184]

When he would visit us, he would have pockets stuffed with money from many lands. He would exchange dollars, English pounds, marks, rubles, promissory notes, checks and various bills of exchange. In a word, he had a whole Bank of Poland in his pockets. It was hard to get him to give to charity and to this day I don't know for whom he needed all that money nor where his money disappeared to. On the contrary, he and his wife lived very poorly and didn't allow themselves to eat or dress well. They lived in one room, like paupers. His fate was that of all the Jews; he died at the Nazis'hands.

"Froyem" and his Goats

Efroyim From was the only one in town who pastured his goats daily on Hage, the Mute's grass–covered hill. Froyem wasn't "all there." Pasturing goats was all he was able to do.

Everyone remembers the tall, thin policeman, Novak. Once, leaving his house he became entangled in the rope with which the goats were tied and fell down flat. He yelled loudly at Froyem and gave him a kick. Froyem was terrified, sat down quietly at a distance and said nothing. His nose was white with fright and he watched the policeman's boots to see if they were again aiming in his direction. Novak turned away, grumbled out a curse in Polish and left.

[Page 185]

When Froyem stood up, the goats were nowhere to be seen, they had run away in fear. When he got home, his mother fell upon him: "What's the meaning of this? You didn't watch the goats. They came running back home by themselves." That made Froyem feel better and he told her the whole true story.

A Premature Death

On August 2, 1964 Khaim Dovid Kozitse died in Israel of a heart attack at the age of 53. Standing at his grave in Ashdod I was reminded of our shared past in Chorzele.

In our youth, we had different outlooks, divided by social class and political leaning. It was difficult in those days to imagine parents letting their children obtain a [secular] education. Thus many of us studied science, literature, and culture on our own. Many talented people were neglected and lost. One of these was Khaim Dovid Kozitse.

His abilities were boundless. He was a talented musician, who expertly played 5 instruments, and wrote his own melodies to his own literary creations. He wrote poems and stories about our little town. Many of his works were devoted to Eretz Yisroel. He longed from afar for our own land. His poems reflected a small town Jewish fear and suffering over the future in the cursed diaspora.

He wrote a rhapsody to the poem "Papirosn" [cigarettes], which depicted a Jewish life from childhood in *kheder* to the deep poverty of old age. He also wrote a rhapsody to the song, "Where is the street, where is the house." In 1939, a few months before the war he wrote a theater play about Jewish life in Chorzele which he and I co–produced in the hall of the Tarbut Library.

His living conditions did not permit him to complete and publish his works. Even though he was an excellent dentist, no matter how much he earned it was never enough, because he spent freely. Money was nothing to him, he didn't appreciate its worth. He wasn't living in the right society, one that could provide him with the opportunity to use his abilities in the right way.

[Page 186]

During World War II, fate brought him to Siberia in deepest Russia. He was one of the war heroes who fought in the Russian army against the German fascists, enduring danger and suffering. After the war he settled in Wroclaw (Poland) and in 1957 he came to Israel.

He left us too soon. His grave in the Ashdod cemetery is in a fitting location, given his past works about Eretz Yisroel, in which he dreamed of dying in the Israeli desert. In that cemetery, not far from the highway, several lonely gravestones can be seen; there are no trees, no plants, no real road, just empty sands with a few graves – the desert of which he dreamed.

The tragedy of death is not so great when it comes at the right time and place. Khaim Dovid left us at the wrong time, but in the right place — much too early, but still, in Israel. How many Chorzele Jews did not enjoy such a privilege...?

Devoted Friends – Yehuda and Rokhl Niborski

Among our most devoted friends we count the family of Yehuda Meyer
Niborski, which did so much to create a social and cultural life for young
people in Chorzele. They emigrated before World War II to Argentina and to
this day have remained faithful to the traditions of our former home. Yehuda
Meyer and Rokhl Niborski see to it that their children absorb all the good
customs of Jewish life that characterized our former community and do
everything possible to maintain contact with surviving Chorzele *landslayt*
[townspeople] all over the world and especially in Israel. The *gemile khesed*
[free loan] fund of the *landsmanshsaft* [association of townspeople] in Israel is
almost entirely their creation.

With great respect for our dear friends' work to preserve the memory of all
Chorzele martyrs and who have contributed greatly to our shared efforts to
memorialize them.

[Page 187]

The first motorcyclist rides into town

During a Polish national celebration May 3, 1921

[Page 188]

The Jewish students of the state (Polish) elementary school

The teachers and students of the state (Polish) elementary school in 1934

[Page 189]

Two Libraries Before the First World War
by Shmuel Lakhower
Translated by Miriam Leberstein

The two libraries differed in both their content and their organization. The first was a socialist library for workers. Its founders were influenced by the first revolution in Russia in 1905. In the bigger Russian cities the fire of that revolution still glowed, but in the smaller towns of Poland it had been extinguished.

Then the young teacher Pinkhes Graubard came to Chorzele. He was the son of a wood merchant and landowner from Sokhatshov [Sochaczew]. Yisroel Leybush Kronenberg had brought him to Rembinek to teach his children Rokhltshe and Pinye. The owner of the Rembolinek farm, Reb Hirsh Kronenberg, Yisroel Leybush's father, was a Torah scholar who sat at his studies all day and let his son run the business. Even though the son was somewhat assimilated, he wanted his children to obtain both a Jewish and secular education.

Any time a teacher came to our town, my parents would also hire him to give us lessons in our home. Our mother wanted her children to be respectable "in the eyes of God and of people." And so my sister and brother Dvoyre and Moyshe took lessons from Pinkhes Graubard, a follower of Poalei Tsion [Workers of Zion, a Zionist–Socialist organization], and a future Yiddish writer and folklorist, and he instilled in them a socialist spirit. Also in the group were: Simkhe Yankev Shafran, the watchmaker; Shmuel Meyer–Khaim; and Miryem Soretshe Zilberman, Yekl the bookbinder's daughter. She was also greatly influenced by her brother Avraml who studied watchmaking with Moyshe Opatavski in Mlave and also got a general education from [Moyshe's brother], the teacher Fayvl Opatavski, who had already published stories in the London [Hebrew language] newspaper *Hadogal* [The Banner], as well as other periodicals. (Both of these were older brothers of [the Yiddish writer] Joseph Opatashu, and were killed by the Nazis.)

As I recall, the workers' library consisted of 300–400 books as well as almost all the pamphlets put out by the publisher "Di Velt" [The World] in Vilna. Among these I recall "The Erfurt Program," by [Karl] Kautsky; biographies of Marx and Engels; works by Sholem Aleichem, Spektor and Mendele Moykher Sforim (from the Hebrew Publishing Committee in New

York); Phillip Krantz's "History of Culture" and his biographies of well–known Jewish figures; the works of Jules Verne and many others. The purchase of the books was entrusted to the Chorzele shipping agent, Reb Shmuel Frenkl, who travelled weekly to Warsaw.

[Page 190]

Rokhltshe Kronenberg

Of course, in Tsarist times the library was illegal. It was located in the children's room and the readers would quickly leave after obtaining their books so as not to attract the attention of the police. All the books were catalogued by author's name and records were kept of the readers.

The library also had a drama society and I remember that they put on Sholem Aleichem's "Mazl Tov" (with my sister Dvoyre in the role of Beyle the cook and Shmuel Meyer Khaim as Reb Alter.) I remember how they rehearsed the recitations of Bialik's "The Last Word", Frug's "Sand and Stars" and Morris Rosenfeld's "The Storm at Sea."

[Page 191]

The library and drama circle did not last long. Someone informed on the leaders and participants and the whole enterprise had to be liquidated.

The first Hebrew public library was more fortunate and had a very different character. It had 500–600 books, mostly fiction (such as "The Agora Books," by Ben–Avigdor and The Hebrew Library of the Tushia Publishing House) and a section for children's literature. The founders were Moyshe Nitskin, Dvoyre and Moyshe Lakhower, Shmuel Meyer Khaim, Rokhltshe Kronenberg and Leye Likhtenshteyn. Leye got her father, Motl Likhtenshteyn, to agree to house the library in their attic.

At that time, Mordkhe Ayznshatadt, the *maskil* [follower of the Jewish enlightenment], began to exert influence on the town. He wanted to extend education to the common people and sought ways to expand the library in a legal manner. With the help of the Jewish Literary Society in St. Petersburg, which had the right to open libraries throughout the Pale of Settlement in Poland and Russia, a branch of that organization opened in Chorzele. In this way, the public library was re–opened in the house of Avromke Akive Noyekh (on Budke Street) and it made a great impression on the town.

Mordkhe Ayznshtadt saw to it that the library would have a section on science, mostly books from the Akhiasaf Publishing House. Among these were: "The History of Humankind," by [Julius] Lippert; "Knowing God," by Shimen Bernfeld; the works of Shloyme Rubin; [Heinrich] Graetz's' "History of the Jews;" "Each Generation and its Scholars," by I.H. Weiss; and the Library of Jewish Science published by [the periodical] *Har Haman* [The Mountain of Time] in Vilna.

The library existed until 1911, when its founders left Chorzele. Moyshe Nitskin and Moyshe and Dvoyre Lakhower went to Warsaw; Mordkhe Ayznshtadt, Simkhe Adler and Eliezer Meyer Khaim made *aliyah* to Israel, the first *khalutsim* [agricultural pioneers] from our town. There was no one else in town at that time to continue the cultural work of the library.

[Page 192]

My Annihilated Home
by Hagar Hertzog (Adler)
Translated by Miriam Leberstein

When we were no longer small children, but had become young adults, we criticized our town and wanted to free ourselves from its old traditions. But whenever people left Chorzele, they would yearn from a distance not only for the town, but for the Arzhits river where we would hold a swimming contest with the Christian boys despite the constant fear that its waters would claim its yearly victim. We missed the Pshonteliner Woods with its berries and laburnum, missed the bushes where we playfully hid and loudly laughed.

My memory takes me to Yosl Meyer Leyb's building with its courtyard, and its many tenants. I remember old Silke who would walk back and forth over the courtyard, talking to herself. We children were afraid of her, because she would mutter about the Messiah and how he had to come soon so that everyone could die and be resurrected.

My brother Aron was the leader of all the children of our and the surrounding courtyards. He was the initiator of all the childish exploits and the organizer of all the games. Once, at Passover, he organized one such adventure: the children uncovered the pits in all the courtyards in which the tenants had buried the utensils that were not kosher for Passover for the duration of the holiday. They brought them to our courtyard and hid them among the stacks of boards. After Passover, when the housewives went to reclaim their utensils they made such an outcry that the whole town was topsy–turvy. Finally, they discovered the instigator and my father administered the appropriate punishment.

*

The first stimulus for the idea of pioneering Zionism among our young people were the talks of the ardent Zionist, Vayser, who called for personal development through emigration to Eretz Yisroel. Quite soon after his first appearance, the first three pioneers made *aliyah*: Simkhe Adler, Leyzer Merheym and Mordkhe Ayznshtadt. The above–mentioned Vayser made a deep impression with his fiery speeches about Eretz Yisroel, which awakened in the young people new dreams about having their own land. But he also left behind the sad memory of his unnatural death. He was living with Christians whose daughter fell deeply in love with him and when he was lying unconscious while sick with typhus, the girl's parents brought in a priest who converted him. He never got up from his sickbed and a rumor spread that the Christians had poisoned him. After his death his family members came to Chorzele and demanded an investigation into his death, but in the meantime, the First World War broke out and the mystery remained buried in Vayser's grave.

[Page 193]

I remember the return of the refugees after the end of World War I. A large number of Jews who had been expelled from town and went to Siberia at the beginning of the war never returned, but those who did return began to rebuild their economic and social lives. A number of young people organized a cultural club which undertook the task of reestablishing the earlier library that Dvoyre Lakhower had organized for the town youth. The activists who undertook to rebuild the library were Alter Tsitrinazh, Itshe Kozhenik, Libe Pshisusker, Hagar Adler and Shloyme Hertzog.

[Page 194]

Another group of young activists decided to reorganize an amateur drama club to perform theater. The first rehearsal took place on Shavuot. While the parents were in synagogue praying they got word that the holy day was being desecrated and that boys and girls were performing theater together [in violation of religious strictures]. So the rabbi ordered that the prayers be interrupted and personally went to find the sinners, accompanied by a large group of butchers, wagon drivers and ordinary Jews.

The Jews in the rabbi's entourage angrily wanted to barge into the house, but Shloyme Hertzog, a student of the rabbi, asked the rabbi to enter alone to assure himself that the whole story was a libel. The rabbi entered, looked around, and saw a group of boys, without any girls, not wearing makeup and not acting on stage, but sitting innocently and reviewing the texts of a forthcoming performance. It thus became clear that the big outcry about the desecration of the holy day and the mixing of boys and girls was greatly exaggerated and there was no reason to get upset.

After this event the young people began to feel a little freer and they began to attract talented girls to the drama club. I was one of the first actresses who appeared on the "Chorzele stage." My father [a ritual slaughterer] was very upset because Hasidim didn't want to eat the meat of the animals he slaughtered while his lewd daughter was involved with theater. They tormented him so much that he decided to see for himself what occurred during performances, and once slipped in through a window to have a look. He watched for a few hours to see how the young people were fooling around, and mumbled to himself, "Children, silly children, it's just childish foolishness." But the fanatic elements in town didn't share his assessment and didn't stop tormenting him in his work as slaughterer the entire time I played theater.

[Page 195]

The Hertzog family

An entire Chorzele family (?) together

[Page 196]

Nakhman Tikulsker

Rifka Herstog

Moyshe Rozenblum

Simkhe Berlinka

[Page 197]

My brother Yoysef had also at that time "gone astray" but in a more serious way. He taught Hebrew to the young people and gave readings on Zionist themes. The young people began to participate in

social and political groups. They were mostly Zionist, but there was also a Bundist group and others even further to the left. There began a struggle among the groups in town over influence and that struggle was reflected in the question of who would have control over the non–partisan library. Except for this, the social and cultural activity of the young people was non–partisan. They brought in lecturers, organized entertainment and excursions, conducted self–educational groups and the like. For example, the Jewish doctor gave lectures on anatomy, Moyshe and Bashke Tsvierkovski devoted themselves to the young people in the field of theater, and Rabinovitsh and Tik taught violin.

*

There were many fine men and women in town who devoted themselves body and soul to various kinds of social and communal activism, caring for the needy, helping the poor. And they did this without any political ideology but simply with a Jewish heart, for their own souls, for God and people, often in unusual and original ways.

Take the two sisters, Sore and Miryem Kalmans. They demonstrated warmth and kindness for the poor and suffering. When our mother died,these two sisters saw to our needs and were our protectors, teachers and care providers in every way.

Take the household of Dovid Koval. Libe, the mother, would share her last bit of kerosene, flour or fat during the German occupation in World War I. Leye was always collecting money for the poor. Shloyme gave to charity generously. Malke would bring shirts or sheets or pillows from home to distribute to the needy.

Take Sore Yukht (from the Koval family). On the coldest days she would drop in, wearing her husband's boots and fur coat, at the houses of her well–off friends (Libe Koval, Gitl Koval, Hagar Hertzog) to collect all kinds of necessities for poor children and women.

Take our stepmother, nicknamed the *khazente* [cantor's wife]. She took care of the sick, applied cupping, gave enemas, assisted in births and, not to be mentioned in the same breath, sewed shrouds for the dead. Her competition in these areas was Melekh Tsitrinazh; he was such a specialist in various "medical" practices that the town doctor would take him along to help with difficult cases. Melekh would say that he was the doctor's "existence" when he meant his "assistant."

[Page 198]

Take my mother–in–law, Haytshe Hertzog. She and her husband Yehoyesh were distinguished not only for their concrete help for the poor, but also for the way they gave that help, modestly, with deep caring, as if they were part of the family.

*

The following episodes offer profound and original revelations about individuals and the community in the past of our destroyed town.

The wife of Yisroelke the Koheyn, Blime, had three weaknesses: 1) Every Passover she would sew a new garment for the Christian Patfor, the town water carrier, and make him put it on when he fetched water for her during the holiday, so as to avoid the possibility of contamination by leavened food. 2) When she went every week to the *mikve* [ritual bath] she would stay there late into the night and immerse herself tens of times to purify herself of traces of unclean animals (dogs, cats, mice) that she had encountered in the course of the week. 3) She would go about singing the then popular song "Borekh Shulman went out" which portrayed the tragic fate of a Jewish boy who sacrificed himself for the community.

Yankev Kozheniak was himself one such sacrificial martyr. When his wife, Yakhtshe, was gravely ill he made a vow that if she recovered he would for his whole life, winter and summer, waken and summon Jews to prayer in the morning. I still remember: on a late Friday night in winter, the windows covered in frost, a deadly silence; suddenly the clock strikes 4:00 and beneath the windows one hears a deep voice: "Wake up, Jews, to worship God." I lay in my warm bed thinking what love, what devotion to God and man are embodied in the religious devotion of this simple Jew.

Mendl Farbarovitsh and Mordkhe Pshisusker are etched in my memory as participants in the ceremony dedicating a new Torah scroll in the synagogue shortly before I left for Eretz Yisroel. Mendl fitted out the Torah in his own home and Mordkhe walked at the head of the procession, dressed in white and blue clothing, like the flag of Zion. The whole town, rich and poor, participated with joy, faith and enthusiasm in bringing in and installing the new Torah, everyone feeling that he was taking part in a great religious and national event.

[Page 199]

*

Finally, a few words about my father, the cantor and ritual slaughterer, Reb Moyshe Shimen Adler â€" an unforgettable father, Jew and man. He was not only an officer in a religious institution but also a social institution all by himself, personally providing food and fuel to all the needy. He himself raised the money for these two necessities; himself delivered bread and wood; himself brought what was needed in such a manner that the recipient would not notice that help had come from a human hand. Many times he returned from the bath house without the shirt that he had been wearing because he gave it away to a poor Jew who had no shirt at all.

Often, he would disappear from home for an entire evening because he was busy with outfitting a poor bride for her wedding or with cheering up the sick child of poor parents. He poured his heart and soul into relief work and the town appreciated and honored him for that. When he was old and had grown weak, he continued his work of collecting money for the poor and when he knocked with his cane on someone's door, they gave generously. When he lay breathing his last on his death bed, tens of poor women opened the door to the Holy Ark in the synagogue to make an accounting to God on my father's behalf.

I see him now before my eyes, as he was on the night before Yom Kippur, wrapped in his snow–white cloak and saying the *Kol Nidre* prayer. Now I feel his gentle hand, which he would place on my head before leaving the house to listen to *Kol Nidre*. Now I see the Chorzele Jews for whom, for many years, he prayed to God for health and livelihood and whom he loved as his own brothers.

[Page 200]

The community has disappeared, the brothers have been wiped out.

[Page 200]

People and Events
by Menakhem Lanienter
Translated by Miriam Leberstein

The Kidush Hashem [martyrdom] of Rabbi Reb Yitshak Meyer Solovani

Reb [respectful form of address] Yitshak Meyer was both a prodigy of Jewish learning and an ardent Zionist in his deeds. His home was always filled with young people. He loved to engage them in discussions that always ended with the conclusion that the only option was to make *aliyah* to Eretz Yisroel.

He kept a diary and would stay up late into the night writing in it, by lamplight, all of the day's events.

He had a wife and children (two sons and two daughters), but they gave him no joy. The children didn't want to study in yeshiva and although that caused him great heartache, he never tried to force them to do so against their will.

He had a fearful nature and was especially afraid of the police and of weapons. Once, on a freezing cold day in the winter of 1929, we were travelling by train to Warsaw. At one of the stations, several Christians who were returning from hunting entered the train armed with rifles. Reb Itshe [familiar form of Yitshak] Meyer immediately disappeared and we searched for him for more than an hour before we found him, half-frozen, at the door to the train car, ready to jump out.

In August 1939, several of us, leaders of the Jewish community, were sitting and talking about the political situation. Reb Yitshak Meyer said that he was certain that there would be a war, and showed us a passage in a certain book that demonstrated that war was inevitable and that it would not be good for the Jews. "We must flee!" he exclaimed.

"So why are you still sitting here?" someone asked.

"I don't want to be the first," he answered.

[Page 201]

Before the war broke out he and his entire family moved to Otvosk, because his son-in-law came from there. When the Germans arrived in Otvosk, someone shot at them. The Germans rounded up all the Jews and announced that if the Jew who had shot at them did not confess, they would burn all the Jews. Reb Yitshak Meyer stepped forward and said that he was the shooter. The Germans tied him to a horse and dragged him along the ground until he died.

The Estate Leaseholder Moyshe Tsvirkowski

Moyshe Tsvirkowski was the only Jew in the area who was the leaseholder of an agricultural estate.[1] Every Saturday his courtyard served as a meeting place for young people who played sports there. He was a theater lover and provided much support for the town's drama circle.

Although he himself was a sympathizer of the Bund he agreed to allow the young people of Agudat Israel establish a *hakhshore* [Zionist training farm] on his estate, where they could prepare themselves for emigration to Israel.[2]

Moyshe Tsvirkowski survived the war and died in Warsaw in 1961.

Reb Avraham Sher

He was the *shofar* blower for the town. He knew a lot of trades but couldn't manage to make a living. (His business was bringing goods from Warsaw). But he was a good humored man, always cheerful.

The Sher family considered itself to be a fine, respectable family. All of the children were very able, but regrettably, no one from the family survived [the war].

Yosef Tik Does Theater

He was a poor shopkeeper and barely provided for his wife and three children. Still, he was a great lover of the theater, especially the plays of [Avram] Goldfaden. He also played the violin for 30 years. He wasn't a professional violinist, but he taught others to play.

[Page 202]

Once, they produced the play, "The Wild Man" [by Jacob Gordin]and the leading role was played by a young man from a neighboring town. When this young man fell ill, Yosef decided to take his place. His wife, who always complained that Yosef was always occupied with nonsense instead of providing for his family, created such a scene during the show that they had to discontinue the performance. On the Saturday night of the second week of performances, they brought in a "wild man" from Krasnoshets and carried on with the show.

Fishl Stolier [the Carpenter] Goes to Eretz Yisroel

FIshl was a very poor man, even though he made furniture for the rich. He always said that he was unable to make plain things: "If you want plain furniture go to Leyzer, because my work is special."

When his wife would demand money to prepare for the Sabbath, he would tell her that he was owed money and would go to collect it. His wife would say that she would go to collect the debts, but he wouldn't let her do that. Once, when she insisted on going to collect money owed by the notary, Fishl yelled at her: "You don't even know how to speak to me, how will you speak to the notary?"

In 1924, it was rumored in the town that they were signing up craftsmen to go to Eretz Yisroel. Fishl decided to go and went to the Tarbut [Hebrew language school] library where the registration was taking place to fill out the necessary papers.

"What's your name?" they asked him.

"Pincus," he replied.

"Your name is Fishl," they told him.

"So why do you ask?"

"What's your occupation?" "Merchant."

"But you're a carpenter," they said.

"So why do you ask?"

And so the conversation continued, but when it came time to sign the papers, FIshl declared he would not do so.

[Page 203]

"Maybe you don't know how to write," someone called out.

"So why do you ask?" he replied.

Fishl didn't go to Eretz Yisroel. "There won't be place in Palestine for both of us", he said.

Translator's Footnotes

1. Jews were generally not permitted to own agricultural estates, but could hold the lease to an estate owned by another. The lease entitled the holder to administer all the business of an estate and could yield a good income.

2. The Bund was a socialist organization that was opposed to Zionism and to religion. Agudat Israel was an orthodox religious organization that initially was opposed to Zionism but later participated in Zionist programs. Here, the willingness of the Bundist sympathizer Moyshe Tsvirkowski to aid the Agudath youth's Zionist program evinces tolerance and generosity.

Two Poems
by Chaim Dovid Kazhitski
Translated by Miriam Leberstein

Our townsman Chaim–Dovid Kazshitski wrote the first of these poems in Chorzele in 1933, when Hitler came to power in Germany and anti–Semitism increased among the Polish population. Aron Koval preserved the poem in his memory, and provided it for publication in this book in Haifa in 1965. At the same time, the author sent us the second poem, which he wrote in Wroclaw, Poland in 1952.

—The Editor

Hear Me Out, Dear God

When I was a child
they sent me to *kheder* [religious
school for young children].
My mother knitted me a sack to
hold my prayer shawl.
I
studied *Chumush* and *Rashi* [first
five books of the Bible with
commentary]
and never thought to question
God.
The crowded classroom did not
oppress me.

I remember how the teacher
would whip me
for using dirty words
but I still loved him, despite his
hot temper.

[Page 204]

I loved that angry man, my
teacher Reb Leyzer;
he was dear to me, my teacher,
Reb Leyzer.

He had a Jewish heart, full of
feeling.
He told us little boys beautiful
stories,

stories of our people
and of God's wonders
and wove a web of lovely dreams
around us.

Then life suddenly changed,
In technology, in culture.
The child stopped weaving
dreams,
already mature at the age of
seven.
The public school soon taught him
to hate;
the children were divided by race.

There's nothing to eat at
home,
so Reb Yankl goes to the fair,
to sell his wares.
But, for God' sake,
what can he do, with his Jewish
nose,
his side locks and his beard.
Waiting for him are pickets,
armed with clubs and sticks.

Her youngest child just three
months old,
Mother pleads with God, God the
merciful,
to bring Father back unharmed.
But the devil impudently laughs
at the pious, naïve woman.

Robbed of what little he had,
Yankl's left with only his prayer
shawl.
Blood drips from his brow.

[Page 205]

Tell us, dear God, what will
happen now.
We will never give in.
We will never betray you.

A star shines in the East,

There you can hear the call of the
pioneers,
a call that thunders.
There the courageous pioneers
plow the bloodied fields.
There they make their bodies
strong.

They help to redeem the earth
there.
We will show the world a wonder
there.
Don't look to politics,
turn your gaze to Zion.
"Our hope is not yet lost."[1]

I Want a Home

I want a home, I long for one.
The wide world has no place for
me.
I long for my small, sweet land,
there, where a lonely wall stands.

I no longer need what I have
here,
Where there remain only tears.
We've given the world enough;
six million of us have
disappeared.

Here there's no one left to
find.
Everyone considers you a
coward;
even when you fight like a lion,
no one sees that, no one
believes…

[Page 206]

I want a home, the time has
come.
My brother has prepared one for
me.

He fought for it, he gave his
blood,
he did not lack for courage.

    I want a house, one that we
build there.
My place now is in the Negev.
I want a home there, where my
happiness lies,
I won't return to a life in exile.

The Kazhitse Family

[Page 207]

The departure of Hadassah Alter for the *hakhshore* [Zionist training farm]

A group of young people at the departure of Sore Aykhboym (first on right) for Erets Yisroel (1933)

[Page 208]

Dine and Sholem Fater

Leye Fater

Hebrew classes at the Tarbut [Hebrew language] School (1936)

Translator's Footnote

1. This quotation is a line from the song Hatikvah.

[Page 209]

The Dear Jews of Our Town
by Y.M. Niborski
Translated by Miriam Leberstein

My wife and I have visited Israel nearly ten times, and each time we had fresh impressions of the Jewish land. Although we would each time meet the same dear *landslayt* [townspeople] and would review the same memories of the past, we would always experience anew the closeness of a shared past.

We would recall the bygone days of our youth, the streets where our parents lived. We recalled our hometown–the marketplace, the Brik Gas [Bridge Street], the rude [a ridge near the river], the *granitshe* [border]. We remembered the shoemaker, the boot maker, the wagon drivers, the miller, the blacksmiths, the hardware and textile merchants, the haberdashery shops, the grain dealers, the *melamdim* [teachers of young children] and other teachers, the cantors, the ritual slaughterers, the fish sellers, the butchers, the simple unlearned Jews, the Zionists, the Bundists, the Hebraicists, the Yiddishists, the Hasidim, the *misnagdim* [opponents of Hasidism].

We recalled the shops where you could buy sugar for a penny, the amateur "diplomats" who squabbled over world politics, the brew houses and taverns where the Christians got drunk, the architect Yankev Pesakh, who had no equal in the world – all of these Jews with their varied personalities – stingy and generous, stubborn and pliant–were our own, our dear ones, blood of our blood, bone of our bone.

I see before me: Hershl Gotyes in the *shtibl* [small prayer house] of the Alexander Hasidim; Yosef Sores, in the old *besmedresh* [study house/synagogue]; Moyshe Shimen the cantor in the old synagogue – these dear prayer leaders who would awaken a thrill in the hearts of their congregations.

None of these dear Jews any longer exist. The town is still there, with its streets, river, fields and woods, but there are no Jews, the hardworking, kind, pious, wonderful Jews.

The following true story shows how deeply rooted were the piety and nobility of the Jews in our town:

[Page 210]

Y.M.Niborski (standing) during a reception for him and his family in Israel, 1963

He, his wife, daughter, son–in–law and grandchild

[Page 211]

My Aunt Etke (Avraham Tsodek's wife) was brought to America by her children and arrived by ship in New York on a Saturday. She was the only one of the passengers who refused to disembark on the Sabbath. The ship's captain had to argue with her for more than an hour until she agreed to leave. But she sat by the ship until nightfall.

When I visited her in 1950, she told me a secret. Before she emigrated to America, Itshe Meyer Rikhter lent her $5 and she had hoped to have the opportunity to repay the debt. When she learned of the murder of the town's Jews, her grief was doubled; not only had she lost her townsmen, she was also burdened with a private debt forever.

During one of my visits to Israel, I looked up Itshe Meyer's son Yehoyesh Rikhter and brought back to my Aunt Etke a written receipt from him stating that the debt had been paid. Her face lit up with joy as she pressed to her heart the tear–drenched receipt and quietly whispered, "Now I can die in peace." That was an example of the kind of Jews we had in our town, and we must remember them as long as we live.

The Summing Up of a Family
by Henye Niborski
Translated by Miriam Leberstein

Before World War I there lived in our town a Jew named Yosl Monkarzh, who was called, as they did in those days, by his father's name –Yosl Meyer Leybs [i.e. Leyb's son]. Yosl was an intelligent man, a religious scholar, and an able and honest merchant. He had a large prosperous store where you could buy anything from a needle to the heaviest metal–working tools for construction and farm work. Peasants and noblemen from the entire region were his customers, and treated him with great trust and respect.

Yosl Meyer Leybs ran a fine well–ordered household, donated to charity, invited poor guests into his home. His wife Silke would prepare rich broths and other dishes for poor sick people and women who had just given birth.

[Page 212]

The couple had three children — Rashke, Yitshak and Henye–Rokhl. Rashke married a young man from another town who (if I'm not mistaken) became a rabbi in Zamosc. The son [Yitshak] also went to live in his wife's hometown. So only Henye–Rokhl remained in Chorzele. She married a young man from Kolne named Kalman Ayznshtadt. He was a refined person, a religious scholar, but had no practical sense for business. Nevertheless he had a weakness for taking on various businesses, believing every person who promised him great fortune.

So it happened that he ran several businesses into the ground, and each time his father–in–law bailed him out. He never got rich but he had a fine home, invited poor guests for the Sabbath, and had a full house of respectful, well brought up children – 7 sons and 2 daughters. When the children got older, they all worked in their grandfather Reb Yosl's business. He married them all off and set up nice households for them. Two of the sons (Binyomen and Shmuel) emigrated to America even before the first World War and there married two sisters from Chorzele.

[Page 213]

By the time the First World War broke out, Kalman Ayznshtadt's wife Henye Rokhl and his mother–in–law Silke had already died. Like all Jews the remaining members of the Ayznshtadt family and the old man, Yosl Meyer Leybs, had to evacuate the town, which was located on the very border with East Prussia.

Leyzer Niborski and his family, wife Henye, children Yosef, Itamar and Yitshak

Yosl Meyer Leybs' granddaughter Sore stayed by his side; she was the only one to remain in her grandfather's business. Her younger and exceptionally handsome husband, Yisroel Yosef Beylovitsh (from Mlawa) was sent to the front. Sore, her 6 month–old child and her aged grandfather were together during the years of wandering. When they returned to the town, Reb Yosef's beautiful house, along with his business and his full warehouse, had become a mountain of ash. What the flames had not destroyed the Christian neighbors had plundered.

They had to begin from scratch, with almost nothing. They managed to rent a small shop with a small room that had to serve as kitchen, dining room and bedroom. They furnished it with borrowed beds, an old table and a cradle, several chairs and a few chests that served as cupboards for their measly few dairy and meat dishes. With their last bit of cash, as well as loans freely granted by some peasants when they learned that old "Yosek" had returned, they bought some merchandise and began to make a living.

In the meantime, letters had begun to arrive from Sore's husband, who was imprisoned by the Germans. Sore began to send packages and did everything possible to alleviate his situation, hoping for the day when he would return. But he did not return. Yisroel Yosef fell ill and died in a German prison camp.

Sore began a different life as a widow. But she bore her fate with dignity, effort and hard work, and provided for her family, which her old grandfather could no longer help to do. Sore took care of him with respect and love until his last day. And she also raised her only child with great care, devotion, respect and love.

[Page 214]

In 1938, Sore's daughter went to Argentina, sure that she would soon be able to bring over her mother. But the law in Argentina provided that newcomers could not bring in another person until they had lived in the country for two years. The murderer Hitler didn't wait that long; Sore remained in Poland and was killed along with our 6 million martyrs.

In addition to Sore, the following family members also died in Poland: Kalman Ayznshtadt's oldest daughter, Miryem, with her husband Avrom Sher and their five children — Hentshe, a manicurist; Royzke, the only bookkeeper and the real head of the town's loan society; Malke, who had completed a course at the ORT [vocational training] school in Warsaw; Yankl, who worked with his father as a shipping agent – an intelligent, humorous, extremely friendly man, the permanent shofar blower in the synagogue; Meyer, the youngest, a student in the Jewish *gymnazie* [academic high school] in Mlawa.

Also killed were Moyshe Ayznshtadt and his second wife Feygl Triumkowski (from Bialystok) who was very active in the community and always willing to provide help anyone who needed it. Moyshe's three sons from his first wife had worked and lived in Warsaw and died there.

Kalman Ayznshtadt's oldest son, Avrom Hirsh, a fanatically religious and quiet person, with a good head, who without the benefit of book learning or teachers was able to keep the business accounts, who required nothing for himself and made do with anything and never bothered anyone – he, his wife and children were also all killed.

Naftali and Dovid, of the same family , thcir wives and children, also died.

These families all perished in the same manner as hundreds of thousands of Jewish families in the age of horror, our greatest destruction.

[Page 215]

The five daughters of Avrom Sher (second from the right, Rivke Katz)

A group of young people (1923).
Sheyne–Leye Sher, Malke Koval, Aron Leyb Gzhebialka, Yosef Safran, Eli–Leyb Fater, Shepsl Frenkel, Rivke Herzog, Avrom Katz, Beyltshe Gliksberg.

[Page 216]

A group of girlfriends (from right) Leye Frenkel, Khane Sakolower,Feyge
Frenkel, Malke Bayshvayger, Rivke Katz

At a farewell banquet for men leaving for military service (1934)

[Page 217]

Ways of Life and Memories From the Past
(Reprinted from *Faroys* [Forward], Mexico, 1963–65)
by Zelik Sniadower
Translated by Miriam Leberstein

I: Leyzer's *"Bude"*

"Leyzer's *bude*" was what they called the narrow, cramped hut that served as Leyzer's workshop and store and most important, the place where our gang of idle, scruffy and rebellious children of well–off families would gather daily for hours. Leyzer himself had chosen the bitterly sarcastic name (in Poland a *buda* is a small wooden shelter for dogs), mercilessly making himself the butt of ironic barbs, just as he made fun of everyone at the slightest opportunity, whether they were his friends or not.

The person who conceived, planned and built the *bude* was a distant relative of Leyzer, Yankl the Bookbinder. Yankl the Budovnik [builder of *budes*], as they also called him, was the eternal engineer who, in addition to binding holy and secular books, would spend sleepless nights exhausting his brain over construction projects to enlarge his fortune.

Leyzer's *bude* came about through strange circumstances. The place where it stood had been for many years a simple gate, 3 meters square, with a small door that let in the autumn winds. Yankl the Budovnik would open the gate only once a month on fair days and the peasants would pay a small sum to drive their wagons through it to the market place.

One evening, when Yankl the Bookbinder was on his way to evening prayers, it began to rain and he had to quickly take shelter under the eaves of a neighboring house that sloped over his gate. In this way, he protected himself from the rain, standing patiently between the neighbor's wall and the rain that flowed from its jutting roof. Standing there an idea occurred to him: if he could fit through the opening of 50 centimeters between the wall and the water flowing from the roof, why did he need the gate? What did he need the few zlotys he earned on fair days, one day a month, when he could build a little shop of 2 ½ meters right in the middle of the market and leave quite a good passageway for those who didn't want to go the long way around but wanted to enter directly into the market. It was so simple, how come he hadn't thought of it years ago, he thought regretfully. And in Yankl the Budovnik's engineer's brain the *bude* was already a done deal. Before long two carpenters were sawing and chiseling blocks and boards and the *bude* began to grow.

[Page 218]

They erected the *bude* on a flimsy foundation of four oak blocks that stood about half a meter above the ground so that rain and the waste water of the countless neighbors could flow under the *bude* to the gutters of the market place. Almost five meters long, 2 Â½ meters wide, a step in the front, a step in the back, a small window like that in a prison bracketed between the front door and the wall and the shop was complete. Another triumph for Yankl the Budovnik!

Leyzer's mother didn't have to bargain hard with her relative Yankl – a *zloty* [unit of currency] more, a zloty less, and they had a deal. Yankl was understanding – the widow, Leyzer's mother, badly needed a means of livelihood and her son Leyzer had "golden hands." From the smallest remnant, the tiniest strip of fabric, Leyzer could make a hat, whether one with a visor, a winter hat with earlaps or a sailor hat, he'd manage to make something. With his golden hands he always found a way.

Because of Leyzer the few town tailors had to put up with a lot from the housewives who vigorously demanded a remnant, even a strip of fabric so that Leyzer could cobble together a hat. And he did cobble together a living for himself, his mother, his sister Ita, and his little brother. And he didn't need anyone to help him; he did it all himself – cutting, sewing, ironing. He could take apart his sewing machine, repair it and reassemble it by himself like the best mechanic.

[Page 219]

But when it came to the monthly fair, Leyzer's golden hands were of no avail. For a few days before the fair he would work like the devil to make the navy blue caps with shiny black visors. He would carry the boxes of merchandise to the stall, lay out the hats, arrange the display, doing this all quickly and enthusiastically. But as soon as a customer approached, Leyzer was lost. When it came to bargaining, to making a deal, it was his mother, assisted by his sister, who had to do it, because Leyzer hated doing business. It just wasn't in his blood. "Commerce is theft and swindle," he would say, and so he wouldn't engage in business.

Leyzer's stall was the poorest among the hat makers' stalls, which were all grouped together. He had the rights to the last stall in the row, at the end of the market, near Rikhter's hardware business, and the most difficult customers found their way to him. The peasants who reached his stall had already spent time bargaining with all the other hat makers without having obtained the bargain they wanted.

But at midday, when Leyzer's mother had to leave the stall to go home for a quick bite to eat, Leyzer became the salesman. He carelessly sat down on his three–legged stool with a book in his hand and prayed to God that no customer would come and disturb his reading.

We, his pals, would take advantage of the midday hour to drop in on Leyzer to at least have a chat. A day when his *buda* was closed or when Leyzer wasn't there somehow seemed unnatural, because we loved him so. His native intelligence, his naturally sharp sense of justice and righteousness, his cheerfulness and willingness to share his last bite of food drew us to him.

One day at the fair, Leyzer was immersed in [Maurice] Maeterlink's "The Life of the Bee," and recommended that everyone read it. "This is a splendid work," he said, "and if you read it closely, we will discuss it later." And Leyzer engaged in discussion his whole life. Debating was a painful necessity for him. Leyzer never agreed with anybody, he had his own way of thinking and his own interpretation of every event and every person. When he was unable to convince his opponent with his Leyzerish eloquence, he would revert to personal attacks, mercilessly annihilating his opponent with his sharp irony and bitter sarcasm. This would often lead to anger and conflict, but you always had to make up with Leyzer.

[Page 220]

But the apparently ironic and pugnacious Leyzer wasn't the real Leyzer. Those who knew him well knew that behind his bitter, sarcastic armor there lay a dreamy, tender soul, and this young man was haunted by a vague, eternal yearning.

One day, he yearned for a mandolin, so he could strum the loveliest melody. His golden hands quickly got used to the instrument and he was happy when he squeezed out some heartfelt folksongs or romantic songs.

But before long, Leyzer would reject the mandolin, and begin to sculpt figures. The clay and plaster and ordinary dough would yield to his long fingers and there came to life beautiful miniatures, little dogs, ducks, horses, the head of an old man masterfully executed. There was nothing Leyzer couldn't sketch or paint.

Then, again, before long, he would grow sick of painting and sculpture and he would return to his books. He read continuously, spent every free minute with a book in hand, ready to discuss it with everyone.

His keenest arguments were with God, and he bitterly mocked the representatives of religion – the rabbis and other religious figures. His persistent blasphemy and his mockery of the Zionist big shots led to serious quarrels and his stubborn refusal to wear a hat [as required by religious law] caused a scandal. But none of this affected our friendship with him. We supported him without reservation even though we didn't always agree with him. We loved Leyzer for his integrity, and his deep belief in humanity.

Leyzer's excessively violent impulses would sometimes be restrained by Aron–Yitzhak's intelligent grey eyes. When Leyzer would lose control during an argument, or, as was his habit, would launch a bitter attack on a comrade or opponent, Aron–Yitshak had only to fix his persuasive eyes on Leyzer and he would restrain himself, sometimes even withdraw from the attack. Aron–Yitzhak's deep intellect, his mature wisdom and knowledge had great influence on all of us, but to overcome Leyzer's rebellious nature and definitively change him was a difficult task even for Aron–Yitshak, because Leyzer went his own way, moving impulsively forward, dreaming his eternally vague dreams.

[Page 221]

*

The center of our group was Leyzer's *bude*. "Let's go to the *birzhe* [stock exchange]," we would pun. There, in the tiny structure that Yankl Budovnik had built we'd get together day in, day out — 4, 6, 8 or even more friends — and Leyzer was always the initiator of our passionate discussions. But when Leyzer's mother appeared at the back door, we would magically disappear.

She was doing right as his mother. In our presence, Leyzer would forget about his work. The unfinished visors would lie about. During our "invasions' there was no room in the *buda* for even half a customer, we took up all the room and they still had to make a living.

But for that reason, Friday (not to mention the Sabbath) was "our day." Leyzer didn't have to work in the *bude*. On Friday, Sabbath eve, Leyzer was no longer a hat maker. Early in the morning he would put on his white coat and start to prepare his cutting instruments, clean the machines, polish the scissors and sharpen the razors. Then he would go off to the attic room that housed the Jewish barber.

In the middle of the room was an upholstered chair, opposite the wall where there hung the usual mirror. And all day, until it was time to light the Sabbath candles, Leyzer would cut, trim and shave Jewish heads. Young and old came to beautify themselves for the Sabbath, some for haircuts, some for a shave.

Religious Jews would come with their children and ask him to be careful of their *peyes* [side locks] , because the Christian barber was not so particular about the matter and would purposely dip into the *peyes* with their instrument while winking amusedly at the Christian customers. But Leyzer's golden hands wielded the instruments deftly over the Jewish heads.

[Page 222]

Everyone knew that even though Leyzer was a non–believer, a real apostate, he still had a Jewish heart, and he wouldn't harm their *peyes*.

The *bude* was known in town as a center for the leftists. Even though none of us belonged to a political party, the *bude* was the only place where you would hear the names Bakunin, Lenin, Trotsky, Marx and Engels, and Plekhanov, for us almost living characters who influenced our naÃ⁻ve imaginations. The socialist works and manifestos we stuffed ourselves with without method and order, gradually affected us, under Leyzer's influence. With his hatred (who knows where it came from) of everything religious and bourgeois, we turned into a naive deeply–believing socialist–anarchist group.

None of us knew who he was or what we actually wanted. It was a strange mixture of Bundist–socialist and anarcho–communist ideas that were never expressed with clarity or consciousness. We were ruled by a chaos of modern ideas and revolutionary slogans all cobbled together. And with the help of our deep belief in a better world and the constant stubborn influence of Leyzer we turned into a militant romantic group that changed the monotonous life of the town.

With his sharp tongue, nimble mind and innate intellect, Leyzer unwillingly became our leader. This leader of the left never rested. We held "box evenings," [where social and political questions were drawn at random from a box], lectures, debates, dramatic groups. The library began to bring in speakers and the town was topsy–turvey.

Here was Leyzer, preparing the chairs [for a play], doing the makeup, prompting, directing and performing the leading role. There was nothing Leyzer couldn't do; he was indefatigable, stubborn to the point of madness. He wanted to bring light to the dark, medieval world.

And there was Leyzer, sitting at his work in the *bude*, running his machine at high speed, pushing on the pedal with both feet and with his long nimble fingers weaving the cardboard strip through the navy blue fabric, while singing a Yiddish song. Suddenly, he stopped the machine, and his eyes fixed on the sad, empty, rainy marketplace, he said to me: "You know, Zelig, I've decided to leave this town.

[Page 223]

I'm going to Argentina. I'm suffocating here, I can't breathe, I can't stay here and rot. This is no life, we're just living corpses here, we're being extinguished before our time, we have to escape, the sooner the better."

That's what Leyzer said and we knew that once Leyzer got an idea in his head, he would act on it. His mother's pleas didn't help, nor could friends or family change his mind. Within a couple of days, Leyzer was already poring over a Spanish–Yiddish dictionary and we would listen to him reading in Spanish. Soon we were accompanying our dear beloved comrade to his departure for the long voyage, together with another friend, Yankev Vayngartn.

A few weeks ago, I received the sad news that Leyzer Niborski, the tireless dreamer, loyal comrade and simple honorable idealist had died. A close relative and *landsman* of his, a good friend of mine, told me how Leyzer, the once modern small town Don Quixote, left the world with a sarcastic smile and a scornful witticism. And as a religious Jew I say: Blessed is the true judge. I will never forget my dear Leyzer.

II. The Strong Man of the Ozhits

The Ozhits was a Jewish river flowing though Polish land. It is very hard to find this little river on a map. You can barely see this sinuous little vessel as it winds its way like a worm through the rich black, green and red stripes of the landscape.

But anyone who had the privilege of bathing in its quiet clean waters, which flowed through verdant meadows and plains, had to ignore the insignificant impression that the Ozhits made on the map. For the town Chorzele, which had pitched its tents on the very banks of the river, the Ozhits was a would–be Volga or at least a Nile. It is hard to imagine how Chorzele could have lived without its river.

[Page 224]

First of all, where would the town have gotten its water? You might think that the big well in the middle of the market place was an adequate source of water, but then what would we have done with our dead cats? Because no matter how many cats died in Chorzele, that's how many turned up in the market place well. And what about the peasants? No one threw them in the well, whether dead or alive, but on market days and especially on fair days, they — young and old alike – would make a "donation" to enrich the waters of the big well. And the well would be actually barricaded by horses and wagons, and go and find someone in charge in the midst of the fair when the police were all drunk and in a tizzy. People didn't even use the water from the market well to water the horses.

Others might have suggested using the small well on the sands [an area of town]. In the first place, how big could it be if a few Christian women would make a single pass of a bucket over the surface, and that would be it for the day. If another few peasant women did the same thing, there would be no water left. The remaining women would have to wait until the white sand at the bottom of the well let in a fresh flow of water and allow them to dip the bucket again, or they would take home a bucket that was half water, half sand.

And on the days before holidays and of the Sabbath, the little well on the sands had to endure all sorts of commotion — pushing and fighting and cursing that resounded in both Polish and Yiddish. And it was the little well itself that was responsible. Because no matter how meager and pitiful it looked, no matter that it was so small it could be filled in with one shovel, it was renowned for its water "as soft as butter," that was the best for washing the women's and girls' hair. So don't ask what went on there on the day before a holiday!

So it remained that the Ozhits and no other was the main source, and did not begrudge its clean water, which the water carrier would carry to and through town and make sure that the barrels in Jewish homes would not go dry.

Then, the question arises, what would Chorzele have done if it had had to carry out the *tashlikh* ceremony [of symbolically discarding sins on Rosh Hashonah] without its beloved river. It would have looked very bad if they had had to resort to the market well. And in the lovely fall evenings when the half-summery sun would still warm with its last powers, the Ozhits took on a holiday charm. The river looked different, as there appeared rows of Jewish men and women, girls and boys of all ages, old people and households, filling the green meadow. They bent over the river with prayer books in hand and finally pulled breadcrumbs from their pockets and threw them in the waters of the patient river.

[Page 225]

Year in, year out, the Christians passing by would shrug their shoulders and wonder at the Jewish crowds that foolishly came to pray at the river. And the quiet and compliant Ozhits didn't make a peep and unquestioningly accepted into its waves the sins of the Chorzeler Jews and carried them far away to the sea.

But no one bullied and abused the river more than the washerwomen, who would array themselves along the river from dawn until late at night, washing, rinsing, wringing, pounding and smacking on their washboards and ceaselessly dirtying the clean sparkling water of the river. The Ozhits could never answer the question, how could such small town accumulate so much dirty laundry. Nor could the river stand the idle chatter, gossip and fantastical stories that the women would engage in every day from morning to night. So the poor Ozhits had to accept into its water the poison of evil tongues and swallow it into its depths.

In winter, when the clear waters of the river would darken and grow cloudy and flow more quickly, it did not long enjoy any rest. As soon as the first dry frosts came, the Ozhits was covered with a thin layer of ice. At Hanukkah, the river still struggled and in places broke through the icy crust with its dark flow. But the struggle was in vain. No matter how bravely the river fought, it had to surrender to the strong pressure of the freezing weather and before long the sparkling river was frozen for months.

You might think that the river was resting during these winter months, as it should have, because who would have the heart to bother and annoy such a fine river, when it lay alone under the ice, unable to see the light? But no, Chorzele Jews were cruel. The river was theirs in summer and in winter, and if the river didn't like it, it could pick itself up and leave town.

[Page 226]

So as soon as the experts gave the signal that it was time, the Chorzelers set off with their crowbars and saws, axes and hammers and mercilessly began tearing pieces of ice from the surface. Then they carried away the living limbs of the martyred river on sleds and stored them in cellars — huge stacks of ice, pressed together, sprinkled with sawdust and straw — so that they could cool themselves off in the summer.

Chorzelers needed a bit of ice in summer so they could refresh themselves with a soda water mixed with sour cherry juice. Ice was also used as a remedy for an overheated head, to cool off a *schav* [sorrel soup] or red beet borsht, not to mention a piece of melted butter in Tammuz [Hebrew month usually occurring in July]. No matter what, the Chorzele Jews needed their bit of ice in summer. So they wouldn't consider whether the Ozhits liked it or not. They extracted ice all winter long.

But there would come a time, only once a year between Purim and Passover, when the oppressed and exploited river rebelled. At the beginning of spring you could not contain the Ozhits. The Jews were frightened by its current, once so mild and humble. You couldn't recognize it. The Ozhits was in revolt, furious, and began to show what it was capable of. With its stubborn actions it tried to take revenge on the town, to get even with it for the many sins and injustices inflicted on it the entire year.

First, the agitated river attacked the bridge with all its power. The Ozhits knew that the beloved bridge was the weakest spot of its opponents – the Jews who abused the river all year. And it was obvious that the bridge was worthy of their love. It was an old ruin, riddled with holes like a used up sieve, a bunch of boards, a patch on a patch. And when Bertsak [the wagon driver] travelled on it with his loaded wagon on his way back from Proshnits, and took his "eagles" [i.e.horses] over the bridge, it shook like a *lulav* [palm branch used in religious rite during Sukkot] in the hands of an old *dayan* [religious judge]. But the oak poles deeply buried in supports along the sides endured the pressure of the heavy wagon as well as the peasants' lighter loads and the carriages of the landowners.

[Page 227]

And it was the poles at which the Ozhits aimed its attack. Rapidly and angrily, as if driven by demons, the rushing waves continuously hammered at the pillars of the bridge. Gathering force from miles around, from all the fields and meadows, the raging Ozhits concentrated its powerful artillery and mercilessly aimed itself against the bridge. The usually quiet river grew impressively from hour to hour and turned into a mighty Sambatyon [mythical turbulent river that was said to rest only the Sabbath].

In the town, the alarm grew. The river had soon reached the Shiltser Highway, then the mill was in danger, and worried and upset, the town's householders and proprietors ran around, each with his own prediction on whether the bridge would survive the attack of the rebellious river.

No greater misfortune could befall the town than for the bridge to give way to the determined river. Chorzele would be finished. Because two kilometers to the east was the East Prussian border, the geo–political belt that connected all communication. To the north, there was the old sand road that led through villages and pathways to Mlawa, but traffic on it was negligible because it was muddy and impassable. To the south lay the distant train station at Rashoyke, and it was not easy to get to the train, you could do it only by going through Budek, with the Vietrak road,which took 3 hours to go a mere 3 *viorsts* [about 3 kilometers].

So only the bridge remained to connect the town with the Prushnits Highway, the only convenient link to deliver anything.

When it came to rescuing the bridge, all religious and racial differences disappeared. The navy blue caps and short jackets of the Poles mixed with the

Jews' black fabric hats and long caftans, and they all worked to protect the bridge. All kinds of tools were brought in and they set to work.

The task was to break up the ice floes into smaller pieces before they could reach the bridge supports. This dangerous job fell to the volunteer fire brigade, made up of the strong men of the town, both Christian and Jewish, although the Christians, of course, were in control. In their able hands the crowbars and axes moved more quickly, and the saws didn't rest. But it wouldn't be appropriate to quote the [Biblical] passage [Genesis 27:22], "... [T]he hands are the hands of Esau [i.e., non–Jewish]". The Jews did not lag behind in their efforts. Whoever could, lent a hand, participated in the fight, and when it was all over and the bridge had been saved, the whole town talked exaggeratedly about the young people who sacrificed themselves for the holy work.

[Page 228]

The Jews never said it out loud, never complained, but among themselves they were secretly resentful that the Christians had to take part in the bridge drama. After all, the Christians of the town didn't have much to do with the Ozhits. The river was almost Jewish. In the summer the Christians would water their horses there, and sometimes bathe them, but so what? And if the [Christian] doctor sometimes brought his dog down there and forced him to swim and retrieve a stick from the waters, was that such a big deal?

If on a summer day a Christian would sit by the river with his fishing rod, burning up in the sun, in the hopes of pulling out a couple of skinny fish, was that such an achievement? Especially since everyone in town and in the surrounding villages had known for years that while the Ozhits wasn't stingy with its water, it was very miserly with its fish. If Chorzele householders wanted fish, they were better off going to one of the fishermen who fished the Prussian lakes and buying as many fish as their hearts desired. The Jews followed the river's advice, left it alone and bought their fish from the fishermen.

Although the Jews of Chorzele could buy fish from the Prussian lakes, they couldn't bathe or swim in those lakes, so for those purposes they had to resort to their own trusty river. Don't ask what the Ozhits had to put up with all summer from its Jews! Magically, people lost their fear of the tragic legend that someone must fall victim on the cool altar of the quiet river and every evening young and old flooded the "*rude.*"

[Page 229]

The *rude* [ridge] was a place far from town where the river made a turn and its banks there were watched over by a row of willows, which dipped their branches in the quiet stream and cast delightful shade.

Jews [i.e. Jewish males] would lie down by the shore on the fine sand near the willows. Little heaps of clothing, mixed in with *tales kotons* [fringed ritual undergarments] lay about abandoned on the ground. Chorzele Jews didn't know about bathing suits or any other such scandalous things. Stark naked they would enjoy God's beautiful world and refresh their bodies in the sweet stream.

Especially on Sabbath eve, on the stifling Friday afternoons when the sun shot out fire from the sky, the ridge would be mobbed. It swarmed with old Jews with wet beards and *peyes*, with children, and especially *kheder* boys and pranksters.

Liberated from the stuffy *besmedroshim* [houses of study] and *shtibls*, from the poor *kheders* and *talmud torahs* [religious schools for children], Jews big and little breathed freely near the quiet river and with pleasure inhaled the fresh meadow air and refreshed themselves in the cool river. They would immerse themselves countless times, just like in the *mikve* [ritual bath]. Others would do the crawl against the stream. The daring would swim off to the opposite bank, the expert swimmers would show off their strokes, do the backstroke or dead man's float on the surface or underwater until they reached the middle.

No one was the subject of more stories and tall tales than Yankl. His full Jewish name was Yankl Frenkel, but the Christians called him Frenkliak [a Polishized version of the name]. Yankl was the best swimmer in Chozele. Frenkliak knew the Ozhits like his own hand. As long and wide as the river was, Yankl was ready to take it on. He was a giant of a boy and as shy as a young girl.

Yankl came from a strict Hasidic family. His father, "Shmuel der Rebe [Hasidic rabbi]," as he was called, was an ardent Gerer Hasid, a religious scholar well versed in Talmud. He was an outstanding arbitrator [in the religious courts], always engaged in debates with rabbis and *dayans* and always had complaints about *shoykhtim* [ritual slaughterers.] He was a firm Agudnik [adherent of the religious organization Agudath Israel] and would zealously persecute the Zionists and go out of his way to annoy the "enlightened."

[Page 230]

And even though Yankl had to behave in a dignified manner, dress like a Hasid in a long coat, and never fail to attend the afternoon and evening prayers, the lad had already gotten caught up in the modern movements. He considered Hillel Zeitlin and [Chaim] Zhitlowski to be the greatest geniuses and he knew [Simon] Dubnov practically by heart.

Because of his modest, simple and goodhearted nature everyone – Jews and Christians alike – loved Yankl. And when they whole town learned what a strong and good swimmer he was, his popularity among the children and young people was unequaled.

The tailor was the only person who suffered because of Yankl. No matter how wide and long the craftsman fashioned Yankl's caftans and coats, his broad athletic shoulders would somehow manage to bulge out. And the sleeves were a big problem. Every piece of clothing that Frenkliak wore looked like it had been turned inside out or else belonged to someone else, because his arms would stick out of the sleeves. His sleeves were never long enough to cover his long and powerful arms. And his Jewish cloth cap with its little visor never seemed to sit properly on his big square head.

But when Frenkliak rid himself of this clothing, his arms and shoulders seemed to grow, spread out, as if his athletic physique had been stripped of its armor, and his muscular limbs would twitch nervously with every movement. The naked Frenkliak was somehow not the same person. The Frenkl who dressed in traditional Jewish garb bore hardly any resemblance to the nude giant who appeared at the Ozhits every evening.

The people on the ridge would be entranced by Frenkliak as he did the crawl, stayed underwater for long periods, and demonstrated his amazing ability to swim against the current. It looked as if he was waving his sturdy arms in the air rather than fighting a current, and the crowd would remark that only Yankl swam with almost half of his body out of the water.

The fellows would envy Frenkliak, but at the same time they were proud of him, and would endlessly recount his feats and heroic acts, many of them exaggerating in their childish naivete.

[Page 231]

That summer a tragedy occurred – the Ozhits claimed a victim. And the death of a young Christian boy caused the name Frenkliak to turn into a legend.

A well–off Christian from a nearby village owned by a nobleman approached the Ozhits and decided to test his strength against the river by swimming across at a secluded spot that was heavily overgrown with shrubbery. Carefree, he jumped in, but he never came out.

The voices of peasants who ran up with scythes and sickles in their hands reached all the way to the ridge. All along the river on that summer evening you could hear their unearthly screams "Help! Help!" Little boys and shepherds pointed to the place where the victim had disappeared among the thick grown water plants.

The sad news spread like lightening along both banks of the river and quickly reached the ridge, the place where the Jews had a monopoly. And all the Jews who were near the river ran off, half naked, toward the grassy area where the tragedy had occurred. When the few dozen children and young people arrived, out of breath, at the place where they were searching for the drowned man, they found quite a few Christian peasants, men, women and children, who had run over from nearby village and fields.

On the river was a lone canoe with two men who were wielding long poles to poke through the thickly tangled plants, barely able to reach the bottom. On the banks, elderly people helplessly ran around, giving advice, shouting loudly and trying to show they knew more about drowning victims than anyone else. Old and young, men and women, quietly wiped away tears and ceaselessly told horrifying stories about drowned people caught up in the water plants who had never been retrieved from the unyielding river and given a Christian burial, these wandering souls who could never be released from sin and remained forever in the depths of swamps and rivers, taking revenge by dragging down innocent victims.

[Page 232]

Old peasants fearfully crossed themselves and prayed to Jesus that the drowned man would at least rise to the surface somewhere after three days, as sometimes happened, because to find him in the river would be impossible. The Ozhits, they well knew, would not readily give up its victim.

When Frenkliak began asking questions in his garbled Polish, trying to find out exactly where and how the drowning had occurred, the assembled Christians answered evasively and looked at the tall youth with distrust and scorn. "Who sent for him and who needs him?" asked the town manager, who had suddenly joined the group. "What gall for a Jew to come and confuse things with foolish questions when such a tragedy has happened among the Christians."

Among the Christians there awoke a feeling of distaste for the Jews who had run over from the rude. "Who needs them, the *zhidkes* [disparaging Polish term for Jews], what did they come here for?" and several of them were ready to sic their dogs on the frightened boys and young men, who were already preparing to flee.

But Frenkliak had already begun to undress, calmly and with determination tossing off his clothes. It didn't bother him that the Christians were murmuring and that women were standing around. In the wink of eye, he was naked, and slowly made his way to the river. Yankl's determination and the fact that a drowned man was lying in the river's depths affected the Christians and a mysterious silence suddenly fell upon the river bank.

A strange smile appeared on Yankl's face as he slowly approached the water. He didn't give a hoot for the Christians, even the weeping women. He was going to drag the drowned man out of the river and show what he could do; that was what he had decided and no one would change his mind.

Before Frenkliak managed to reach the water, an old peasant holding a long string approached the young giant and insisted that he put on the peasant's belt and tie it to the string, so that if he got caught somewhere, they would be able to pull him out onto the bank.

[Page 233]

But Frenkliak refused to put on the belt.

The boy instantly disappeared from the surface of the water. His naked athletic body shone in the last rays of the setting sun as he nimbly sank into the dark blue water. At that moment, the setting sun turned red and twilight slowly began to cover the meadows with its grayness and the river began to reflect the leaden glow of night.

But no one noticed that night was already falling. Hundreds of eyes were staring at the surface of the water, and Jews and Christians with bated breath quietly counted the seconds – seconds that felt like hours – as they anxiously waited for a miracle, or God forbid, another catastrophe. A painful mood reigned over all. From the distance, the croaks of a pair of frogs interrupted the fearful silence; then they too became mute.

Christian women murmured prayers and nervously crossed themselves. Off to the side, young Jewish boys who had come over from the ridge huddled together fearfully waiting for Yankl to appear on the surface of the river. The Christian boys from the canoe had long ago taken their poles out of the water and let their boat float with the current, hunching over as they kept their eyes glued to the river.

And Frenkliak did appear. His square head with its closely cropped hair sprouted out of the dark water quite a distance from the shore and his open mouth hastily and greedily swallowed streams of air. With his right hand he wiped his face and rubbed his eyes. This lasted several seconds. Then, in the blink of an eye, the young man turned over and dove down again, disappearing into the now almost black water.

Frenkliak's appearance had lasted only a moment and the crowd could not figure out what was happening. Only when he disappeared for the second time, did every one exclaim a collective "ah!" And again it grew deathly quiet in the dark night and everyone's hearts beat faster in astonishment.

[Page 234]

But this time it did not take long. Off to the side, from the very midst of the thickest growth of water plants, where the current was the strongest, Frenkliak swam with one hand and boldly headed for the shore, and you could clearly hear his voice shouting in Polish – "I'm holding him by his foot."

As if electrified the crowd ran to the river. Frenkliak's daring act made them forget that the dead body of a young man that he had just dragged out of the river lay before them, half submerged between the sand and the river, his deathly pale face shining in the dark. The lamenting parents and family of the drowned man ran to him but most of the crowd respectfully surrounded the naked giant.

Yankl smiled oddly at the people surrounding him, shook himself several times to dry himself off and slowly went to his bundle of clothes, lying on the dewy grass, to get dressed. He slowly began pulling his shirt and underwear onto his half wet body, patiently pulled his *tales koton* over his square head and said not a word. How long had he been underwater, how did he find the body, where did it lie, and other many such questions remained unanswered.

When Frenkliak had put on his coat, he picked up his shoes and socks and set off barefoot on the path that lead to Chorzele, accompanied at a distance with the gang from the ridge. The hero of the Ozhits was late that night for prayers.

[Page 235]

I Remember!

by Nomi Kahan (Zisl Gershanovitsh)

Translated by Miriam Leberstein

Reb Yosef Shoykhet

I was born in Chorzele

and lost my whole family there.

There on the high hill

there on the green grass

I dreamed in childhood of happiness.

I did not even know what I wanted then

but now I know one thing – it will never return.

[Page 236]

You were too short, my childhood dream

You disappeared as quickly as a soap bubble

I remember the day my grandmother took me to *kheder*

She told everyone, "I'm bringing you a bright one"

but I did not make a fuss.

I remember my uncle Moyshe Mendl Koheyn;

he played an important role in town,

but only trouble came of it.

I remember when they would not let us walk outside

after 10 o'clock at night.

I was still a child then.

You could walk only to the border, and no further

I remember Fat Ostashewski;

everything was crushed under his heavy tread.

everyone trembled when he appeared.

The sight of him meant misery for all.

An Encounter in Bukhara
by Malke Plishun (Bayshvayger)
Translated by Miriam Leberstein

It happened in 1942, in faraway Russian Uzbekistan, in Bukhara. There was a place there, where all the Polish Jews [war refugees] gathered and I stood there every day, hoping to meet someone I knew, a friend or relative.

So it was that after many days of standing there one day I saw hundreds of people vying to obtain some kind of white drink. I heard something about some Polish Jew with an Uzbeki son–in–law who had produced the drink himself and called it "*pianke*."

I thought to myself, how lucky were the people who were drinking it, and I was impelled toward the kiosk where it was being sold. I pushed my way through, even though I had no money, and suddenly my blood froze: In the kiosk I saw Yosef Tik. "Herr Tik," I shouted, but he did not hear me because of all the people trying to get a drink. "Herr Tik" I shouted again, with all my strength. He noticed me and leapt to my side. He embraced me like a father and we both burst into tears.

[Page 237]

"Come," he said to me. "I'll introduce you to my son–in–law, my Yehudes" husband. And Yosef Tik led me into the kiosk introduced me a tall Uzbek and handed me a glass of "*pianke*." After the second glass, he boasted that this was his own creation and his son–in–law (an NKVDist [member of the secret police]) smiled. He already understood a little Yiddish; Yehudes was teaching him. Yosef said, "Come tomorrow morning and you'll see Yehudes." The next morning I ran to the kiosk, where Yehudes was already waiting for me, holding a pretty little blonde girl in her arms. It was odd, because all the Uzbeki children were dark and dirty and here was such a pretty child with Jewish blue eyes.

We rejoiced and cried and rejoiced again, and week and months went by. One day I came to the square and found no sign of the kiosk. I was greatly surprised, but I had no way of finding out what had happened.

Some time later, I happened across a man lying face down on the ground in the town park, groaning. Such sights were common at that time, but my instincts drove me to approach the man to get a closer look. It turned out to be Yosef Tik, bloodied and beaten.

Before I left Bukhara, I managed to find Yehudes. I asked her what had happened with her father. She said that he had left Bukhara, intending to go to Poland. "And you, Yehudes, what are you planning to do?" I asked. "My husband won't let me leave," she answered. "Even now, I had to sneak out of the house, he loves me so much. He promises me that we will go to Persia."

That was the end of my encounter with Yosef Tik and his daughter Yehudes.

[Page 238]

Before My Eyes
by F. (B.) Malka
Translated by Miriam Leberstein

Chorzele was as small as a yawn.

Near the German border stood our town

With its narrow little streets

And its little Jewish shops.

You could count everyone on your fingers

But its youth accomplished wonders

Turned themselves into artists

And made fun of young lovers.

Nor did we girls limit our chatter —

Feyge, Rivka, Leah and I, with Khantshe our leader—

We met every Friday for the blessing of the candles

And began talking about everyone we knew.

But our joy was short–lived, for Shmuel soon arrived

And when we heard him coming, we fled the kitchen.

For we were afraid of Shmuel Frenkl

If we had stayed, he'd scream at us,

"You girls are acting like *shikses*." [1]

I remember one winter night,

when there was a ball.

We all went there to dance,

What harm was there in that?

But the boys rebelled, springing up in anger

"We won't let our girls behave this way."

It wasn't because they wanted to defend us,

But they begrudged us our freedom, they just couldn't stand it.

They ran off and came back, bringing Hodes Kats with them

In the middle of the best dance, she dragged Rivka away

[Page 239]

> The rest of us just stood there, didn't move from our places
>
> Our blood rushing up, flooding our faces.
>
> And there constantly hover before my eyes
>
> Images of those bygone Chorzele lives
>
> May they never be forgotten
>
> As long as we shall live.

Translator's Footnotes

1. Shiksas – non–Jewish women

There Once Was a Home, a Town
by Rokhl Nives (Tikulter)
Translated by Miriam Leberstein

> My dear childhood was full of beauty and honor
>
> The Sabbath table in all its splendor
>
> My father making the *kiddush* blessing
>
> My face aglow like the candles Mother lit.
>
> For my mother, God decreed
>
> That her body would rest in the earth of Kfar Saba[1]
>
> Standing at her grave, as if lulled by a dream,
>
> I remember the life that once blossomed
>
> When I come and stand here,
>
> A prayer arises, of its own accord.
>
> A twig moved by a gentle breeze
>
> Quickly awakens memories
>
> My eyes glitter and a tear falls.
>
> Who, oh who, can comfort me?
>
> There once was home, a town

All that remains is a sorrowful leaf.

*

The bright window of my grandmother's house
Looks charmingly out upon the little street
Grandmother's house is full of spirit and warmth
She herself a woman of honor.
On every Rosh Khodesh Sabbath [2]
Grandmother prepared a feast and invited guests
Like the seven days of the week,
Seven candles stood in their holders.
Grandmother lit them and shed a tear.
When the Sabbath ended, and stars sparkled in the sky
Grandmother said the prayer, God of Abraham
Her sorrowful prayers in those days
Are eternally etched in my memory.

*

My brother Nakhman left home during the First World War
And went across the border with his dreams and shining vision
His heart was drawn to the land where he longed
To renew his life in any way that he could.
But the hand of fate ruled otherwise
My brother, I honor your memory.

*

There was a home, there was a town
All that remains is a sorrowful leaf.

Translator's Footnotes
1. Town in Israel
2. Rosh Khoydesh – first day of the month

[Page 240]

Natives of Chorzele who Fell Fulfilling their Duty
Translated by Jerrold Landau

Alter – a female soldier, daughter of Chaim

Beishwinger, Nathan the son of Esther

Gorman, Nachman the son of Shmuel

Weingort, Avraham the son of Meir–Yaakov

Cygenbojk, Avraham the son of Moshe

Sniadower, David the son of Shimon

Elisha Shmueli the son of Frimet (Kaszeniak)

[Page 243]

Bulletin, The Hechalutz Hatzair [Young Pioneer] of Chorzele
(Number 1, November 25, 1932)
(transmitted exactly as in the original)
Translated by Miriam Leberstein

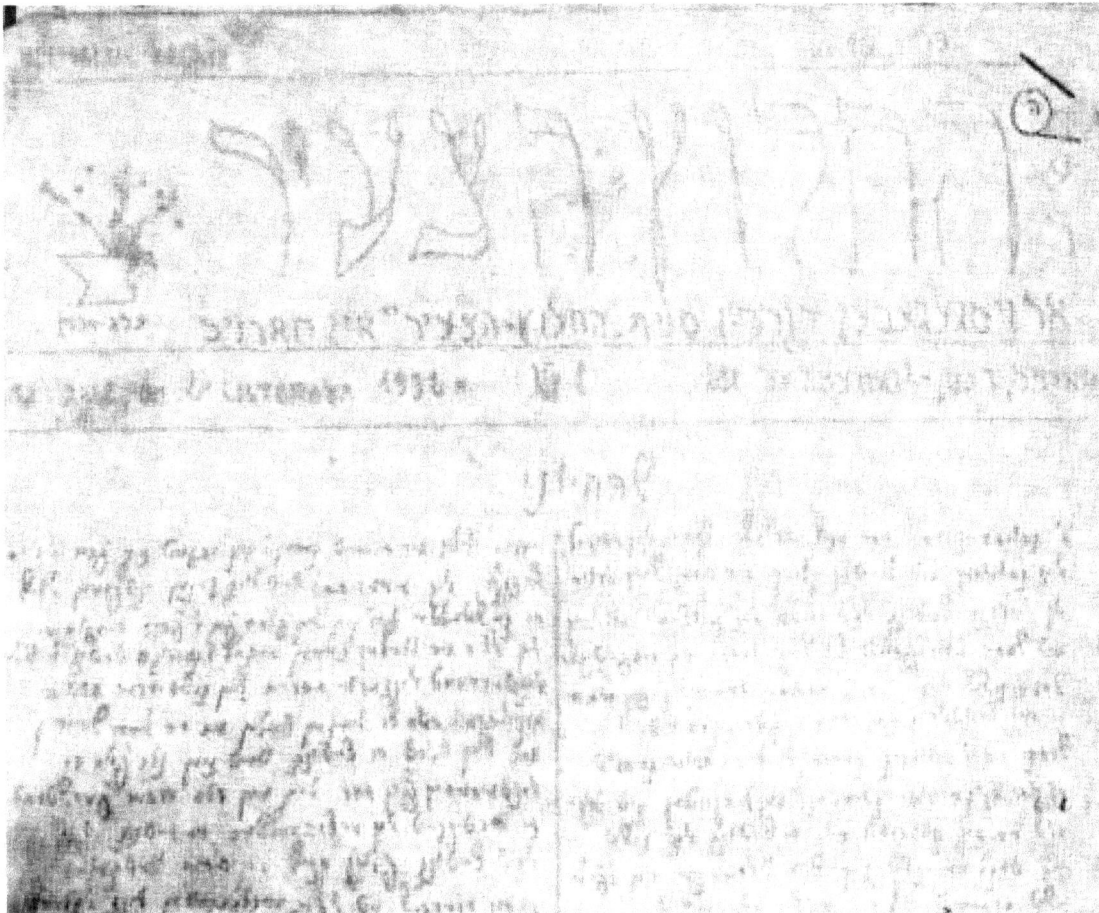

The Bulletin of Hechalutz Hatzalr (first page)

Shehechayanu! [prayer of thanks to celebrate special occasions]

Important news! The Hechalutz Hatzair branch in Chorzele is now the equal of other branches. We, too, are now publishing our own newspaper. This news has suddenly spread joy among members and sympathizers.

But some, while blessing the initiators of this achievement, have made the *shehechayanu* in a sad mood, because they doubted that it could continue to exist. It was good, they thought, that the newspaper wasn't a daily or a bi-weekly, and that it wasn't even printed by machine, but was handwritten, and written out by a friend, to boot.

[Page 244]

But even that entails certain expenses, which given our current financial means, are very difficult to obtain, and requires enormous patience.

And most important, do we have members with some kind of journalistic abilities? And who will be the editors? Isn't that so?

But, comrades, that is not our task. We don't intend simply to boast that we too are publishing our own newspaper from time to time. Our goal is this: Every member of an organization and especially a youth organization has his or own specific demands and opinions about various events in the movement or about relations between members, or concerning the local committee and the executive board.

We want to provide the means for our members to freely express themselves about these questions, which trouble our members. And every member will be able to answer the questions in the form of an open discussion.

And if we find somewhere a published article that interests our members, which not everyone has access to, we will republish it.

In a word, the newspaper will serve only the interests of our members. I believe that everyone understands the importance and educational value of such a paper for the branch. And everyone will certainly support us energetically and as much as they can to make publication possible.

And finally, I want our dear members to note that each of you should make an effort during the week to write at least one article for the paper. No one should think: Who am I to write, I have no journalistic talent. Let the initiators deal with such foolishness.

Comrades, know that this will have great significance for the growth of our branch, both in numbers and in quality. And no one should be afraid to write because we the initiators are no more talented than you are.

Y.L.

The "Shushanim" *kivutsa* ["Roses"group] sends wishes for success on the publication of our members' paper, Hechalutz Hatzair.

[Page 245]

Hello, members!

Here we have taken the first steps to open wider the gates to our development. Our committee worked hard to put out the members' publication Hechalutz Hatzair. We all bear the title of member of Hechalutz Hatzair and now we are getting an additional member, which may also be called Hechalutz Hatzair. This member will be our superior; of course, it depends on our will. It will penetrate into all the secret corners of our souls, because its task is to understand our life. It will awaken all of our sleepy thoughts and for that reason, dear friends, do not refuse this member when he comes to you seeking entry to your thoughts. Wake up and pick up your pens!

Tell him, friends, your thoughts and opinions. Tell him what you don't understand, give him your stories and poems. Then he will pass these on to all the members and you will receive the answers you require.

In this way, we will get along better. No hidden issues will rule us, and our road in life will be beautiful.

Won't you be happy when you pick up our publication and find in it the ideas of others, as well as your own? The intellectual world of each member will be clear and understandable to all. In addition, we will have a mirror which will reflect our lives and the life of the branch.

So, dear friends, get to work! Don't let this new member get away because only he can fulfill this task and have such significance.

Sore Eykhler (Alon)

[Page 246]

The new work year is beginning. During the summer months our work slacked off, and it is now necessary, at the beginning of the new work year, that we increase our efforts in order to make up for our neglect. The only way to succeed is through concrete actions, and that is where we can and must direct our efforts. The efforts of those who are in the organization for the workers of Eretz Yisroel in general and for Hechalutz Hatzair in particular bring us closer to the achievement of Zionism.

What does Zionism mean? It is the revolutionary reconstruction of Jewish life, the construction of our national home.

Those who will bring about this radical change in Jewish life are the Jewish workers in Eretz Yisroel. Therefore, comrades, let us work energetically to achieve our goal, that is, to enter Hechalutz Hatzair with the requisite physical and intellectual resources, so that we can be worthy of carrying the flag of the Jewish workers in Eretz Yisroel and successfully continue to put workers in the forefront.

Gefen (Z.V.)

[Song in Hebrew –not translated]

[Page 247]

No! Such things must not be permitted!

What can we say about the recent events in Eretz Yisroel?[1]

We don't want to wage war. That must not happen, because the great work of construction that we have undertaken has not yet ended; it is perhaps not even half finished, and under the circumstances threatens never to be finished.

We cannot remain indifferent that the future of the Jewish working masses should be subject to strike breaking, and that the strike breakers are none other than the innocent members of Faction B, incited by their Lag b'Omer general – brothers of a single people!

The Revisionist movement appeared on the Zionist stage, talking about renewing and developing new forces, showing new ways toward construction, but in the end they showed their true faces.

At a time when not a single worker of any other people living in the land went to work, the members of Betar, under the protection of the British police, came to work in the factories. This open strike breaking will hasten the end and open the eyes of those young workers who have been captured by the Revisionist liar. They will again take their place in the ranks of Histadrut, the ranks of the working people of Eretz Yisroel.

Nor should it be permitted that the Jewish colonists from Zikhron Yaakov and Nes Tziona and Jewish entrepreneurs from Tel Aviv and Jerusalem boycott Jewish workers who are members of HIstadrut. The colonist fears Histradrut which is fighting for a 7 hour workday and higher wages when he can get Arab workers for a few piaster less.

No! We cannot permit such things. Without Jewish workers there is no Jewish Eretz Yisroel!

Even–Moreh (A.L.)

[Page 248]

Oasis

On the cobblestone streets, the blood that's been spilled

Will call out and appeal to God.

Perhaps heaven will hear its cry

And the city of stone will weep

Only a few will abandon the noise

The poisonous noise of the city

And sing the song of their heart's true desire

The desert, so vast, so vast

Only a few put one hand to a plow

While holding a gun in the other

And their eyes are aflame with a holy courage

And the difficult road becomes easy.

In the desert, a silvery spring will burble

And a village will be covered in greenery

And the sun glowing between trees and sand

And golden sheaves will flow

And people, like the blossoming sheaves, stand in rows

With the fire of faith in their hearts

And will celebrate the blessing of their own effort

And curse the noise of the city

Those who mock will continue to mock

Those who build will keep on building

Our faith is a luminous tower

That reaches to the clear blue sky

[Page 249]

Hands that break stone will harrow and sow

And singing will harvest the fruit of years of strife

Blood and marrow offered up with glowing faith

Will transform the barren land

Into a paradise.

Avrom Shturmak

Our Impressions

It has been a short time since we joined the branch of Hechalutz Hatzair. But that has sufficed for us to have been entirely taken up by the goal of fulfilling the task of being true comrades. Until now, we didn't know that there exists a world of comrades that is entirely different from the world in which we have lived until now. This is a world of ardent comradeship that carries everything along in its current.

As soon as we entered the office of our branch, a wave of joy swept over us, we were surrounded by an atmosphere of brotherhood, people were singing and dancing, everyone joined together.

In addition, all these people were bound together by a goal toward which they all strived. Their hearts call out with one cry and one idea rules their minds. Their future lies in Eretz Yisroel. We were drawn by the amazing force to this entire tribe of people and a small revolution took place in our hearts.

The Hechalutz way, of which we had known nothing until now, became clear to us. Now we will make a great effort to learn the way and to help those who are in it.

Kivutsa Shoshanim [Roses Group]

[Page 250]

Prizes for the Readers of Hechalutz Hatzair

In order to enable the members of Hechalutz Hatzair to wear badges we will give badges as prizes. Every member who sends us 5 coupons, that will be printed in 5 issues of Hechalutz Hatzair, will be entitled to win a badge. The first coupon is provided in this issue.

About Party Discipline

Last week, the Hechalutz brought the renowned actor Jaques Levi to perform in Chorzele. We thought our act would be welcomed by all the local groups, because how could it be otherwise? A small town which has no theatrical group of its own, without the means to bring in a fine speaker, not to mention an actor like Jacques Levi.

A town that has no movie theater, no place for young people to enjoy their free time and especially to enjoy an intellectual experience. So the Hechalutz, with the help of the Proshnitser League for the Workers of Eretz Yisroel, tried to break the sad tradition of lethargy and provide the young people with a little cultural entertainment.

But we encountered opposition. The Peretz Library (the Bund, in other words)[2], the ostensible provider of culture for local youth, whose cultural activities consists of outdoor gatherings and denouncing Zionist events, began to sound the alarm about the terrible disaster threatening Chorzele. Like the fools of Chelm [fictional town in Jewish folklore], they quickly called a meeting, at which they decided not to allow Levi's performance and to boycott it. They complained that the Halutzim don't come to their outdoor gatherings or dance with their girls, and not all the Halutzim come to a lecture that they arrange once in five years.

[Page 251]

The two ostensible leaders of the Bund – full–fledged losers and intellectual boors — made every effort to prevent the event.

It is also interesting that through the delegation they announced that if their members were given discounted tickets, they would stop their holy fight against us. That is, the fight that they were presumable fighting for its own sake, was really a fight over financial interests. This is their true face – speaking of God while holding a serpent in their hand.

But reason triumphed. Despite their boycott, the evening was a big success and the hall was packed.

But let it be known: All those who yelled so loudly in support of the boycott were not ashamed to stand under the windows and in this original and hidden manner spared themselves the cost of even discounted tickets. That's the morality of the Bund. It is regrettable that the sensible Bund members of the Peretz Library who wanted to take this opportunity to have a little cultural enjoyment were prevented from doing so by the decision of their leaders. Let us hope that this fact will open their eyes and they will see the true nature of their cultural providers and will join our ranks.

S.L.

News from the branch

On November 2, 1932, by decision of the committee, Comrade Zlate Frayman was admitted as a member of Hechalutz Haboger [Adult Pioneers]

Recently there was formed a *kivutsa* group named Shoshanim [Roses] which consists of 7 members 13 years old. They are carrying out their work very energetically.

Four men from Hechalutz Haboger have been certified for *Aliyah.*

Support the Fund for Tarbut [Hebrew language school system] of Hechalutz Hatzair

Support the Fund for Hechalutz

Join en masse in the League for Workers of Eretz Yisroel

Support the Jewish National Fund of Israel

Provided by A. Likhtenshteyn

Translator's Footnotes

1. The events referred to concern a conflict in Palestine between Histadrut [Labor Federation], with which Hechalutz Hatzair identified, and the Revisonist Zionists, led by Vladimir Jabotinsky. The workers affiliated with Histadrut conducted a labor strike, and the Revisionists fought to suppress the strike. Faction B and Betar were Revisionist organizations led by Jabotinsky.

2. The incident reported in this article reflects the rivalry between the Bund, a Socialist, anti–Zionist organization, and the Hechalutz Hatzair.

[Page 252]

Minutes of the Gemiles Khesed [free loan] Fund
January 22–23, 1938
(provided exactly as in the original)
Translated by Miriam Leberstein

The minutes of the Gemiles Khesed fund of January 22, 1938

Minutes No. 1

In Chorzele, on Saturday, 20ᵗʰ day of Shvat, 5698, January 22, 1938, at 7 P.M. the general meeting of the Gemiles Khesed Fund took place, with the following agenda:

1) Opening; 2) Election of Chairman for the general meeting; 3) Reading of the [governmental] authorization of the fund, and regulations and statutes of the Gemiles Khesed fund; 4) Report of activities to the present time; 5)

Determination of the terms and amount of loans; 6) Election of the board of directors and oversight committee; 7) Motions

1. The founder of the Gemiles Khesed fund, H. [Herr = Mr.] M. Fridman, opened the meeting.

2. H. Avrom Mikl Adler was unanimously elected chairman and he invited the following to join him on the presidium: Herrs Shmuel Frenkl and Avrom Siniak, with Hirsh Grinberg as Secretary.

3. H. Shabti Frenkl read aloud the authorization from the voivode [provincial government] and the accompanying letter from the *staroste* [county government], as well as the regulations and statutes of the Gemiles Khesed fund. The meeting took note of these.

4. H. M. Fridman gave his report. He indicated that the critical conditions in the town and the difficulties of obtaining credit even with interest, had led him to think of founding the fund. Through the fund every tradesman and merchant can receive an interest–free loan and that will certainly substantially alleviate their poverty. He has appealed to townspeople living abroad, and wrote five letters. As of now, he has received one response from Reb [respectful form of address] Yehuda Walershteyn from Canada, with a check for $200.This gift laid the foundation on which to establish the fund. H. Fridman appealed to everyone at the meeting to support this important institution as much as possible.

5. It was decided that the limit on the loans will be 50 zlotys, with the terms being 10 weekly payments.

6. The number of attendees was 65 (all with the right to vote.) Seven people were elected to the Board of Directors: Shepsl Frenkl (41 votes); M. Fridman (40); Avrom Siniak (27); M. Sokolower (23); Khaim Igler (21); Ziskind Berliner (19); Mendl Kats (18).

   As alternates: Itsik Meyer Slovne; Moyshe Mendl Kohan and Dov Brener.

   On the oversight committee: 1) A.M. Adler 2) Zev Gutlezer; 3)Zalmen Milshteyn. As alternates: Moyshe Ayznshtat and Oser Orntshteyn.

H. Fridman made a motion that the general meeting should authorize the board of directors to decide on all unforeseen questions until the next general meeting. The meeting considered the motion and expressed its full confidence in the board of directors.

Signed:

Chairman: A.M. Adler   Assistants: Sh. Frenkl, Avrom Siniak

[Page 254]

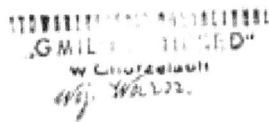

Minutes of the Gemiles Khesed Fund of January 23, 1938

Minutes No.2

Chorzele, Sunday, 21st of Shvat,5698, January 23, 1938. At 7:00 P.M., a general meeting was held with the following agenda:

1. Constitution of the Board of Directors

2. A letter to Yehuda Walershteyn

3. Designation of the amount of loans

4. Designation of terms of office of the Board of Directors

5. Announcement about applying for loans

6. Weekly fee for the town's Jewish population

7. Open for motions

Resolutions

1. The Board of Directors is constituted as follows:

   a. President: Mordkhe–Menakhem Fridman

   b. Vice President: Avrom Siniak

   c. Treasurer: Shepsl Frenkl

   d. Secretary: Menakhem Dov Kats

    e. Board Members: M. Soklower, Z. Berliner, H. Igler

    f. Alternates: Itsik Meyer Slovne, Moyshe Mendl Kohan, Dov Brener.

    g. Oversight Committee: Avrom Mikhl Adler, Zalmen Milshteyn, Zev Gutlezer.

2. To send a letter of thanks to the donor H. Yehuda Walershteyn for his donation, which enabled us to open the Gemiles Khesed fund, attaching a certificate and a copy of the official receipt.

3. To remain in contact with Herr Yehuda Walershteyn and appeal to him to persuade Chorzele townspeople in Canada to also contribute to the Gemiles Khesed.

4. To publicize the charitable donation of Yehuda Walershteyn in the Jewish press.

5. It was decided that the amount of each loan will be 50 zlotys, to be paid in weekly installments.

6. The meeting times of the Board of Directors shall be twice a week, on Sunday and Thursday, from 6–8 in the evening.

7. Anyone can apply for a loan from Sunday to Thursday; money will not be distributed until Thursday.

8. The members of the Board of Directors – M. Fridman, A. Siniak, Sh. Frenkl and Mendl Kats – will visit the town residents and obtain contributions for the Gemiles Khesed.

9. H. M. Fridman proposed that the philanthropist Yehuda Walershteyn be elected an honorary member of the Gemiles Khesed in Chorzele and that a plaque with the name of Yehuda Walershteyn and also the names of all donors to the Gemiles Khesed should be mounted in the hall of the Gemiles Khesed. The Board took the motion under consideration.

All resolutions were passed unanimously. The meeting was closed.

On behalf of the Board of Directors, we attest that these minutes accurately reflect the original

Chairman M. Fridman

Treasurer Sh. Frenkl

Secretary Menakhem Dov Kats

Page 256]

A Letter to a *Landsman* [fellow townsman]
(From March 3 1938)
Translated by Miriam Leberstein

[Hebrew dates, etc. – not translated]

To: The Honorable Mr. Khaim Noyekh Kuzniak, New York

We are honored to inform you that there has been officially established in our town a Gemiles Khesed fund, to alleviate the conditions there by providing whatever aid we can, so that each tradesman or shopkeeper can obtain credit interest–free.

It is impossible to describe the critical situation in Chorzele.

The first person to respond to our appeal was Herr Yehuda Walershteyn (Wilson) of Toronto (Cananda.) He sent a check for $200 for the Gemiles Khesed fund. That is our foundation. But it is like a drop of water in the ocean of needy Jews. The respected philanthropist Herr Walershtyen was born in Chorzele, his father was called Reb Aron "Grayesk;" he had a hardware business in the market place. Your father knew him well.

As the president of the Gemiles Khesed, Herr M. Fridman reports, you, as a person born in Chorzele, are connected by a long thread to our town and you are a social activist in the place where you live.

We therefore urgently ask you to appeal to Chorzele *landslayt* to contribute to the Gemiles Khesed. At the same time, we ask you to announce the formation of our Gemiles Khesed in the Jewish press in your country. We here will publish in the press the name of every person who contributes, and the amount of the contribution. We do not consider it necessary for us to advise you how to organize the task, for example, by establishing a founding committee. You know better than us how to proceed in your community.

We ask you to send aid as quickly as possible, because it takes so long to correspond with you. It has been 8 months since we sent a letter about the Gemiles Khesed to our *landslayt* at the address of your uncle, Herr Itsik Kozheniak, but regretfully we have not received an answer.

We hope you will take our appeal under consideration, because of the importance of the Gemiles Khesed these days, particularly in Chorzele, and that you will devote your effort for this cause. In this way you will play a part in the existence of the Gemiles Khesed in Chorzele.

[Page 257]

The Philanthropist Yehuda Walershteyn (Wilson)

Even before World War II, Yehuda "Grayeskes" (the son of Avrom Walershteyn), living in Canada, was well know for the generous support he sent to the Gemiles Khesed and other social causes.

Yehuda Walershteyn (Wilson), one of the young people in our town who followed the Jewish enlightenment, left Chorzele in 1914, along with his brother. In 1921, he brought his mother and sister to Canada and there the family laid down roots.

An important and busy tobacco merchant, Yehuda, despite his many business activities and respectable status, did not forget his hometown and over the years maintained contact with his friends and acquaintances there. He always generously provided support to Chorzelers who made aliyah [emigrated to Israel] and to the work of the Chorzele *landslayt* association in Israel, especially for the publication of the yizkor book and for the writing of a Torah scroll for the synagogue in Ra'anana [Israel] in memory of the holy martyrs of Chorzele.

A heartfelt thanks to our friend Yehuda Walershteyn (Wilson).

The Committee

Reb Meyer Yakov Zayngurt lights a candle during celebration upon completion of the Torah scroll in memory of the martyrs of Chorzele in the synagogue in Ra'anana

[Page 258]

Torah scroll in memory of the Chorzele martyrs in the synagogue in Ra'anana

[Page 259]

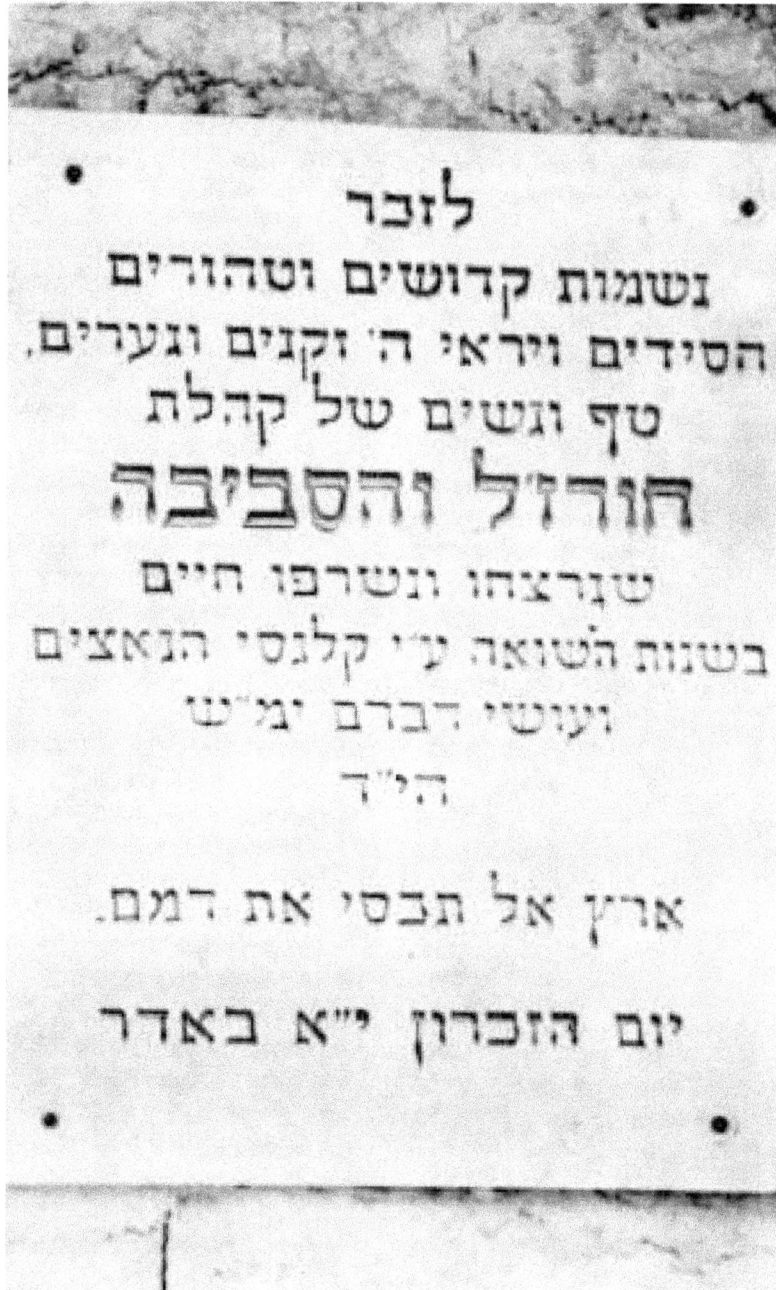

לזכר
נשמות קדושים וטהורים
החסידים ויראי ה' זקנים ונערים,
טף ונשים של קהלת
חורזל והסביבה
שנרצחו ונשרפו חיים
בשנות השואה ע"י קלגסי הנאצים
ועושי דברם ימ"ש
הי"ד

ארץ אל תכסי את דמם.

יום הזכרון י"א באדר

The Memorial stone in *Martef Ha Shoah* [Museum of the Holocaust] on Mount Zion in Jerusalem

[Pages 260-263]

Necrology – Chorzele, Poland

Transliterated by David Sosnovitch

Edited by Ann Harris

Family name(s)	First name(s)	Sex	Father's name	Mother's name	Name of spouse	Page
ADLER	Avraham Michael	M				260
ADLER	Gitel	M				260
ADLER	Moshe Shimon	M				260
ADLER	Rashke	F				260
ALTER	Ela	F				260
ANUSEWICZ	Akiva	M				260
ARTENSZTEJN	Asher	M				260
ARTENSZTEJN	Avraham Mordechal	M				260
ARTENSZTEJN	Berel	M				260
ASZ	Matel	M				260
ASZ	Meir	M				260
BACHRACH	Avraham Yosef	M				260
BACHRACH	Bat Sheva	F				260
BACHRACH	Hana Rahel	F				260
BACHRACH	Meir Moshe	M				260
BACHRACH	Miriam	F				260
BAJLOWICZ	Sarah	F				260
BAUMGARTEN	Haya	F				260
BEILSWEIGER	Esther	F				260
BEKERMAN	Aharon Matel	M				260
BERENT	Michael	M				260

BERGER	Feivel Berel	M				260
BERLINER	Binyamin	M				260
BERLINER	Ziskind	M				260
BERLINKA	David Ber	M				260
BERLINKA	Yohanan	M				260
BLANKITNER	Itzhak	M				260
BRENER	Berel	M				260
BRENER	Berel	M				260
BRENER	Berel	M				260
BRENER	Dan	M				260
BRENER	Fishele	M				260
BRENER	Shifra	F				260
BRENER	Simha	M			Zisa	260
BRENER	Zalman Meir	M				260
BRENER	Zisa	M			Simha	260
BULMAN	Shlomo	M				260
CHIECHANSKI	Berel	M				262
CHIECHANSKI	Gershon	M				262
CHIECHANSKI	Moshe	M				262
CHIECHANSKI	Shalom	M				262
CYTRYNIARCZ?	Melech	M				262
DAWIDSOHN	Glike	F				260
DZEBIELKA	Aharon Leib	M				261
DZEBIELKA	David Hersh	M				261
DZEBIELKA	Eliyahu	M				261
DZEDZIC	Feivel	M				261
DZEDZIC	Henech	M				261
DZEDZIC	Moshe Zerah	M				261
DZEDZIC	Yishaya	M				261

EDELSZTEJN	Koppel	M				261
EICHLER	Yehuda Nehemya	M			Beila Rivka	261
EIGLER	Berel Leib	M				261
EIGLER	Haim	M				261
EIZENSZTADT	Moshe	M				261
ELBAUM	Pinhas	M			Sara Hana	262
ELBAUM	Sarah Hana	F			Pinhas	262
FATER/PUTER?	Eli Leib	M				262
FATER/PUTER?	Moshe	M				262
FATER/PUTER?	Shalom	M				262
FATER/PUTER?	Tevil	M				262
FISZERUNG	Yehiel	M				262
FREJMAN	Yishaya	M				262
FRENKEL	Shalom	M				262
FRENKEL	Shmuel	M				262
FROM	Matel	M				262
FRYDMAN	Esther	F				262
FRYDMAN	Hanah	F				262
FRYDMAN	Mordehai Mendel	M				262
FRYDMAN	Simha Bunim	M	Yaakom	Rivka		262
FRYDMAN	Yaakov	M			Rivka	262
GARBOWICZ	Rashke	F				260
GARDI?	Haim	M				260
GERLICZ	Hershel	M				260
GERSZTEJN	Sarah Hana	F				260
GIWELB	Natan	M				260
GIWELB	Shalom Itzhak	M				260
GIWELB	Yudel	M				260

GLIKOWSKI	Yihezkel	M				260
GLIKSBERG	Hershel	M				260
GOLDSZLAK	Hersh	M				260
GORMAN/GURMAN	Aharon	M				260
GORMAN/GURMAN	Aidel?	M				260
GORMAN/GURMAN	Avraham	M				260
GORMAN/GURMAN	Miriam	F			Shmuel	260
GORMAN/GURMAN	Nachman	M				260
GORMAN/GURMAN	Shmuel	M			Miriam	260
GRAJCER	Avraham	M				260
GROSKIND	Mendel	M				260
GROSKIND	Shalom	M				260
GROSKIND	Sheindel	F				260
GRYNBERG	Esther	F				260
GRYNBERG	Hershel	M				260
GUTLEZER	Velvel	M				260
GWIAZDA	Moshe Aharon	M				260
HACOHEN PENCZAK	Yehezkel	M			Hana Dvroa	262
HACOHEN PENCZAK	Yehezkel	M			Hana Dvroa	262
HECHT	Haim	M				261
HENDLER	Moshe	M				261
HENT	Leah	F				261
HERZOG	Haya	M				261
HERZOG	Rahel Zisel	F				261
HERZOG	Zalman	M				261
HOCHMAN	Shlomo	M				261
JABLONKA	Herzke	M				261
KAMINISKI	Eliyahu	M				262
KATZ	Leib	M				261

KATZ	Mendel	M				261
KITNIK	Itzhak	M				262
KLATSHEWSKI	Yohan	M				262
KNOP	Avraham Itzhak	M			Malka	262
KNOP	Malka	F			Avraham Itzhak	262
KNOT	Gitel	F			Moshe	262
KNOT	Moshe	M			Gitel	262
KODZITSA?	Itzhak Meir	M				262
KOHEN	Haim	M				261
KOHEN	Hanah	F				261
KOHEN	Moshe Mendel	M				261
KOHEN	Tova	F				261
KOHEN	Yehiel	M				261
KORN	Zadok	M				262
KORZENIAK?	Avraham	M				262
KORZENIAK?	Matel	M				262
KOWAL	David	M				262
KOWAL	Hanah	M				262
KOWEL	Feivel	M				262
KRYSZTAL	Haim Shmuel	M				262
LAKRYC	Moshe	M				262
LANIENTER	Itzhak	M				262
LANIENTER	Motel	M				262
LANIENTER	Natan	M				262
LANIENTER	Simha	M				262
LERNER	Avraham	M				262
LEW	Mendel	M				262
LEW	Zalman	M				262
LICHTENSZTEJN	Artshe	M				262

LICHTENSZTEJN	Hershel	M				262
LICHTENSZTEJN	Matel	M				262
LINDENBERG	Leibel	M				262
MAKOWSKI	Frimet	F				262
MAKOWSKI	Leah	F				262
MAKOWSKI	Velvel	M				262
MALINIK?	Gabriel	M				262
MARGOLIS	Meshulam	M				262
MILSZTEJN	David Arye	M				262
MILSZTEJN	Hana Mindel	F				262
MILSZTEJN	Itzhak Meir	M				262
MILSZTEJN	Zalman	M				262
MONDERDZITZKI?	Israel Shalom	M				262
MONDERSZTEJN	Shlomo	M				262
MONDERSZTEJN	Yaakov Israel	M				262
NADEL	Itzhak Meir	M				262
PENCZAK	Esther Rahel	F	Yehezkel	Esther Rahel		262
PENCZAK	Noah	M	Yehezkel	Esther Rahel		262
PENCZAK	Yosef	M	Yehezkel	Esther Rahel		262
PINDEK	Hersh Itzhak	M				262
PINDEK	Yosef	M				262
PLUDA	Avraham	M				262
PRZYSUSKIER	Avraham Yehuda	M				262
PRZYSUSKIER	Haya Feige	F				262
PRZYSUSKIER	Karsa?	F			Pinhas	262
PRZYSUSKIER	Menahem Mendel	M				262

PRZYSUSKIER	Pinhas	M			Krasa	262
PRZYSUSKIER	Sheindel	F			Yaakov Meri	262
PRZYSUSKIER	Yaakov Meir	M			Sheindel	262
PSZENICA?	Natan	M				262
PSZENICA?	Shlomo	M				262
RABINOWICZ	Naftali	M				263
RABINOWICZ	Wolf	M				263
RICHTER	Fruma	F				263
RICHTER	Izhak Meir	M				263
RICHTER	Matel	F			Yoheved	263
RICHTER	Yoheved	F			Matel	263
ROGEN	Israel Yakov	M				263
ROGEN	Shlomo Asher	M				263
ROSENBLUM	Itzhak	M				263
ROSENSWEIG	Haim	M			Perl	263
ROSENSWEIG	Perel	F			Haim	263
ROSTOKER	Feige	F				263
ROSTOKER	Sarah	F				263
ROZEM?	Hersh Itzhak	M				263
RYTERBAND	Izak	M				263
RYTERBAND	Leizer	M				263
RYTERBAND	Natan	M			Zirul	263
RYTERBAND	Tzirel	M			Natan	263
RYTERBAND	Yehiel	M				263
RYTERBAND	Zisa Haya	F				263
SCHLAMOWICZ	Haim Yosef	M				263
SCHROTT	Avraham	M				263
SCHROTT	Keila	F				263

SCHROTT	Matel	M				263
SCHROTT	Meir	M				263
SCHROTT	Miriam	F				263
SEGEL	David	M				262
SEGEL	Itzhak	M				262
SEGEL	Yerahmiel	M				262
SHNIDOWER	Shimon	M				263
SHULTZ?	Zalman	M				263
SLAVNE	Itzhak Meir	M				262
SOKOLOWER	Ben Zion	M				262
SOKOLOWER	Leiba	M			Mordehai Haim	262
SOKOLOWER	Mattisyahu	M			Sara Rivka	262
SOKOLOWER	Mordehai Haim	M			Liba	262
SOKOLOWER	Sarah Rivka	F			Matityahu	262
SPADNIK?	Moshe	M				262
STUDENT	Haya	F				262
STUDENT	Natan	M				262
SZAFT	David Beer	M				263
SZER	Avraham	M				263
SZER	Israel	M				263
SZKOP	Moshe Hersh	M				263
SZMIER	Malka	F				263
SZTEJN	Haya Rivka	F	Leib Hersh			263
SZTEJN	Haya Rivka	F	Leib Hersh			263
SZTEJN	Israel Natan	M				263
SZTEJN	Lieb Hersh	M	Leib Hersh			263
TAUB	Gedaliya	M			Sara	261

TAUB	Sarah	F		Gedalya	261
TEHILIM	Dvora	F			263
TEHILIM	Naomi	F			263
TEHILIM	Yosef	M			263
TYK	Yosef	M			261
TYKULSKER	Dvora	F			261
TYKULSKER	Golda	F			261
TYKULSKER	Hana Rahel	F			261
TYKULSKER	Itzhak	M			261
TYKULSKER	Leah	F			261
TYKULSKER	Leiba Royan?	M			261
TYKULSKER	Mindel	F			261
TYKULSKER	Nahman	M			261
TYKULSKER	Rivka	F			261
TZVIRKOWSKI	Moshe	M			262
WALD	Israel Menashe	M			261
WARSHOWSKI	Yitzhak	M			261
WEILAM	Mendel	M			261
WEILAM	Yaakov	M			261
WEINGARTEN	Hana	F			261
WENGEL	Malia?	F			261
WERGROWSKI		M			261
WINERSZTEJN	Michael	M			261
WINERSZTEJN	Yitzhak Meir	M			261
WINO	Aharon	M			261
WINO	Binyamin	M			261
WINO	Yosef David	M			261
WONSIEK	Liba	M			261
YOCHT	David	M			261

	Hersh					
YOCHT	Golde	F				261
YOCHT	Haim Wolf	M				261
YOCHT	Hershel	M				261
YOCHT	Hershel	M				261
YOCHT	Yaakov	M			Sara	261
ZAGACKIER?		M				261
ZAGACKIER?	Yitzhak David	M				261
ZAKOWER MAKOVER	Baruch	M				262
ZELAZNE?	Haim	M				261
ZEMEL	Avraham	M				261
ZEMEL	Hanah	F				261
ZEMEL	Haya Beile	F				261
ZEMEL	Zalman Moshe	M				261
ZILBERBERG	Shmuel	M				261
ZILBERMAN	Haim Avigdor	M				261
ZILBERMAN	Menachem	M				261
ZILBERMAN	Rahel	F				261
ZILBERMAN	Yaakov	M				261
ZILBERMAN	Yaakov Moshe	M				261
ZIMAN	Matel	M				261

[Page 264]

List of Deceased from Chorzele

From the State of Israel and in other countries

Translated by Jerrold Landau

Eisenstadt, Mordechai
Eichelbaum, Pinchas
Alter, Tauba
Alter, Tzvi

Baharab, Zeev
Baharab, Leah
Biren (Przysusker),
Mordechai
Beida, David–Hirsch
Beida, Chana
Berlinka, Simcha
Brener, Berel
Brener, Chaya–Tzirel
Brener, Yaakov

Gewelb, Nathan
Gewelb, Leah

Davidson, Yisrael

Silverman, Yisrael

Tyk, Yisrael and wife
Tykulsker Zalman
Tykulsker, Sara
Tykulsker, Nachman
Tykulsker, Perl

Katz, Rivka

Lachower, Shlomo–
Yehuda
Lachower, Chana–Breina
Lachower, Fishel
Lachower, Dvora
Lachower, Leib–Hirsch
Lachower, Moshe
Lanienter, David
Lew, Chava–Neche

Mar–Chaim, Yosef–
Chaim
Mar–Chaim, Golda

Mar–Chaim, Shmuel
Mar–Chaim, Fishel
Mar–Chaim, Yissachar

Niborski, Leizer
Neier, Rivka

Piekasz, Dvroa
Farberowitz, Mordechai–
Mendel
Farbberowitz Sara–Beila
Freiman, David
Freiman, Zlata

Cwyrkowski, Moshe

Kazszica, Chaim–David
Kazszeniak, Yosef
Kazszeniak, Beila
Kazszeniak, Yaakov

Rustiker, Keila

Shafran, Mendel and wife
Shafran, Feivish

———

[Page 265]

List and Chorzele Natives in the World
(1966)

Translated by Jerrold Landau

United States (America)
Canada
Argentina
Mexico
Uruguay
Australia
France
Scotland
and
Israel

List of Chorzele Natives (1966)
(In various countries and in the State of Israel)

United States (America)

Eisenstadt, Freda
Eichelbaum, Avraham
Baharab, Aryeh
Berger, L.
Goodman, Abba
Goodman, Louis
Genbard, S.
Handelman, Ruth
Silverstein, D.
Lazari, Jeman
Laker, Harry
Levinson, Helen
Morrison, Anna
Margolis, Henry
Mehlman, L.
Nitzki, N. and Louis
Staar, R.
Silverberg, Louis, and Yosa
Snyder, Esther
Segal, F. D.
Edelson, M.
Friedland, Sh.
Cohen, Harry and Philip
Kowal, Y.
Kittner, L.
Klein, Nathan
Rosen, Saul and Rivka
Riba, Golda
Regent, K.
Stein, Eva
Sirota, Juan and Reva

Canada

Brovner, Hersch
Wilson, Yehuda

Argentina

Artenstein, Lazar
Weingarten, Yaakov
Tykulsker, Leon
Niborski, Yehuda and
Rachel (sons Melech and
Yosef, Daughter, son–in–
law, and grandchildren)
Niborski, Ephraim
Prusan, Paula
Frenkel, Yehuda–Aryeh

Mexico

Artenstein, Fishel
Teifeld, B.
Lew, V.
Lew, Y.
Nitzkin, Chiel
Simon, Mottel
Kaszeniak, M.
Sniadower, Zelik

Uruguay

Artenstein, Lazar and Gil
Hoffman, Golda
Przenica, Shmuel
Koszeniak, Noach and
Yitzchak

[Page 267]

Australia

Gmelnik, Heina
Katz, Yaakov
Niwes, Rachel

France

Edelstein, Ch.
Kogan, Perl
Kaluszinski, Riva
Romelsburg, Tzila

Scotland

Greenhil, Anna
Lewiner, Sara

Germany

Sniadower, Izak

In the State of Israel

Eistenstadt, Elisheva
Eichelbaum, Hinda and Tzipora
Eichelbaum, Shragav
Eichler, Yaakov
Alberstein, Dvora and Tzvi
Alter, Meir
Alter, Chaimv Alter, Naomi
Anachowicz, David
Anachowicz, Yisrael
Erez, Rachel
Artenstein, Yitzchak

Barlas, Tzipora
Burtnik, Tzilav Birenhak, Rivka
Bahir, Yaakov
Baharav, Moshe
Beida Y.
Biren, Pnina
Blenitner, Rachel
Ben–Yosef, Meir
Bar–Natan, Yeshayahu
Beker, Yehudit

Berlinka, Chasia
Berent, Mordechai
Branrat, Yaakov
Bronstein, Sara

Ganot, Shimon
Gewelb, Noach
Gerszonowicz, Rachel
Greenberg, Malka

Davidson, Moshe–Leib
Degani, Tzvi
Jedzitz, Yechiel
Drezner

Hamburger, Hadassah
Helfgot, Freda
Hendler, Shlomo–David

Woloczer, Bilhah
Wolk, Sara
Weichman, Bela
Weingort, Miriam and
Meir–Yaakov

[Page 268]

Wengerowski, Eliahu

Zoger, Tova
Zahavi, Eila

Tykulsker, Rosa
Tykulsker, Dov
Tykulsker, Gedalia
Tykulsker, David
Tykulsker, Pinchas
Tal, Alexander
Tliszewski, Tova

Jabrow, Pnina
Judengloiben, Bela
Jochet, Moshe
Jochet, Menachem
Yismach, Mina

Kochavi, Sara
Chmelnicki, Yitzchak
Katz, Chaim
Katz, Shlomo

Katz, Shimon
Carmi, Moshe
Carmi, Shraga

Lachower, Menachem
Lachower, Shmuel
Lanienter, Nachman
Lanienter, Yosef
Levavi, Shlomo
Leviatan, Golda
Litauer, Dora
Lewenberg, Sara
Lach, Dina
Lach, Yisrael
Lefel, Bronia

Markowicz, Bracha
Monderstein, Tzipora
Milstein, Moshe
Mlawski, Tirtza
Mar–Chaim, Eliezer
Mar–Chaim, Yeshayahu
and Fruma
Mar–Chaim, Avraham
Mar–Chaim, Yechezkel

Nisenbaum, Pnina
Neuer, Shmuel
Nafcha, Aharon
Nesher, Simcha
Nesher, Yosef
Nesher, Bunim

Sokolower, Rabbi
Ephraim
Sokolower, Avraham (Tel
Aviv)
Sokolower, Moshe
Sokolower, Simcha–Eli
Sokolower, Avraham
(Afula)
Sokolower, David
Slawni, Shimon
Slawni, Chaim
Segal, Chaya

Ivri, Eliezer
Edelstein, Sara

Azrieli, Sara
Etingen, Rivka
Etzioni, Rivka
Erlich, Rivka

[Page 269]

Pindik, Yisachar
Piekasz, Chaim and
Eliahuv Perlowicz, Tzila
Peretz, Rivka

Fater, Dov
Fater, Matityahu
Fater, Meir
Fater, Menachem
Fiszrig, David
Fliszun, Malka
Fried, Nisan
Freiman, Eliezer
Freiman, Chaya
Frenkel, David
Frenkel, Yaakov
Frenkel, Malka
Frenkel, Moshe

Ciechanowski, Malka
Ciechanowski, Yitzchak

Kowal, Moshe
Koszik, Moshe
Koszik, Shmuel
Koszeniak, Moshe
Koszeniak, Yakel
Koszeniak, Reuven
Kotliar, Esther
Kotliarski, Hadassah
Kalina, Chaim
Kantorowicz, Miriam
Kaufman, Chava
Kinel, Freda
Krau, Sender
Krawiecz, Rachel
Kranszak, Meir

Rawicki, Mina
Rudek, Yitzcak
Rom, Rivkav Rustiker,
Moshe

Raz, Reuven–Moshe
Riterbant, Leibel
Richter, David
Richter, Yehuda
Richter, Yeshayahu

Shaft, Michael
Shafran, Yosef
Shafran, Yitzchak
Shachori, Chinka
Stigletz, Zisel
Shmueli, Frimet
Sniadower, Gershon
Sherpski, Leah

———

[Page 272]

Chorzele (Choszel)

Translated by Jerrold Landau

A Jewish community that was destroyed in the storm of the Holocaust during the Second World War, and was swept away in the deluge of blood and fire by the impure hands of the Satans of our generation; A holy community that was destroyed in the midst of its flourishing, destroyed and razed to its foundations, erased from the book of life, wiped out as if it never was, nullified and is no more.

We will light an eternal light to its memory, and guard it so that it is never extinguished!

INDEX

This index does not include those names listed in the Necrology starting on page 289 nor the lists starting on page 299, so please also review those names separately.

Rozenblum, 228

Rozencwajg, 12

Rozenstrauch, 31, 48

Rozenzwajg, 25

Rudek, 306

Rustiker, 299, 306

S

Safran, 248

Sakolower, 249

Samsonow, 197, 198

Samuel, 83, 84

Sar, 101

Scher, 67

Schneider, 41

Segal, 15, 17, 82, 175, 176, 186, 200, 204, 301, 304

Shaar, 15, 17, 145

Shachori, 306

Shafran, 151, 152, 222, 299, 306

Shaft, 306

Shapira, 133

Sher, 47, 204, 233, 247, 248

Sherpski, 306

Shimon, 8, 9, 12, 13, 15, 18, 28, 70, 71, 74, 95, 100, 272, 289, 296, 302, 304

Shimony, 129

Shmuel der Rebe, 260

Shmueli, 272, 306

Shniadover, 7

Shochet, 79

Shoyme the butcher, 209

Shturmak, 277

Shufman, 115, 117

Silbersztajn, 180

Silverberg, 301

Silverman, 299

Silverstein, 301

Siniak, 282, 283, 284

Sirota, 64, 101, 301

Slawni, 304

Slovne, 282, 284

Smolenskin, 30, 57

Snell, 89

Sniadever, 191

Sniadower, 100, 204, 205, 250, 272, 301, 302, 306

Snyder, 301

Sochaczew, 9, 95

Soklower, 284

Sokolow, 30, 87, 107, 112, 122, 123, 124, 125

Sokolower, 4, 12, 14, 15, 17, 78, 79, 80, 98, 99, 101, 103, 144, 145, 189, 209, 282, 304

Sopieski, 64

Sosnovitch, 289

Sporn, 28, 29, 30

Staar, 301

Stein, 301

Stigletz, 306

Stolier, 190, 234

Student, 12

Szafran, 18

Szar, 81, 82

Szer, 56

Sziniak, 12

Szirota, 15

Szirota's, 15

Szniadower, 7, 9, 12, 13, 14

Szulcz, 101

T

Tal, 95, 304

Tchernichovsky, 109, 112, 117

Teifeld, 301

Tenenbaum, 95

Tik, 209, 229, 233, 267, 268

Tikulsker, 47, 228

Tishbi, 111, 112, 117, 118

www.ingramcontent.com/pod-product-compliance
Lightning Source LLC
Chambersburg PA
CBHW080149310326
41914CB00090B/989